SEXUALITY IN GREEK AND ROMAN SOCIETY AND LITERATURE

With numerous original translations of ancient poetry, inscriptions and documents, this fascinating volume is the first major sourcebook to explore the multifaceted nature of sexuality in antiquity.

The detailed introduction provides full social and historical context for the sources, and guides students on how to use the material most effectively. Themes such as marriage, prostitution and same-sex attraction are presented comparatively, with material from the Greek and Roman worlds shown side by side; this approach allows readers to interpret the written records with a full awareness of the different context of these separate but related societies. Commentaries are provided throughout, focusing on vocabulary and social and historical context.

Marguerite Johnson is a lecturer in the School of Humanities at the University of Newcastle, New South Wales. Her main research interests are in Latin poetry, especially Catullus, Ovid and Martial. She is also researching the history of ancient magic, particularly the role of women as practitioners.

Terry Ryan is a senior lecturer in the School of Liberal Arts, University of Newcastle, New South Wales. His main research interests are Greek and Roman erotic literature, Catullus and Augustan Age literature.

SEXUALITY IN GREEK AND ROMAN SOCIETY AND LITERATURE

A Sourcebook

*Marguerite Johnson
and Terry Ryan*

Routledge
Taylor & Francis Group

LONDON AND NEW YORK

First published 2005
by Routledge
2 Park Square, Milton Park, Abingdon, Oxon OX14 4RN

Simultaneously published in the USA and Canada
by Routledge
711 Third Avenue, New York, NY 10017

Routledge is an imprint of the Taylor & Francis Group, an informa business

© 2005 Marguerite Johnson and Terry Ryan

Reprinted 2006
Transferred to Digital Printing 2008

Typeset in Garamond by
Keystroke, Jacaranda Lodge, Wolverhampton

British Library Cataloguing in Publication Data
A catalogue record for this book is available from the British Library

Library of Congress Cataloging in Publication Data
Johnson, Marguerite, 1965–
Sexuality in Greek and Roman literature and society : a sourcebook /
Marguerite Johnson and Terry Ryan.
p. cm.
Includes bibliographical references and index.
1. Classical literature—History and criticism. 2. Sex in literature.
3. Sex customs—Greece—History—To 500.
4. Sex—Greece—History—To 500. 5. Sex customs in literature.
6. Sex customs—Rome. 7. Sex—Rome. I. Ryan, Terry. II. Title.
PA3014.S47J64 2005
880′.09—dc22
2004012722

ISBN 10: 0–415–17330–2 (hbk)
ISBN 13: 978–0–415–17330–8 (hbk)
ISBN 10: 0–415–17331–0 (pbk)
ISBN 13: 978–0–415–17331–5 (pbk)

CONTENTS

INDEX OF PASSAGES CITED

III MARRIAGE

ILLUSTRATIONS

PREFACE

The focuses of this sourcebook are the sexual practices, mores, ideals and realities of the ancient Greeks and Romans. The most abundant and informative
sources are to be found in literature[1] and these provide the majority of the
selections. Inscriptions, especially graffiti, and some visual material are also
included. Each source has been chosen on the basis of its capacity to contribute
to the diversities of approach to matters of sexuality and sexual expression and
to illustrate the integral relationships between these issues and key components
of ancient society and culture. The selections range from the era of Homer and
Hesiod through to the Graeco-Roman world of the Second Century AD. This
timeframe, from the poetic output of the early Greek world through to an era
still relatively free of Christian influence, establishes socio-historical parameters
within which to work. Within each segment, an effort has been made to
establish a sense of authorial chronology in the development of literary and
societal attitudes towards any given aspect of sexuality.

Each chapter begins with a short introduction. The sources are dealt with
thematically and chronologically under appropriate sub-headings and commentaries are provided on individual passages. The chapter introductions set
the scene for the treatment of respective themes, literary and personal insights,
as well as cultural and historical considerations. In view of the overlapping
nature of the subject matter, there is a significant amount of cross-referencing
between and within chapters. The pieces chosen within each chapter reflect a
process that aims to ensure that, given the breadth of the topic in general, the
major elements of ancient sexuality are introduced. The substantial scholarship
available on many of the areas treated in this book provides a valuable adjunct
to the sources and interpretative material contained herein.

How to use the sourcebook

Our intention is to provide documents that will serve as illustrations of specific
aspects of sexual life in Greece and Rome. In addition to the passages, the
introductory material and the notes are designed to augment the reader's
understanding of a given topic. The bibliographical references in many of the
notes are to direct readers to undertake independent research.

For effective results, readers should keep the following in mind when using the sourcebook:

- The historical and social environment that provides the context for a particular passage.
- The author's cultural heritage, style and tone.
- The genre within which the author is working.
- The author's use of certain words or phrases and the need for an awareness of the importance of terminology (the Glossary of Authors and the Glossary of Greek and Roman terms are, therefore, an integral part of the book.[2]
- Areas of cultural similarity and difference in relation to the attitudes, mores and practices of the Greeks and Romans.
- The use made of mythology: the extent to which stories, myths and fables are informative in regard to the sexual attitudes of the ancients.
- The relevance of academic material available to stimulate interpretations of a given author and passage and the importance of the divergence of scholarly opinion.

There is a focus on the use of Greek and Latin words throughout this sourcebook, particularly in the notes, which is intended to provide an understanding of concepts that cannot be fully appreciated within the context of a translation. For easy reference of repeat words, see the 'Glossary of terms' at the end of the sourcebook.

Notes

1 In addition to scholarly analysis of ancient sexuality both in respect of individual writers and specific themes, there has been quite a deal of recent attention paid to collections of sources and analyses; cf. McLure and also Hubbard. There has also been an increasing amount of material on sexuality in Greek and Roman art. Cf., for example, Boardman and La Rocca; Johns; Mountfield; Kilmer 1993; Koloski-Ostrow and Lyons; Stewart 1997.
2 On the methodological approaches required to analyse ancient sources on sexuality, cf. H. N. Parker 2001. On the use and significance of ancient vocabulary, cf. Adams 1982; J. Henderson 1991.

ACKNOWLEDGEMENTS

We offer our sincerest thanks to our former colleague, Dr Rhona Beare, for her lively and invaluable advice and insights especially in the realm of Greek poetry. Professor Harold Tarrant, of the University of Newcastle, offered much assistance, in particular his discussions of Greek literature and philosophy. Thanks also must go to Professor Brian Bosworth (University of Western Australia) and Associate Professor John Penwill (La Trobe University) for their constructive comments on the Introduction. Colleagues from the University of Newcastle provided invaluable assistance with teaching relief and their constant encouragement; special note should be made of the research assistance provided by Kay Hayes and proofreading by Letitia Waller. Without the tangible and generous support of the Department of Classics and the Schools of Liberal Arts and Humanities at this university we could not have completed the project. Finally, an immense debt is owed to our students, who have proved a deep well of inspiration. From these delightful teaching experiences this book was born.

At the personal level, heartfelt thanks are owed to Helen Poirier, Nicholas Talbot, Emma Lindsay, Holly Marlin, Sarah Gibbs and Kathleen Stephenson. No words are adequate recompense.

ABBREVIATIONS

The abbreviations of journals follow the practice of *L'Année Philologique*.

Collections

AP	W. R. Paton (ed.), *Palatine Anthology* [*Greek Anthology*] (Cambridge, Mass., 1916–1918).
CIL	*Corpus Inscriptionum Latinarum* (Berlin, 1863).
EG	G. Kaibel (ed.), *Epigrammata Graeca*, Vol. 1 (Berlin, 1878).
L&S	C. T. Lewis and C. S. Short (eds), *A Latin Dictionary* (Oxford, 1879).
LSJ	H. G. Liddell and R. Scott (eds), *A Greek–English Lexicon*, 9th ed. (Oxford, 1940).
OLD	P. G. W. Glare (ed.), *The Oxford Latin Dictionary* (Oxford, 1982).
ORF	E. Malcovati, *Oratorum Romanorum fragmenta liberae rei publicae*, 2nd ed. (Turin, 1955).

Ancient authors and works

Ach. Tat.	Achilles Tatius
Ael.	Aelian
Aeschin.	Aeschines
Alc.	Alcaeus
Alcm.	Alcman
Anacr.	Anacreon
And.	Andocides
Apollod.	Apollodorus
	Epit: *Epitome*
	Lib: *Library*
A.R.	Apollonius of Rhodes
Apul.	Apuleius
	M: *Metamorphoses*
Ar.	Aristophanes
	Ach: *Acharnians*
	Ec: *Assembly Women*

	Eq: *Knights*
	Lys: *Lysistrata*
	N: *Clouds*
	Pax: *Peace*
	Pl: *Wealth*
	Ra: *Frogs*
	Th: *Women at the Thesmophoria*
	V: *Wasps*
Archil.	Archilochus
Arist.	Aristotle
	Prob: *Problems* [pseudo-Aristotle]
	Rh: *Rhetoric*
Asclep.	Asclepiades
Ath.	Athenaeus
Cat.	Catullus
Cato	Cato the Elder
Cic.	Cicero
	ad Att: *Epistulae ad Atticum* [*Letters to Atticus*]
	Cael: *Pro Caelio*
	de Fin: *De Finibus*
Cyran.	Cyranides
Dem.	Demosthenes
E.	Euripides
	Hipp: *Hippolytus*
Gallus	Gallus
Herod.	Herodas
Hdt.	Herodotus
Hes.	Hesiod
	Fr: *Fragments*
	Th: *Theogony*
	WD: *Works and Days*
H.H.	*Homeric Hymns*
Homer	*Il*: *Iliad*
	Od: *Odyssey*
Hor.	Horace
	E: *Epodes*
	O: *Odes*
	Sat: *Satires*
Hyg.	Hyginus
	F: *Fables*
Ibyc.	Ibycus
Juv.	Juvenal
Liv.	Livy
Luc.	Lucian

Lucil.	Lucilius
Lucr.	Lucretius
Lys.	Lysias
Mart.	Martial
Max. Tyr.	Maximus of Tyre
Mimn.	Mimnermus
Ov.	Ovid
	AA: *Ars Amatoria*
	Am: *Amores*
	Fast: *Fasti*
	Med. Fac: *Facial Treatments for Ladies*
	Met: *Metamorphoses*
	Tr: *Tristia*
Parth.	Parthenius
Paus.	Pausanias
Petr.	Petronius
	Fr: *Fragments*
	Sat: *Satyricon*
Phld.	Philodemus
Pl.	Plato
	Lg: *Laws*
	Parm: *Parmenides*
	Ph: *Phaedrus*
	R: *Republic*
	Smp: *Symposium*
Plaut.	Plautus
Plb.	Polybius
Plin.	Pliny the Elder
	NH: *Natural History*
Plin.	Pliny the Younger
	Ep: *Epistles*
Plut.	Plutarch
	Ant: *Life of Antonius*
	Caes: *Life of Caesar*
	Cat. Ma: *Life of Cato the Elder*
	Cic: *Life of Cicero*
	Lyc: *Life of Lycurgus*
	Mor: *Moralia*
	Pel: *Life of Pelopidas*
	Per: *Life of Pericles*
	Pomp: *Life of Pompey*
	Sol: *Life of Solon*
	Thes: *Life of Theseus*
Prop.	Propertius

Quint.	Quintilian
Rufin.	Rufinus
Sall.	Sallust
	Cat: *War with Catiline*
Sapph.	Sappho
Semon.	Semonides
Sen.	Seneca the Elder
	Con: *Controversies*
Sol.	Solon
Str.	Strabo
Strat.	Straton
Suet.	Suetonius
	Caes: *Julius Caesar*
	Tib: *Tiberius*
Tac.	Tacitus
	Ann: *Annals*
Theoc.	Theocritus
	Id: *Idylls*
Thgn.	Theognis and *Theognidea*
Thuc.	Thucydides
Tib.	Tibullus
Tyrt.	Tyrtaeus
Varr.	Varro
	RR: *Res Rusticae*
Verg.	Vergil
	Aen: *Aeneid*
	Ecl: *Eclogues*
	Geor: *Georgics*
X.	Xenophon
	An: *Anabasis*
	HG: *Historia Graeca* (*Hellenica*)
	Lac: *Constitution of the Lacedaemonians* [pseudo-Xenophon]
	Mem: *Memorabilia*
	S: *Symposium*

INTRODUCTION
A socio-sexual background to Greece and Rome

Greece

The ancient Greeks enjoyed a variety of sexual experience. To them *eros* was a primal force, which permeated all life and experience in the cosmos, from gods to mortals, to the animal world. They found the topics of love and lust in their varying forms suitable for discussion and inquiry in works that ranged from epic to drama, from love poetry to philosophical discourse. In devoting so much attention to *eros* these writers provide detailed information about their attitudes towards sexuality and its importance within their respective societies.

While it is true that some artwork and literature taken in isolation can give the impression that the Greeks lived in an uninhibited sexual environment, there were strict social and ethical codes in operation, with variations depending on historical context and the mores of the individual community or *polis*.[1] An important consideration about the cultural traditions and representations of sexuality in the ancient world is that, with very rare exceptions, they are conveyed to us by the thoughts and viewpoints of men.

From Homer onwards, the primary focus of Greek literature is the world of the male. A man was expected to be successful, to contribute to the life of his community and to protect his household and all its dependants. Only men could be active citizens, only men could provide leadership within and defence of the community. In regard to sexuality, being a man was equated with taking the active part in any relationship. While marital fidelity was essential for the female and ideally expected of the male, examples taken from literature consistently highlight sexual freedom for men. From the world of religion and mythology, Zeus and Odysseus could and did take lovers at will, while in the real world a married man could form a liaison with a prostitute.[2] The hiring of a *hetaira*, a female prostitute of the finest quality, was acceptable for the satisfaction of the male's need for sexual gratification as well as companionship and even intellectual discourse. Demosthenes writes: 'We have *hetairai* for delectation, slaves to see to our daily sexual needs, and wives to bear legitimate

1

offspring and to be faithful protectors of the households.'[3] This social reality explains why many of the ancient sources deal with sexual activity, lust and love between a male and a prostitute rather than between a husband and wife. The major deterrent to seduction of girls or adultery with women was the risk of reprisal from an aggrieved male party. Male same-sex relations have generated controversy (among ancient as well as modern writers) but there is universal agreement concerning the opprobrium incurred as a result of sexual relations between two adult males. Rape is occasionally alluded to in non-bellicose circumstances, and in literature there are frequent representations of the vulnerable girl who becomes the target of the male libido. The unprotected girl was regularly regarded as fair game, and in mores and legislation, the primary response to rape was presented in terms of the damage to the husband, father or guardian.

Women in Greece from the Archaic age (c. 800–480 BC) through to the Classical age (c. 480–323 BC)[4] could not participate directly in politics and rarely owned land or controlled inheritance.[5] Marriages among the aristocracy were usually arranged to ensure that familial, political and economic ties were maintained and promoted. The main functions of married women were to be dutiful wives, bearers of legitimate heirs and effective managers of households. Such a clear definition of the female's role was not restricted to the aristocracy. Even though the sources largely reflect the lifestyles and values of the upper class, Hesiod, for example, makes it clear that a wife was a necessity for the production of male offspring within lower socio-economic groups.[6] Not surprisingly, therefore, in a society that placed such importance on legitimacy,[7] women's lives were restricted in regard to what they could and could not do outside the *oikos*.[8] Similarly, contact with men other than one's husband or immediate kin was limited to the greatest extent possible.[9] The care a husband took in ensuring his wife's good behaviour reflected the basic premise that women needed to be supervised as much as possible.

The sexual dichotomy that stressed a woman's need to be chaste and maternal[10] while a husband could have sex with a variety of partners is not to suggest that all Greek marriages were devoid of love and desire. Homer's depictions of Hector and Andromache and Odysseus and Penelope illustrate intense and loving relationships within marriage.[11] The wedding hymns of Sappho, with their idealisation of the beauty and desirability of the bride and groom, while reflecting a similar romanticism, also indicate the importance of desire within wedlock. It is necessary, however, to note the impact of cultural, social and generic issues on such representations.

While it was socially acceptable in Archaic and Classical Greece to depict sexual congress with prostitutes in works of art and literature, it was not the case when it came to the respectable relationship between husband and wife.[12] For the ancient Greeks marriage represented duty to one's *oikos* principally through the provision of heirs. This in turn ensured that the family unit served the needs of the *polis* in the provision of citizens, soldiers, politicians and religious leaders. It should be pointed out, however, that in some non-personal literature there is evidence of sexual attraction within marriage: the *Lysistrata*, for example, is structured primarily around the theme of intense conjugal desire, but the conventions of the comic, with its emphasis on irony and parody, must be considered.

The Greeks recognised a clear division between one's private sex life and one's duty to the *oikos* and *polis*. One of the standard views of the state of being in love or desiring someone, denoted by the term *eros*,[13] was the possible danger of its destabilising consequences.[14] An obvious example of this is the story of the Trojan War. The attraction Paris had for Helen, inspired by the goddess Aphrodite, led to the abduction of another man's wife and a ten-year siege in which thousands of men died. Greek literature depicts the forces of *eros* as frightening, socially destructive and physically, emotionally and mentally debilitating. In this sense, the separation of the wife and children from the sexual activities of the slave-quarters, the brothels and the male drinking parties or *symposia*[15] ensured that the *oikos* and its most important members were protected from the potentially damaging forces of uninhibited sexual expression. The fear that a woman, if left unsupervised, would fall victim to the powers of *eros* is further reason to maintain this social and familial system. Ironically, men were able to enjoy a variety of sexual activities within a range of culturally ordained environments and with socially specified partners, but women were regarded as more wanton. Aristophanes' comedies provide images of the sex-addicted female,[16] while the myth of Tiresias gives an aetiological justification for the belief that women enjoyed sex far more than men.[17]

As a result of expansion during and after the foundation of Alexander's empire, families sometimes experienced dislocation and the *polis* began to change in composition and structure.[18] In view of the social changes of this age, it has been argued that in comparison to the women of the Archaic and Classical eras, those from the Hellenistic era (323–30 BC) enjoyed more freedom in the areas of politics, law, property and sexuality.[19] However, one should be wary of interpreting such advancements as indicative of a widespread change in attitude towards women and a movement away from the negative stereotypes that dominated the literature of the Classical age.

Male same-sex relationships were widespread in antiquity. There is an abundance of evidence taken from sources as diverse as Late Archaic and Early Classical poetry, Attic comedy, Plato, Aeschines' oratory and the *Greek Anthology*.[20] These sources depict a variety of attitudes and approaches towards the theme, ranging from intensely personal admissions, to comic mockery, to philosophical examination.

Relationships between males were structured around socially ordained behavioural patterns. Of key importance were the related issues of age and the sexual dynamics of the active and passive partner. These relationships usually occurred between an older youth or mature citizen and a *pais*[21] between twelve and seventeen.[22] The older male assumed the active role, designated by the

3

term *erastes* or lover, while the *pais* was passive and was called the *eromenos* or beloved.[23] Such a relationship is referred to as *paiderastia*, and the customs and laws associated with this varied throughout the Greek world.[24] The sexual boundaries and etiquette associated with the active and passive partner also applied to male–female relationships as is widely attested in artwork, with the male dominant and the female subordinate.[25] This does not mean, however, that the *pais* was regarded as a female substitute in terms of sexual activity. What was important was the maintenance of the active and passive roles. The Greeks made sure to depict, particularly in their artwork, the social differentiation between a *pais* – as potential citizen – and an inferior object of sexual gratification. Because of his future role in the *polis* the *pais* is depicted with respect in art. In Athenian red-figure pottery, for example, there are no conclusive examples of the *eromenos* as the recipient of anal or oral penetration,[26] for such demeaning roles are reserved in artwork and literature for prostitutes and slaves.[27]

Erotic relations between males were part of the educational process in many Greek societies, including Sparta[28] and Athens. Idealised depictions from Athens, literary and artistic, portray a careful courtship, in which the *pais* proved himself appropriately chaste and somewhat cautious, before the relationship progressed along spiritual and intellectual lines with the *erastes* instructing the youth in matters ranging from philosophy to the citizen's role in serving the state. The relationship between *erastes* and *eromenos* may thus be interpreted as part of the process of transforming a boy into a man. Although the relationship could sometimes entail a physical dimension, when the *pais* became a man, that side of the bond was expected to end, while the emotional attachment, ideally speaking, endured.[29] Following marriage, if he chose to, he could continue to pursue and love young men.

There is a paucity of source material about same-sex relations between females. Sappho's poetry is an intense and insightful presentation of love among women, her lyrics strengthened by the fact that we hear a female voice expressing female emotions. It has been posited that she was part of a female group or *thiasos*[30] at Mytilene on Lesbos. As part of such a circle, Sappho is sometimes envisaged as an educator who taught certain skills relating to married life, religious observance and literary and musical accomplishment.[31] Indeed, some of Sappho's lyrics[32] address the young women in the language of an *erastes* to an *eromenos*. Hence, in the Second Century AD, Maximus of Tyre compares her relationships with girls to those between Socrates and his *paides*.[33]

In the Classical age we have few female sources that deal with intense or erotic love for other females.[34] While Plato presents a positive glimpse of such female relationships in the *Symposium*,[35] he seemingly reneges in the *Laws*,[36] where he disapproves of sexual relations between two men as well as two women.[37] Asclepiades in the Third Century BC and Lucian in the Second Century AD continue to represent sexual relations between women as something either abominable or exotic and therefore intriguing, perverted and titillating.[38]

4

Finally, by way of background to the issues explored in Chapters III, V and VI, the importance of legislation on matters pertaining to sex, choice of partners and related issues needs to be addressed.[39] Due to the nature of the evidence, the focus will largely be on Classical Athens. The Greeks were wary of *eros* and the possible negative side effects it could unleash, particularly if its pleasures were over-indulged.[40] For this reason certain regulations, often in line with non-statutory moral traditions as well as law, were enforced to ensure that men and women acted with restraint and thereby were productive and helpful contributors to the wellbeing of the *polis*.

Greek laws were particularly harsh when it came to *moicheia*.[41] In Classical Athens a husband could kill an adulterer caught in the act or, alternatively, he could take him before the appropriate magistrates; if the adulterer admitted to the crime, he could be put to death, and if he denied the charge, he would be subject to a trial.[42] The woman involved would be punished through divorce and debarment from public religious activity.[43] The act was regarded by the Athenians as a crime, not on moral grounds explicitly, but because it was a potential source of public disorder and violence.[44] The importance the Greeks placed on *hubris*, the meanings of which range from an outrage in the eyes of gods and men, to the infliction of shame or humiliation upon an individual, is therefore often connected to laws dealing with rape and adultery.[45] In the case of the latter crime, it is the cuckolded husband who is the victim of *hubris*. Also of importance, however, are the sentiments contained in 'Xenophon's comment in the *Hiero* that the *moichos* destroys the *philia* between husband and wife.'[46]

It has been argued that rape might not have been regarded as a serious offence in comparison with adultery: the degree of *hubris* that the husband of the victim suffered was not as great as that endured by the man whose wife had allowed herself to be seduced by an adulterer.[47] Keuls, for example, argues that the act was 'committed not for pleasure or procreation, but in order to enact the principle of domination by means of sex,' and further that there was 'an unusual moral and legal tolerance of this offence'.[48]

To illustrate contrasts in sexual behaviour an obvious choice is to consider the case of Sparta. According to Xenophon, it was legal in Sparta for a man who decided not to cohabit with his wife but wanted offspring to choose a woman of good family and high birth and, if granted consent by the husband, to have children by her.[49] Xenophon claims this was instituted by Lycurgus in Archaic times, and he presents it as surviving as a feature of Spartan practice in the Classical era. He notes the importance of the husband's permission in such an instance and though the Spartiates' fellow Greeks were sceptical, one must be careful not to conclude that institutionalised polyandry existed within the Spartan community. The complexities of this particular community, with its focus on military discipline and preparedness, male leadership and the pressure to bear children to maintain cultural and social traditions, provide a context in which to assess wife-exchange. The unique circumstance of the

Spartans illustrates the perceived differences and overt tensions in the moral and associated cultural systems of various *poleis*.

Laws also governed same-sex male relationships and, as with all other legislation in Classical Athens, it applied to members of citizen families. Slaves could not court *paides*;[50] teachers and athletic trainers could not attempt the seduction of their students;[51] citizens could not seduce a *pais* under the age of twelve without incurring social opprobrium and, possibly, legal action;[52] prostitution was illegal for freeborn males of all ages (cf. 77).[53]

Rome

Roman attitudes, customs and institutions relating to matters sexual have many similarities to those of the Greeks, but there are marked differences. Much Roman literary source material was generated by the upper class (or their Italian and provincial counterparts), representing aristocratic and well-to-do values and lifestyle, although the voices of the lower classes can still be heard.[54]

The ideals of the *matrona* (a married woman, usually with children) and the *univira* (she who has known only one man, her husband) were held up for Roman wives to emulate, although, as in Greece, it was often an impossible image to attain and sustain.[55] Women from the aristocratic circles were expected to marry young,[56] sometimes to an older partner chosen for political, social, financial and family reasons,[57] and to produce heirs to continue the family or *gens*. They were expected to remain chaste and behave in a way that would not draw attention to themselves or bring disrepute to their husbands.[58] In the Early and Middle Republican eras the power of the husband and father as head of the household (*domus*) was total. The *pater familias* had ultimate authority (*patria potestas*) that extended to the power of life and death over the entire household, including his wife, children and slaves. The influential and powerful position men had in relation to their wives in the Middle Roman Republic is illustrated in the following words of Cato:

> If you had apprehended your wife in the act of adultery (*adulterium*),
> with impunity you could take her life without a trial; she, if you were
> committing adultery or if you were being adulterated, would not dare
> so much as touch you . . . (*ORF: Fr.* 222M)

Despite the power of the *pater familias*, Roman women did have more freedom compared to their counterparts in Classical Athens. While levels of independence depended on individual households and their heads, it appears that, among the aristocracy, *matronae* were allowed to socialise at mixed gatherings, exert control over their children's upbringing and, occasionally, but indirectly, influence politics. This autonomy was particularly characteristic of the *matronae* from the Second Century BC onwards and was essentially a consequence of Rome's expansion into Greece and the East. With husbands away on military and diplomatic service for extensive periods of time, women from all levels of the citizen classes had to take control of the *domus*, albeit temporarily in the majority of instances, thereby contributing to the erosion of the life and death authority of the *pater familias*.[59]

During this time, contact with Hellenistic culture had an impact upon Rome's social and cultural traditions, affecting the lives of men and women. Wealth poured into the city and along with it an increase in luxury items, slaves and a general love of things Greek.[60] As the leading families acquired more wealth through their involvement in military campaigns, the dowries that went with the women of these families ensured that they continued to live lives of luxury in their husbands' homes. They also enjoyed a social and financial independence that in turn ensured the continuation of a new trend towards quasi-personal autonomy.[61]

Instability caused by civil and foreign conflict from 90–30 BC had an impact on social as well as political and economic life. Many marriages were formed then broken on the basis of short- and long-term political allegiances. There are few cases cited of enduring marriages among the upper classes in this era. Some of the distinguished families of previous generations had died out or were in danger of extinction in this period. Heavy loss of life in aristocratic and Equestrian ranks in the Sullan Civil War (88–82 BC), the aftermath of Caesar crossing the Rubicon (49–44 BC), and the bloody purges following his assassination (44 BC) and the Triumviral regime (43–31 BC) had a devastating effect upon the great families. It is an era in which the names of upper class women are mentioned frequently in the writers. While some are mentioned simply as marriage partners, others are presented as strong minded and liberated women who appear not to have been dictated to by the will of husbands or guardians.

Poets, as well as legal and historical writers, describe extra-marital relationships across the class divide.[62] In the case of women, this sexual freedom was rarely recorded in a positive vein. At the core of Catullus' poetry is a relationship between a freeborn male and a freeborn married woman: the poet himself and his beloved Lesbia. Although still a subject of scholarly controversy, there is evidence within the corpus (especially Poem 79) that suggests that Lesbia is a sister of the controversial political figure, Publius Clodius Pulcer. The strongest candidate of his three sisters is the woman known as Clodia Metelli,[63] wife of the Consular, Metellus Celer. This woman was the subject of a virulent attack on her character and sexual morality in a speech delivered by Cicero, the *Defence of Caelius Rufus*, in 56 BC. This oration reveals a world of freethinking, free moving and independent upper class women who took lovers at will and who frequented pleasure resorts such as Baiae in Campania. In Lesbia we have the representation of a woman possessing the status of an aristocrat along with the sensuality of a female object of desire; in Cicero's Clodia Metelli we have the representation of aristocratic woman as slut.

Other writers provide further examples of the type. Sallust's portrait of Sempronia depicts a sexually liberated woman of high birth who 'had often committed many crimes of masculine audacity' (*Cat.* 25.1) and while references to Julius Caesar's list of affairs with married women (Suet., *Caes.* 50) are designed to impugn his reputation, they are further testimony to female sexual freedom. But we must remember that these are male views of a perceived increased female freedom and it is highly unlikely that women such as Clodia, Sempronia, let alone Fulvia[64] (wife of Clodius Pulcer, then Curio, and later the Consular and Triumvir, Marcus Antonius), are representatives of the majority of *matronae* at this time.

Such representations and anecdotes reveal male anxiety at any increased freedom of women. This apprehension is persistently depicted in Roman literature as dangerous and monstrous. The rhetorical style that regularly characterises accounts of such women reflects the fear or at least partial confusion that existed in the minds of some men when confronted with an exceptionally powerful woman. The moral reforms initiated during the Augustan Principate (28/7 BC–AD 14) also reflect increased trepidation about feminine sexual licence as well as concern for the general movement away from the austere values that typified pre-Hellenised Rome. In an attempt to restore the traditions of the past and to promote Senatorial and Equestrian eugenics, Augustus initiated moral and marital legislation that, in part, was designed to affect the private lives of men, women and the family in general.[65] These reforms also had an impact upon the literary expression of unacceptable *amor* in the form of censorship.[66]

The most significant legislation in terms of Roman sexuality and its expression in the Augustan age was the *Lex Julia de adulteriis* introduced in 18 BC. Under this law *adulterium* was a punishable crime, which incorporated *stuprum*; this entailed disgrace or defilement in connection with sexual activity.[67] The *Lex Julia* was not a novel development in Roman moral legislation. The Second Century BC had witnessed a succession of laws and edicts that attempted to address the growing moral turpitude overwhelming the Republic, culminating in the legislation of Sulla in 80 BC. Such legislation, by the very fact that it was imposed from above, was doomed to failure.

The *Lex Scantinia*, dating from the Republican age,[68] was designed to regulate sexual contact between men. The two main activities thought to be punishable were: (i) *stuprum* with a boy[69] and/or (ii) adult passivity.[70] Punishment of the active partner in an adult relationship may have also been part of the legislation.

These laws clearly forbade certain sexual acts and strictly regulated choice of partner: a married woman could only have sexual contact with her husband and an adult male could not 'have sex with another adult male'.[71] Domitian revived the laws around AD 85, indicative of the fact that they had been openly unobserved. Even during the reign of Augustus, the laws were flouted, as evidenced by the activities of the emperor's own daughter, Julia. Under the Julio-Claudians, sexual activity outside marriage by women of the aristocracy could and did lead to formal criminal trials at which the offences drew the additional charge of treason (*maiestas*). The celebrated trial of Aemilia Lepida in AD 36 involved one of the most powerful (and disliked) female members of the regime being arraigned on charges of sexual relations with slaves, based on reports by informers (*delatores*).[72]

Male citizens could visit brothels and have sex with slaves without breaking either the *Lex Julia* or the *Lex Scantinia*. Roman laws on morality only applied to relations between freeborn men, women and children. Even so, husbands could seek either immediate sexual relief or a long-term sexual relationship outside marriage.[73]

There are important differences between the male same-sex cultures of Greece and Rome. There was no initiatory or educational aspect in Rome compared to what existed in some parts of Greece. It was not legal for a Roman citizen to engage in a relationship with a freeborn youth. Under the *Lex Scantinia*, it was most likely illegal for a freeborn male to engage in a relationship or act with another freeborn male despite his assumption of either the active or passive role.[74] What was legally tolerable was the Roman citizen seeking gratification as the active partner with male prostitutes, slaves or foreign youths.

There is sporadic information about female same-sex relationships and practice in Rome and, apart from the scandalous episode of the Bacchanalian crisis of the 180s BC, there is no close female equivalent of the Greek *thiasos*. While we do not possess any eroticism penned by a Roman Sappho, there is inscriptional evidence that may indicate same-sex female contact (cf. 98). Male views generally reflect contempt or voyeuristic interest in this aspect of female sexuality.[75]

Modern theories and approaches to ancient sexuality

An introductory discussion of the various forms of modern research on ancient sexuality and interpretative methodology is almost as daunting as outlining certain historical and cultural developments in antiquity. It is necessary, however, not only to better understand the scholarly analyses themselves, but also to gain further insight into specific aspects of Greek and Roman sexuality. Two theoretical schools of interpretation have been selected on the basis of their incomparable contribution to the field: feminist and Foucauldian theory.

To define feminist theory can be a difficult task because of its ever-expanding sub-groups. In 1973 a special issue of the journal *Arethusa* was devoted to studies of women in Greece and Rome. Pomeroy's *Goddesses, Whores, Wives, and Slaves*, first published in 1975, also motivated feminist scholarship in the Classics to a significant degree, although the work was not overtly political in either approach or agenda.[76] Others soon followed and continued to elaborate on Pomeroy's work by furthering our understanding of women's lives in antiquity. In more recent times, the early feminist scholarship of Pomeroy and Lefkowitz has been augmented by the more candid application of feminist critique and theories to ancient texts by scholars including duBois, Hallett, Keuls, Loraux, Richlin and Skinner.[77]

Richlin writes of revisionist and activist feminist scholarship. The first continues to make women in antiquity 'visible' in as truthful and rigorous a way as possible.[78] The second utilises information about women and the representation of them in antiquity to challenge accepted canons of historical belief[79] and to promote such research in the teaching of Classics.[80] Both approaches have had an impact on related fields, most notably Gender Studies, which, in relation to Classical Studies, examines 'ways in which the nature of women and men was imagined, constrained, and to a degree determined in ancient Greek and Roman culture'.[81] The electronic age has seen the arrival of scholarly and accessible internet sites that focus on gender in antiquity: by way of example, *Diotima: Materials for the Study of Women and Gender in the Ancient World*, launched in 1995.

To better understand the hesitation some scholars exhibit towards feminist research in the field of Classical Studies, note the cautionary advice of Nikolaidis, who suggests that feminist readings 'sometimes seem to distort the historic realities by retrojecting . . . conditions and understandings of our own era – more specifically of the western societies of our own era – to an ancient culture more than two millennia back.'[82] While such cultural agglomerations are not the exclusive domain of feminist scholars (as Keuls has demonstrated with examples of those who could not be regarded as feminists),[83] it calls to mind the works of those researching such volatile topics as matriarchy who have at times produced distorted views of ancient societies.[84] As Pomeroy has observed, one must be careful about reaching conclusions about women's lives in antiquity based on the presence of goddesses in belief systems and the various ritualistic roles of women in worship.[85] Culham adds that 'it has recently been noted that the depiction of goddesses and similar figures might be evidence for contemporary fantasy and nothing else.'[86] Despite the cautions of Pomeroy and Culham, these more unruly approaches (sometimes of a populist nature) may have contributed (in part) to reactions described by Richlin as 'ranging from bemused to hostile'.[87] Such works, and those that assume overly idealistic or negative positions in regard to facets of Greek and Roman culture, and which do not address cultural and historical specificities, have at times marred acknowledgement of the academic rigour of (the best) feminist and gender studies. The latter include works that have placed significant emphasis on (particularly) women's experiences in antiquity, be they of a literary or mythological nature, such as stories of rape and violence, or sociological and legal documents. Feminist research in the discipline of Classics has changed the way both scholars and undergraduates now approach the representations of women, establishing (and urging) readings that do more than explicate philological concerns in order to lay emphasis on the realities of ancient woman's 'lived' experience.

The theories of sexuality espoused by the French poststructuralist[88] Foucault (1926–84) require attention. Foucault's three-volume work, *The History of Sexuality*,[89] has had a profound and controversial impact on the Humanities, especially in his native France and, in the English-speaking world, most notably in the United States. His second volume, *The Use of Pleasure*, deals with the ancient world and further explores the theory postulated in the first volume that 'sexuality' is a modern construct that had no social or cultural reality before the beginning of the Nineteenth Century. 'Homosexuality,' 'heterosexuality' and 'bisexuality' are equally as modern and equally meaningless when applied to the sexual experiences of ancient Greece and Rome. A culturally created sexuality (the constructionist theory) is one removed from nature, from the individual and his/her inner-self (the essentialist theory). Attraction, courtship and the physical expression of desire in Classical Athens were, according to the constructionist theory, motivated and conditioned by the cultural, political and social institutions in place. Halperin, a leading exponent of Foucauldian theory, writes:

> Sex in classical Athens . . . was not . . . simply a collaboration in some private quest for mutual pleasure that absorbed or obscured, if only temporarily, the social identities of its participants. On the contrary, sex was a manifestation of personal status, a declaration of social identity; sexual behaviour did not so much express inward dispositions or inclinations (although, of course, it did also do that) as it served to position social actors in the places assigned to them, by virtue of their political standing, in the hierarchical structure of the Athenian polity.[90]

Other Classicists who have utilised Foucauldian theory include Zeitlin and Winkler,[91] and much criticism has been directed against their varying schools of (Foucauldian) thought, with Richlin (perhaps) the strongest opponent in terms of Classical Studies.[92] Richlin is of the opinion that Foucauldian scholars, while inspired by feminist research in the formulation of ideas and arguments, have either ignored or downplayed its role in and significant contribution to postmodernism. Related to this issue is the Foucauldian focus on male sexuality: homosexuality in Halperin's book, according to Richlin, is male homosexuality, just as sexuality in Foucault's work is equated with male sexuality.[93] Richlin also argues that Foucault and subsequent scholars tend to bracket 'off cultures with an explicit valorization of the studied culture, as opposed to our own.' Richlin identifies this theoretical problem as particularly prevalent in the work of Winkler 'which blurs Athens into what he calls variously "ancient" or "Mediterranean" culture, positing its structural identity with modern "Mediterranean" culture and its opposition (and superiority) to what he dubs "NATO" culture'[94] (a criticism of some feminist studies voiced by Nikolaidis). This is related to a third area of contention, namely the almost

11

exclusive focus on Greek, especially Athenian, culture without significant application of Foucault's theoretical premise to the Roman world. Finally, Richlin rejects the underlining premise of the constructionist argument that 'homosexuality and heterosexuality . . . are modern, Western bourgeois productions. Nothing resembling them can be found in classical antiquity.'[95]

This is not to suggest, however, that there are two opposing camps endorsing the incompatibility of Foucauldian and feminist research, although Richlin would argue otherwise.[96] Foucauldian theorists, for example, have worked in both an academic and political manner akin to the revisionist and activist methodologies underpinning feminist scholarly objectives. In regard to the approach of academic activism in relation to Gay Studies, both Winkler and Halperin have donated proceeds from each of their books to the San Francisco AIDS Foundation.[97] Foucauldian scholars have also generated new approaches to feminist interpretations as evidenced in the work of Zeitlin, Skinner and Konstan.[98] Furthermore, as Skinner argues, both 'Halperin and Winkler proclaim themselves intellectually indebted to the feminist critique of gender difference' and when 'dealing with the asymmetrical organization of power relations between the sexes in Greek culture, each explicitly adopts a feminist viewpoint.'[99] Such an acknowledgment, albeit knowingly controversial, is made with caution for although Skinner does not address claims of Foucault's scholarly and personal misogyny,[100] she does address both Winkler's and Halperin's own admissions of interest in 'phallic issues'.[101]

Foucauldian scholarship has not only come in for attack by feminist writers and researchers. Thornton, for example, in his work on Greek and Roman sexuality has pointedly contested aspects of this particular school.[102] Despite the contentions endemic in Foucault's work and the work it has subsequently inspired, it has provoked a notable increase in scholarly interest in the area of Greek and Roman sexuality, particularly in feminist and gay studies (more so than Lesbian Studies),[103] which in turn has produced some exciting endeavours in the field.[104]

Notes

1 It is unwise to generalise about Greek culture, as there are significant variations in each state, particularly in pre-Hellenistic times. In the Archaic era, for example, the literary sources are almost exclusively non-Athenian, while in the Classical age, Attic sources dominate.

2 Prostitution flourished in Greece from the early Archaic period. On male and female prostitution, cf. Dover 1978 (19–109); Keuls (153–203); Halperin 1990 (88–112); Kurke (106–50).

3 Dem. 59.122.

4 For an introduction to women in ancient Greece and Rome, cf. Pomeroy 1975; Cantarella 1987; Lefkowitz and Fant; Fantham et al.; Blundell.

5 There are exceptions: Spartan aristocratic women did have access to land and inheritance; likewise, the women of Gortyn (also from Dorian stock) enjoyed a less restrictive lifestyle to women in other parts of Greece. The latter inherited property and possessed various economic rights, especially in relation to land.

6 Cf. *Th.* 603–12. Hes. warns would-be bachelors that they will face old age without a son to care for them and inherit their property.

7 One example of the social and political importance of legitimacy is the issue of citizenship in Periclean Athens. Likewise, in Sparta, the rigid three-tiered social system meant that the proven legitimacy of Spartiate children was of paramount importance to the survival of the culture.

8 This is not to argue that women lived unhappy, entirely secluded lives. The ancient sources, while specifying what women were not permitted to do in Athens, also indicate a range of permitted activities. These activities included the daily tasks of women from the lower socio-economic groups meeting to draw water from public wells, which could have augmented social discourse (but also sexual harassment). Women also participated in religious rites as well as familial activities such as weddings and funeral processions.

9 Note the caution offered by Halperin: 'the seclusion of women was more likely to have been an upper-class ideal than a social reality, however' (1990: 92).

10 Pericles' 'Funeral Oration' (Thuc. 2.45.2) presents a powerful image of the role the wife (in this instance, the war widow) and mother is expected to play in the Athenian *polis*: she is to be neither praised nor criticised.

11 While there are no references to prostitutes in Homer there are concubines (captured in war).

12 Cf. Bing and Cohen: 'nowhere in Greek antiquity is love poetry addressed to a spouse' (3).

13 For a concise discussion of *eros*, cf. Dover 1978 (42–54). The definitive exploration of *eros* and its diverse meanings (as primarily applied to male–male relations) is Pl.'s *Smp.*

14 Cf. Carson; Thornton 1997; Calame.

15 Prostitutes were present at the *symposia*. On this topic cf. Murray 1983 (257–72); Bowie; Murray 1990; Percy (116–21). Cf. also **Illustrations 7 and 10**.

16 Cf., for example, *Lys.* 133–35; *Th.* 477–96; *Ec.* 877–1111. Cf. also, Anonymous, *AP* 10.120:

> Every woman loves sex more than a man does. Out of sense of shame [*aidos*]
>   she conceals the goad of *eros*, even though she is maddened by desire.

17 When Zeus and Hera wish to resolve an argument about which gender enjoys sex the most, they call on Tiresias who had spent seven years of his life as a woman. Tiresias explains that if sexual pleasure were divided into ten parts, one part would be allocated to the male and nine parts to the female (Apollod., *Lib.* 3.6.7). Cf. also Hyg., *F.* 75; Ov., *Met.* 3.318–38. On Tiresias, cf. Loraux 1995; Gantz 528–30.

18 Admittedly, this era was one of immense political and social upheaval but, nevertheless, certain parts of Alexander's empire maintained the traditional *polis* system. States like Rhodes, for example, experienced the retention of autonomy and traditional institutions.

19 On Hellenistic Greece, cf. Burnstein; Pomeroy 1990.

20 Based on Dover 1978 (9). For the categories and an excellent discussion of them, cf. Dover 1978 (9–15). Much of the source material comes from Athens in the Classical period. Consequently, the main points herein refer to this *polis* in the Late Archaic, Classical and Hellenistic eras, unless specified otherwise.

21 Dover notes that the word *pais* means much more than 'boy' and can denote "'child,' 'girl,' 'son,' 'daughter,' and 'slave'" (1978: 16). Cf. also Golden 1985.

22 Dover states that the *pais* had usually 'attained full height' (1978: 16). Cf. also Cantarella 1992 (37–44) for a discussion of age and its upper and lower limitations; Golden 1984; Halperin 1990 (55).

23 For discussion of active and passive roles, cf. Halperin 1990 (30–33).

24 X. (*Lac.* 2.12–14) notes that the Greeks were aware of the variation in the rules and regulations of pederasty in individual states. Cf. Bremmer; Halperin 1989; Shapiro.

25 Cf. **Illustrations 7 and 8**.

26 Cf. Dover 1978 (99–102); Kilmer 1993 (22–25); Shapiro (55–58). Likewise, Dover points out that 'the protection afforded to freeborn boys by the law on hubris is reflected by the rarity of homosexual assault in the visual arts' (1978: 93). Intercrural copulation between males is represented in artwork; cf. Dover 1978 (98–99); Kilmer 1993 (16–21).

27 As with the paucity of written and pictorial information documenting sexual activities between husband and wife, there are limitations when it comes to the depiction of the same between males. Cf. Cantarella 1992 for a brief discussion of the possibility that anal intercourse was part of male–male relations. A pertinent comparison is made with sex between husband and wife and its literary and artistic expression: 'when one thinks about the iconography of heterosexual relationships . . . penetration is only represented when the woman is a courtesan. Relations with "respectable" women leave out all reference to the sexual act. Would anybody dream of thinking, on this basis, that Greeks had sex only with courtesans, and not with their wives?' (25). Cantarella 1992 (25–27) also discusses the graffiti of Thera, the comedies of Ar. and homoerotic verse contained in the *AP* where there are specific references to anal intercourse.

28 In addition to Attic comedy and the works of Pl., X. (*Lac.*) and Plut. (*Lyc.*) are major ancient sources on Spartan pederasty. Cf. also Cartledge 1981a; Percy (73–92).

29 As Dover observes: 'Homosexual relationships are not exclusively divisible, in Greek society or in any other, into those which perform an educational function and those which provoke and relieve genital tension. Most relationships of any kind are complex, and the need for bodily contact and orgasm was one ingredient of the complex of needs met by homosexual eros' (1978: 203). There are instances of long-term male–male relationships; Aristogeiton and Harmodius (Thuc. 6.53–59) and Pausanias and Agathon (*Smp.* 193c) are two examples of lasting couples.

30 On the *thiasos*, cf. Cantarella 1992 (78–86); she (79) observes that these were present in other parts of Greece, including Sparta. On female–female relations in Sparta, cf., Plut., *Lyc.* 18; also Brooten.

31 There is, however, no conclusive evidence within the context of her poetry to sustain the theories concerning Sappho's role as either a member of a *thiasos* or as an educator. Cf. H. N. Parker 1993; Bennett.

32 Sapph.'s poetry is, like much ancient lyric, the subject of some debate over whether or not it is autobiographical.

33 Dover 1978 (174); cf. Max. Tyr. 18.9.

34 Cf. Erinna (97).

35 *Smp.* 191e.

36 *Lg.* 636c.

37 Such an apparent turnaround is not necessarily the undoing of earlier views (cf. Winkler 1990b: 173). Winkler writes on the rejection of pederasty as 'unnatural' in *Lg*: 'It was clearly a thought-experiment of the same order as censoring traditional poetry in the *Republic*, one that went utterly against the grain of the values, practices, and debates of Plato's society. These speculations of Plato are unrepresentative – not the opening move in a new game of moralizing sex – and hence are only obliquely useful for writing the history of sexual mores and practices.' (173).

38 Cf. 100 and 102.

39 Cf. Harrison; Dover 1973 (61–62); Dover 1978; Cohen 1984; Winkler 1990b; Cohen 1991.

40 As Winkler writes in relation to the image of the destructive eros as symbolised in his example from X., *Mem.* 1.3.11 (the man who kisses Alcibiades' son will become a slave and will spend much money on harmful pleasures): 'The hyperbolic features of this cultural image make it easier for us to detect its unreality and to see its use as a weapon of self-discipline' (1990b: 189 n. 53).

41 The term *moicheia* is not limited to adultery, nor is adultery always defined by the term in the sources (cf. Cohen 1991: 98ff.).

42 Cohen 1991 (113). If he were found guilty after a trial, the adulterer was then executed. Cf. Cohen 1991 (122ff.) for an examination of the law against adultery as it applied to the adulterer who is not caught in the act.

43 Dem. 59.87. Cf. Cohen 1991 (224).

44 Cohen 1991 (124).

45 Arist. (*Rh*. 1378b) defines *hubris* as an act that dishonours or humiliates the victim for the offender's pleasure.

46 Patterson (124). Cohen (1991) also notes the passage from X., *Hier.*, relating it to the case of Euphiletus, accused of murdering his wife's lover, Eratosthenes (Lys. 1).

47 Cf. Cole; Harris.

48 Keuls (47, 54); cf. also Harris. For relevant passages and a fuller bibliography on what is a controversial debate, cf. 105–107.

49 X., *Lac*. 1.8.

50 Aeschin. 1.138–39; Plut., *Sol*. 1.3.

51 Aeschin. 1.9–12.

52 Aeschin. 1.15–16. Cf. Cohen 1987; Cantarella 1992 (42–44).

53 The prosecution speech against Timarchus by Aeschin., delivered in the Late Classical age (346 BC), is the most informative source on this issue (cf. Dover 1978: 19–109).

54 As in Classical and Hellenistic Athens, at Rome the exception is the writers of comedies who come the closest to capturing the world of ordinary citizens and their families.

55 As noted in Fantham et al. (211), unlike Archaic or Classical Greece, Rome had no written record of its history until the mid-Third Century BC. When women of the first 500 years of Roman history began to be written about, they were regularly fitted into types, namely the ideal or role model – women such as Lucretia (cf. Liv. 1.57–58) and Cornelia, mother of the Gracchi – and those who represented the bad examples of womanhood. On Roman womanhood and the family, cf. Dixon 1988; Dixon 1992.

56 Cf. Hopkins; Treggiari 1991 (398–403).

57 Cf. the example of Pompey the Great (Plu., *Pomp*. 48, 53, 55).

58 Cf. Prop. 4.3, the story of Arethusa waiting faithfully and anxiously for the return of her husband, Lycotas; 4.11, the Cornelia Elegy, where all the womanly virtues of chastity, motherhood and maintenance of a blameless reputation for herself and the house are epitomised.

59 Cf. Fantham et al. (288–89).

60 Plb. (31.25.4–7) traces the passion of young men at Rome for boys and courtesans, banquets and riotous living to the impact upon society of contact with the Greek world from the Third Macedonian War down to the Sack of Corinth and Carthage (167 to 146 BC); Calpurnius Piso (Consul 133 BC) argued that the overthrow of modesty (*pudicitia*) could be traced from the Censorship of Messala and Cassius, 154–149 BC (cited by Pliny *NH* 17.244); Liv. (39.6.7–9) attributes the decline to the return of Vulso's army from Asia in 187 BC, from which time luxury household items, modes of dress, flute-players, cooks and the like led to excessive *luxuria*.

61 Cf. Fantham et al. (263) on dowries in the Second Century BC and later.

62 On the 'new woman' of the Late Republic, cf. Fantham et al. (280–93); Lyne (13–17).

63 Cf. Neudling 97–98; Rankin 1969; Wiseman 1969; McDermott; Hillard; Wiseman 1974; Wiseman 1975; Levens; Skinner 1983.

64 On Sempronia, cf. Sall. *Cat*. 24.3–25. Unlike Clodia, Fulvia married several times and was active not only in politics, but even in military matters in the turbulent years of the early Triumvirate. Her legendary cruelty matched that of her husband, Antonius the Triumvir, especially her mistreatment of prominent women appealing against severe taxation in 42 BC. When Antonius was engaged in an affair with the *hetaira* Glaphyra (whose son he made ruler of Cappadocia), she attempted to seduce Caesar Octavian (Augustus); his reaction is contained in a poem by him, related by Mart. (11.20.3–8):

> Because Antonius fucks Glaphyra, this penalty on me
>> Fulvia imposes: that I should now fuck her.
> That I should fuck Fulvia? What if Manius were to implore me
>> that I bugger him, would I do it? I don't think so, not if I'm wise.
> "Either fuck, or let us fight," she says. What is there dearer than life
>> itself than this cock of mine? Let the trumpets sound!

The subsequent war Octavian waged against her and Lucius Antonius resulted in her defeat and retirement to the East.

65 As Fantham et al. (212) note, the changes were apparent as well as genuine. Cf. Treggiari 1991 (509–10).

66 On the whole, the outpouring of amatory poetry by Gallus, Tib. and Prop. preceded the introduction of the moral legislation. There is a marked change of tone in the fourth book of elegies by Prop., published *c.* 16 BC (cf. n. 58). Scholars disagree about the date of the first edition of Ov.'s *Am* (possibly 25 BC) but Holzberg 2002 (32) puts a cogent case for it being around 15 BC with the revised edition possibly as late as 1 BC. Ov., therefore, publishes all of his amatory poetry in the climate of the aftermath of the Augustan moral reform. Ov.'s exile to Tomis on account of 'two crimes, a poem and an error' (*Tr.* 2.207) is evidence of Augustus' intolerance to poetry such as the *AA* (although written before the legislation) and its alleged promotion of immoral acts. Some scholars suggest that the erotic poetry of the Late Republic and Augustan ages was written in defiance of various social traditions and attempts at moral reform; cf. Lyne (65–81); Hallett 1984b (246). Cf. also G. Williams.

67 On *stuprum*, cf. Fantham 1991 (267–91). Cf. Adams 1982 (200–201); C. A. Williams 1995 (532–35); C. A. Williams 1999 (96–24).

68 Possibly 149 BC but this is contentious. Cf. Broughton with Patterson (459, 460 n. 3). Cf. also Boswell (65); Fantham (285–87); Cantarella 1992 (110–11).

69 Veyne (29) specifies the act of sex with a minor. Cf. also Gray-Fow (450); Richlin 1993a (528–29, 533).

70 Richlin 1992a (224); Richlin 1993a (530). For further contributors to this hypothesis, cf. Cantarella 1992 (245 n. 72).

71 Richlin 1993a (571).

72 Cf. Tac., *Ann.* 6.40.4.

73 For the discussion of the age of Roman men and women at marriage (which may be insightful in ascertaining the possibility of age-gaps between partners as a consideration in, particularly, male infidelity), cf. Saller; Shaw. Cf. also Hopkins.

74 Again this illustrates a difference between Athenian and Roman attitudes for, as Cohen notes: 'most scholars would agree that, in general, Athenians would have regarded the idea of sexual intercourse between two middle-aged male citizens as disgusting. Such conduct, however, was not felt to transgress the public sphere which the law protects' (1991: 175).

75 Cf. Hallett 1989; Brooten.

76 Cf. also Richlin 1992b, who notes that the study of ancient women as a legitimate academic pursuit 'began to happen in the 1960s' (xiii).

77 This note can obviously not list all works by these scholars. Of particular importance are the following: duBois 1988, 1995; Keuls; Hallett 1984a, 1989; Loraux 1993; Richlin 1992a, 1993b; Skinner 1985, 1986, 1987, 1993 (on the important issue of feminist critique and gender studies). Cf. also McManus.

78 Richlin 1992a (xxi) Cf., for example, Pomeroy, Lefkowitz, Fantham. Cf. also Rabinowitz 9–10.

79 Cf., for example, Skinner, Richlin.

80 Cf. Richlin 1992a (xxi). Cf. also Culham, who writes of activism and the need in feminist scholarship for the clear communication of information otherwise the work 'will be unable

to support modern women either by supplying them with validation of their own experience and interpretation or by bringing women into contact with their own past. The scholarship would also be much less immediately and directly applicable to the undergraduate curriculum, where the study of women in antiquity is so popular' (11).

81 Konstan 1992 (5). Yet, cf. Rabinowitz 10–11 for the critique of gender versus women's/feminist studies.
82 Nikolaidis (27).
83 Keuls 9–11. It should also be pointed out that Nikolaidis does not provide specific examples of allegedly recalcitrant feminist scholars.
84 Cf. Passman's essay in *Feminist Theory and the Classics* and Goldhill's review. In contrast, in the same work, cf. S. Brown's astute analysis of Gimbutas' 'soft' archaeology (254–56). For an objective view of the scholarly tradition of matriarchy, cf. Georgoudi.
85 Pomeroy 1975 (9).
86 Culham 14.
87 Richlin 1992a (xxxi).
88 Halperin refers to Foucault as a 'philosopher and historian' (1990: 6).
89 Foucault 1978, 1985, 1986.
90 Halperin 1990 (32).
91 Cf. Halperin, Winkler and Zeitlin 1990; Winkler 1990a.
92 Richlin 1991, 1992a (xxii–xxvi), 1998. Cf. also Foxhall. For a response to Richlin and to the whole constructionist/essentialist debate among Classicists, cf. Skinner 1996.
93 Richlin 1991.
94 Richlin 1992a (xxv).
95 Halperin 1990 (7).
96 Cf. Paglia who attacks Foucault and his academic advocates, particularly Halperin.
97 Cf. Skinner 1996. Cf. Winkler 1990a; Halperin 1990.
98 Zeitlin (with Halperin and Winkler); Skinner 1993; Konstan 1994.
99 Skinner 1996.
100 Cf. Macey (55, 455).
101 Winkler 1990a: 206. Cf. Skinner 1996.
102 1991a, 1991b.
103 'Literally inaudible. The word "lesbian" does not appear in Halperin's Index, nor is there a discussion of lesbianism per se anywhere in his text, despite the title of his book' (Richlin 1991: 176).
104 Cf. Larmour et al., *Rethinking Sexualities: Foucault and Antiquity*.

I

THE DIVINE SPHERE

Representations of the gods in both Greek and Roman literature serve a variety of functions, from explaining such diverse issues as racial origins and conquest through to providing aetiological explanation and justification for sexual mores and behaviour. This is not to argue, however, that their worship as credible and omnipotent beings was irrelevant: as figures of cult, the gods held a revered presence in the lives of the ancients.

This chapter treats the literary depictions of the gods and reveals that, when it comes to sexuality, they are not so much figures of worship as characters in works of art that encapsulate and symbolise psychological and emotional conditions.

The major gods of the Greek and Roman pantheon embody significant facets of sexuality, ranging from states of virginity (Artemis/Diana) to mindless sexual ecstasy (Dionysus/Bacchus). The most potent representatives of sexuality, however, are Zeus/Jupiter; Aphrodite/Venus and Eros/Amor. Passages 1 and 2 are chosen from epic and set the scene for the chapter from both a Greek and Roman perspective. In 1 Homer depicts Zeus, the all-powerful being, as displaying seemingly total freedom in the field of amatory pursuit. Yet despite his list of conquests (*l.* 312–28), he is still capable of being held accountable by his wife and falling victim to her womanly wiles. 2 illustrates the continuing influence of Greek mythology and symbolism in Roman epic: Jupiter is the Roman equivalent of Zeus whose powers in erotic matters are all encompassing. This second passage demonstrates the ability of male gods to seduce, abduct and rape immortal and mortal women alike.

The gods also provide aetiological examples for same-sex relations between males, as illustrated in the stories of Zeus' desire for the mortal boy, Ganymede. These have been utilised by authors to explore the nature of attraction and sexual preference and to provide a justification for boy-love, as will be seen in the introduction to Chapter 5.

Aphrodite/Venus is the embodiment of sexuality. Though depicted in some literature, such as *Odyssey* Book 8 and *Homeric Hymn* 5, as daughter (of Zeus) and wife (of Hephaestus), she nevertheless displays a sexual behaviour and freedom befitting a male. She is eternally 'laughter-loving', a testimony to the joys of love and desire she inspires, and is at times a champion for the despondent mortal as shown in the poetry of Sappho (4) and Tibullus (9). Hesiod (3) and Euripides (6) reveal the more threatening side of the goddess' gifts of desire with emphasis on the potential for disaster and destruction inherent in unbridled love and passion.

18

While Eros/Amor/Cupid is often closely aligned with Aphrodite/Venus, in the earliest extant account of his birth (3), Eros is displayed as a majestic, mysterious force, born at the dawn of creation. In subsequent works he becomes the child of Aphrodite and eventually assumes the characteristics of the cherub-like Cupid. This boyish representation is deceptive for, despite his state of perpetual childhood, he is ruthless when it comes to inspiring desire. Like his mother, this god is responsible for intense emotional pain as well as joy.

Setting the scene

1 Homer *Iliad* Book Fourteen Extracts: The Deception of Zeus

This is the earliest, genuinely erotic piece of literature from the Greek world (*c.* Eighth Century BC). (1) Such is the nature of its content, it provides a programmatic introduction to the collection as a whole. There are many elements in evidence: the cunning of the woman as user of her allure for gain rather than for erotic pleasure; distrust between husband and wife within a long-established relationship; jealousy and resentment; adornment; incest; rape and seduction; male promiscuity and insensitivity; the essential power of *eros*.

The gods have taken sides in the Trojan War. Zeus has been favouring the Trojans, while his wife (and sister) Hera has been supporting the Greeks. At this juncture Hera pursues a course of action to exploit Zeus' weakness for sex in order to distract him from the war.

Golden-throned (2) Hera, standing on a peak, gazed outwards
from Olympus. Immediately she recognised Poseidon,
bustling up and down the battle in which men win glory,   155
Poseidon, her brother and brother-in-law, (3) and she was glad
    in her heart.
And she saw Zeus sitting on the topmost peak of many-fountained
Ida, and he was hateful to her in her heart.

Then the ox-eyed lady Hera considered
how she might deceive the mind of aegis-bearing Zeus.   160
In her heart this seemed to her the best counsel:
to go to Ida, after appropriately adorning herself.
If he were of a mind to lie in love beside her body,
she might pour a harmless and warm
sleep upon his eyelids and crafty mind.   165

She went to her bedroom, (4) which her dear son Hephaestus
had made for her, and she fastened the strong doors to their posts
with a secret bolt which no other god could open.
There, upon entering, she closed the bright doors.
With ambrosia she cleansed all stains from her   170

lovely skin, (5) and she anointed herself richly with olive oil,
ambrosial, sweet, a fragrant oil which she alone possessed.
If this oil were but shaken in the house of Zeus, bronze thresholded,
its fragrance would reach both heaven and earth.
With this she anointed her beautiful (6) skin,   175
and after combing her hair she plaited it, bright,
beautiful, ambrosial, the hair from her immortal head.
Around herself she put on an ambrosial dress which Athena
had made for her and had placed on it many intricate decorations;
and on her breast Hera pinned it with brooches of gold.   180
She adorned herself with a girdle of a hundred tassels
and in her pierced ears she put earrings, each with
three gems like mulberries, and much grace shone from them.
The bright goddess covered herself with a veil,
beautiful and newly made, which shimmered like the sun.   185
Under her shining feet she bound beautiful sandals.

When she had adorned her body with all these splendours,
she left her bedroom and, calling Aphrodite
away from the other gods, said to her:
"Dear child, would you obey me, whatever I command?   190
Or would you refuse me, angry at heart,
because I help the Greeks and you help the Trojans?"
Then Aphrodite, daughter of Zeus, answered her:
"Hera, queenly goddess, daughter of great Cronus,
say what you think. My heart tells me to do it,   195
if I can do it, and if it is a thing that can be done."

With deceitful thoughts queen Hera said to her:
"Give to me the powers of love and desire (7) with which
you subdue all immortals and mortal men.
For I go to the end of the all-nurturing earth   200
to see Ocean, father of the gods, and mother Tethys,
who nursed and cherished me well in their house,
receiving me from Rhea, when far-sounding Zeus
dispatched Cronus below the earth and the unharvested sea.
I go to see them and bring an end to their continual quarrels,   205
since for a long time now they have kept away from each other,
from bed and love, since anger has fallen upon their hearts.
If by words I were to persuade the heart of those two,
and send them to bed united in love,
I should always be called dear and be honoured by them."   210

Laughter-loving (8) Aphrodite answered her again:
"It is not possible or proper that I should deny your request,

for you sleep in the arms of Zeus most mighty."
She spoke, and from her breast she unfastened the many-coloured
embroidered girdle in which for her are contained all allurements;   215
in it is love, in it is desire, in it is lovers' conversation,
and persuasion that steals the wits even of the wise. (9)
She put this girdle in Hera's hands and addressed her:
"Take this and put it in your bosom, this many-coloured girdle,
in which all things are worked. I say that   220
you will not return unsuccessful in whatever you desire in your heart."

So she spoke, and ox-eyed queenly Hera rejoiced,
and smiling put it in her bosom.

Hera visits the god, Sleep, and persuades him (with the promise of one
of the Graces as his bride) to assist her in the deception.

Hera quickly came to Gargarus,
at the top of high Ida, and cloud-gatherer Zeus saw her.
Sexual desire (10) enfolded his cunning heart,
as when first they mingled in love, going to bed,   295
escaping the notice of their dear parents.
He stood before her and addressed her:
"Hera, where are you hurrying, having come journeyed down from
    Olympus?
The horses and chariot, on which you might ride, are not here."
Lady Hera thinking cunning thoughts addressed him: 300
"I go to the ends of the all-nurturing earth
to see Ocean, father of the gods, and mother Tethys,
who nursed and cherished me well in their house.
I go to see them and bring an end to their continual quarrels,   305
since for a long time now they have kept away from each other,
from bed and love, since anger has fallen upon their hearts.
My horses stand at the foot of many-fountained Ida,
my horses that will carry me over dry land and watery sea.
But now I make this journey down from Olympus because of you,
lest somehow you should be angry with me afterwards,   310
if I went to the house of deep-flowing Ocean without telling you."

Zeus the cloud-gatherer answering, said to her:
"Hera, you can go there another time.
As for you and I, let us enjoy ourselves, let us go to bed in love.
For never yet did sexual desire for goddess or mortal woman   315
pour round me and tame the soul in my breast, (11)
not even when I fell in love with Ixion's wife (12)

who bore me Peirithoos, counsellor equal to the gods;
nor when I loved Acrisius' daughter, Danae of the beautiful
    ankles, (13)
who bore Perseus, most glorious of all men;   320
nor when I loved the daughter of far-famed Phoenix, (14)
who bore to me Minos and godlike Rhadamanthys;
nor when I loved Semele, (15) nor Alcmene (16) in Thebes
who bore Heracles her strong-hearted son,
and Semele bore Dionysus, the joy of mortals;   325
nor when I loved queen Demeter of the beautiful hair; (17)
nor when I loved glorious Leto; (18) nor when I loved you. (19)
    Never yet did
sexual desire pour round me the way I love you now, and sweet
    desire seizes me."

Thinking cunning thoughts, the lady Hera addressed him:
"Most dread son of Cronus, what words you have uttered?   330
If right now you desire to go to bed in love
on the peaks of Ida, where everything is exposed,
how would it be if one of the immortal gods
saw us lying together, and went and told all the others?
I could not get up from the bed and return   335
to your house; it would be a shocking thing.
But if you really want to, and if it is dear to your heart,
you have a bedroom which your dear son Hephaestus
made for you, and fitted strong doors upon their posts.
Let us go there and lie down, since bed appeals to you."   340

Answering her, Zeus the cloud-gather said:
"Hera, don't be afraid that any god or man will see.
I will cover you with such a golden cloud
that through it not even the sun could see us,
the sun whose light is clearest for seeing."   345
He spoke, and the son of Cronus took his wife in his arms.
Under them the divine earth grew fresh grass
and dewy lotus and crocus and hyacinth,
thick and soft, which raised them up from the ground.
On that they lay and were clothed with a beautiful golden   350
cloud from which glittering dewdrops fell.

Notes

1 Cf. F. N. Forsyth; Lindberg (76–78).

2 *chrusothronos*: golden-throned; first of several epithets applied to Hera. She is also *boopis*: ox-eyed (*l.* 159, 222); *dia*: bright (*l.* 184); *meidesasa*: smiling (*l.* 223); elsewhere in Homer, she is *leukolenos* (white-armed).

3 Poseidon and Hera are siblings of Zeus.

4 This action sets in train the beautification process. Hera subsequently seeks the aid of Aphrodite and borrows her potent girdle or *kestos* (*l.* 214–23).

5 The adj. *himeroentos* is derived from *himeros* (desire for sex); cf. also *l.* 198, 216.

6 The adj. *kalos* is a constant in the depiction of beauty in Greek erotic literature; it carries connotations of goodness as well as attractive physical qualities.

7 The weapons of Aphrodite are *philotes* (love) and *himeros*. The former conveys notions of affection and friendship as well as love, while the latter is largely confined to sexual desire.

8 *philommeides* (laughter-loving) is a common epithet for Aphrodite.

9 The *kestos* contains erotic powers: *philotes*, *himeros* and *oaristus* (lovers' conversation), which augment *parphasis* (persuasion). On the *kestos*, cf. Cyran. 1.10.49–100 (Waegeman 195–221); Faraone 1990; Faraone 1992.

10 *eros* is a powerful, sometimes mindless, sexual desire. At the sight of Hera, Zeus is immediately seized by *eros*. The passion was the same as their first occasion of sexual union, a significant comparison, since it entailed incest between brother and sister and the deception of their parents (*l.* 294–96). The issue of incest vexed the ancients. Goodman notes that 'most of the Greek words referring to specific close-kin unions are . . . later in date and no general word for incest is found before the Byzantine period . . . Sexual relations involving parent and child were forbidden everywhere we have evidence; their occurrence in Greek myth generally evokes horror, yet the participants are sometimes marked as numinous by their transgression of the limits of human conduct. Siblings of the same father could marry at Athens, of the same mother at Sparta.' (753).

11 The Catalogue of Prior Conquests by Zeus (*l.* 317–27) is in tune with the behaviour of the heroes of the *Il.*, who narrate their ancestry and achievements on occasions both of confrontation and amity. Note that Zeus makes no distinction between those seduced and those taken in rape and conflates falling in love, being in love, with making love.

12 Dia. This is the only reference to Zeus being the father of Peirithoos; cf. Gantz (278, 718 ff.). On Ixion's attempted rape of Hera, cf. Apollod., *Epit.* 1.20.

13 Cf. Apollod. (*Lib.* 2.4.1) who says Zeus took the form of a shower of gold that streamed into her lap. Cf. 2 n.8.

14 Zeus assumed the shape of a bull to lure Europa, daughter of Phoenix, King of Phoenicia, then carried her off to Crete.

15 Semele was the daughter of Cadmus, King of Thebes. Desirous of making love to Zeus in his transcendent form, she was consumed by fire; cf. Gantz 472–79.

16 Alcmene, daughter of Electryon, King of Mycenae, and wife of Amphitryon, originally from Tiryns, later King of Thebes; cf. Gantz 374–78.

17 Demeter is a powerful deity of agriculture and, like Zeus and Hera, an offspring of Cronus and Rhea. On the incest, cf. n.10.

18 From the union with Leto (daughter of Coeus and Phoebe) came Apollo and Artemis.

19 Cf. Hes. (*Th.* 886–923) who places Zeus' union with Hera as the last in a series consisting of Metis, Themis, Eurynome, Demeter, Mnemosyne and Leto.

2 Ovid *Metamorphoses* 6.103–28: Divine Lusts

Ovid tells the tale of Arachne, a Maeonian (Lydian) girl, outstanding in the skill of weaving, who challenges Minerva (Pallas Athena), goddess of weaving and womanly skills, to a contest. She weaves stories of divine lusts, featuring seductions and rapes by Jupiter, Neptune, Apollo, Liber (Bacchus) and Saturn. Minerva, enraged at the perfection (and perhaps the content) of Arachne's work, tore it to shreds: the girl, in despair, attempted to hang herself, but the goddess transformed her into a spider. (1)

The Maeonian portrays the girl who was deceived by the image
   of a bull –
Europa. (2) You would have thought the bull a true one, the sea
   true as well, as
the girl was gazing back upon the land already left behind   105
and shouting to her companions, fearing the touch
of the leaping water and drawing up her timid feet.
Arachne also fashioned Asterie (3) in the grip of the wrestling
   eagle;
she fashioned Leda (4) reclining beneath the wings of the swan;
she added how, concealed in the form of a satyr,   110
Jupiter filled the beautiful Nycteidan (5) with twofold offspring;
how he was Amphitryon when he took possession of you,
   Tirynthia; (6)
how made of gold he dallied (7) with Danae; (8) as fire the
   daughter of Asopus; (9)
as a shepherd Mnemosyne; (10) a multi-coloured reptile the
   daughter of Deo. (11)
You, too, Neptune, changed into the shape of a fierce young
   bullock,   115
she placed next to the Aeolian maiden; (12) appearing as Enipeus
you begot the Aloidae; (13) as a ram you deceived the daughter
   of Bisaltes; (14)
and the golden-haired, most gentle mother of the corn
experienced you as a horse; (15) as a bird the serpent-haired mother
of the winged horse experienced you; (16) as a dolphin Melantho
   (17) experienced you.   120
All of these women she depicted with exact likenesses, and an exact
   likeness
of the locations. Phoebus is there in the image of a rustic farmer,
   (18)
and how now with the feathers of a hawk, now the skin of a lion
   (19)
he fared; how as a shepherd he dallied with Isse, (20) daughter
   of Macareus;
how Liber deceived Erigone (21) by means of false grapes;   125
how Saturn, in the form of a horse, begot Chiron endowed with a
   twofold nature. (22)
The outermost edge of the web, surrounded by a slender border,
consisted of flowers interwoven with clinging ivy.

Notes

1 On the myths and their variants, cf. Gantz; Robson; on the passage, cf. Anderson (151–71).
2 Cf. 1 n. 14.
3 Asterie, daughter of Coeus and Phoebe, was the sister of Leto (cf. 1 n. 18).
4 Wife of Tyndareus of Sparta who was seduced by Jupiter in the shape of a swan. Her children included Helen and the Dioscouri.
5 Antiope, daughter of Nicteus (or Asopus, *Od.* 11.260); she gave birth to twins, Amphion and Zethos, the builders of Thebes.
6 On Alcmene, cf. 1 n. 16. She is called Tirynthian after the epithet commonly applied to her son, Hercules (stepson of Amphityron of Tiryns).
7 The verb *ludere* means to dally with someone in an erotic sense, to sport, frolic; to deceive; also at *l.* 124.
8 The daughter of Acrisius and Eurydice. Delphi predicted that her son would slay Acrisius, who thus locked Danae in a chamber to prevent her impregnation. Jupiter lusted after her and visited her in the form of a shower of gold, begetting by her the hero, Perseus.
9 Aegina. Jupiter carried her off, begetting by her Aeacus, the ancestral hero of the island named after his mother.
10 Daughter of Uranus and Tellus (Gaia). A sister of Saturn (Cronus), therefore aunt of Jupiter (Zeus), her name means 'Memory'.
11 Here Proserpina (Persephone) is the daughter of Deo, but more commonly Ceres (Demeter) and Jupiter (cf. 1 n. 17). He came to her by night in the form of a dragon: the offspring of their union, Zagreus, was destroyed by Juno.
12 Canace, the daughter of Aeolus, bore Neptune some five sons. Ov. is the only author to mention the deception in this form.
13 Disguised as the Thessalian river god, Enipeus, Neptune mated with Iphimedeia and begot Otus and Ephialtes, the so-called Aloidae. Anderson notes that Arachne may have been mistaken, for 'their putative father was the giant Aloeus' (166).
14 Theophane. Neptune transformed her into a ewe, himself into a ram; from their union came the ram with the Golden Fleece, object of the expedition of the Argonauts.
15 Ceres (Demeter). Apollod. (*Lib.* 3.6.8) says that after intercourse with Poseidon (in which she assumed the form of a Fury), she gave birth to a horse, Arion.
16 Medusa. She was famed for her beauty (*Met.* 4.794–95) prior to being raped by Neptune in a temple of Minerva. Shamed by the pollution of her sanctuary, the goddess turned Medusa into a monster. When beheaded by Perseus, from her blood sprang Pegasus, the winged horse she conceived by Neptune.
17 The only allusion to this story.
18 Apollo was forced by Zeus to spend a year in the service of a mortal, Admetus, King of Thessaly, guarding his sheep.
19 No other source informs us of these escapades of Apollo.
20 Daughter of Macareus, King of Lesbos. Ov. appears to be the only source.
21 Daughter of Icarius of Sparta. 'These tantalizing details are unknown in any other source' (Anderson 167).
22 Phillyra, daughter of Ocean, lay with Saturn (Cronus) and gave birth to the centaur, Chiron. Ov. suggests neither rape nor deceit and none of the other versions contain these elements.

Aphrodite and Venus

3 Hesiod *Theogony* 188–206: The Birth of Aphrodite

Hesiod is the first extant source to tell of the birth of Aphrodite from the severed genitals of the sky god, Uranus. Gaia (Earth) bore her son and consort, Uranus (Sky), and together they produced the Titans, including the conniving Cronus. In addition to the Titans, Gaia bore monsters, creatures so hated by Uranus that he kept them in Gaia's womb by continual penetration. Gaia eventually persuaded Cronus to castrate his father, thereby severing Earth from Sky and establishing a new divine reign. (1)

. . . cutting off the genitals [of Uranus] with steel
[Cronus] threw them from the mainland into the surging sea,
and it carried them for a long time; around them a white   190
foam arose from the immortal flesh and from it a maiden
was born. To holy Cythera (2) she first
drew near, and from there came to sea-girt Cyprus.
She emerged, an awesome and beautiful goddess, (3) and all around
    grass
grew beneath her slender feet. (4) Gods and men call her
    Aphrodite   195
[and goddess foam-born and crowned Cytherea] (5)
because in the foam she was born.
And they call her Cytherea because she came to Cythera.
And they call her Cyprus-born because she was born in sea-girt
    Cyprus.
And they call her genital-loving because she was born from
    (severed) genitals.   200

Eros went with her (6) and beautiful Desire (7) followed her
immediately after her birth and as she entered the company of the gods.
From the beginning, among men and immortal gods
she possessed this honour and obtained this portion: (8)
the whisperings of girls, smiles, deceits,   205
sweet enjoyment, love and kindness. (9)

Notes

1 Cf. Sale; Thornton 1997.
2 The shrine of the goddess at Cythera was among the oldest and most renowned in Greece.
3 In this early representation of Aphrodite, she is endowed with two significant qualities. At the moment of her birth, she inspired awe (*aidoia*, deserving of respect), a term derived from **aidos** (that which causes shame or respect; dignity); cf. 6. She is also beautiful (*kale*), the quality for which she remains renowned in all subsequent literature.
4 The reference to the spontaneous growth of grass symbolises Aphrodite's role as a goddess of sexuality, intercourse and fertility.
5 Some regard this line as an interpolation.
6 Here Eros is not the child of Aphrodite.
7 Here Himeros is the deification of the concept of desire.
8 The honour (*time*) and the portion (*moira*, also fate, destiny), applying both in the eyes of gods and men, are the powers outlined in *l*. 205–06; cf. the description of their consequences in 5.
9 Cf. 1 (*l*. 214–17) for the powers embroidered on the *kestos* she lends to Hera.

4 Sappho *Poem* 1: A Hymn to Aphrodite

Sappho calls on Aphrodite and asks for her help. The goddess is presented – despite
the artistic or artificial nature of the piece – as a benevolent patron of her devotees,
amoral, approachable (yet still awesome), and willing to oblige an individual in the
successful pursuit of another. (1)

Seated on your multi-coloured throne, Aphrodite, deathless,
guile-weaving child of Zeus, I beseech you,
do not with satiety or pain conquer
my heart, (2) august one, (3)   4

but come to me here, if ever at other times as well,
hearing my words from far away,
having left your father's house,
golden you came   8

having yoked your chariot. Beautiful swift
birds (4) directed you over the black earth,
frequently beating their wings, down from the sky
then through mid air   12

and quickly they arrived. You, blessed one,
smiling with your deathless face,
asked what I had suffered this time, why
I was calling yet again   16

and what I wished most to happen for me
in my mad heart. "Who is it this time that I am to
persuade to take you back into her heart? Who,
Sappho, wrongs you?   20

And if she (5) flees now, she will soon be chasing you.
If she does not accept presents, she will give them. (6)
If she does not love you now, soon she will,
even if she is not willing." (7)   24

Come to me now, also, and release me from harsh
care. All the things that my heart
desires for me – fulfil. You yourself, be my
ally in this enterprise. (8)   28

Notes

1 Cf. Page 1955 (3–18); Castle; Segal 1974; Stanley; Friedrich (107–28); Marry; Giacomelli;
   Winkler 1981; Snyder 14–16; Winkler 1990a (168–76); Petropoulos; Robbins 1995;
   Wilson (21–34).

2 *thumos*: the heart as the seat of emotions, thoughts, passions; also soul or spirit; at *l*. 18 it is described as 'mad'.

3 Sapph. addresses Aphrodite as *potnia*; a formal title for goddesses and women, it emphasises the speaker's status as a suppliant.

4 *strouthoi* (pl.): Roman writers equate the *strutheum* with a bird known as the *passer*, famed for salaciousness and love of carnal pleasure (cf. Festus 410.17L; Cic., *De Fin*. 2.75; Cat. 2 and 3). It is later used as a euphemism for the penis (Adams 1982: 31–32). The image of these birds drawing her chariot adds a comic and erotic tone.

5 The gender of the object of desire is indicated only by the fem. participle *etheloisa* (willing).

6 Here *dora* refers to the gifts exchanged between lovers.

7 The imagery of hunter and hunted is indicative of the active and the passive in the love relationship. This situation is usually seen in male–female unions and in male–male ones (between the *eromenos* and the *erastes*). What to the modern eye may seem unequal is emphasised in the final image of the stanza, the girl loving even when unwilling.

8 The use of *symmachus* (ally) is a clear echo of the Homeric relationship between suppliant hero and patron divinity.

5 *Theognidea* 1386–89: The Power of Aphrodite

The poems known as the *Theognidea* are seen primarily 'as a representative cross-section of the elegiac poetry written for sympotic and other social settings in the sixth and early fifth centuries' (West 1994: xv). A common feature of the collection is poetry devoted to love and its effect. Here, the goddess is saluted as the beneficiary of Zeus' generosity and acknowledged as having power over the minds of mortals.

> Bred on Cyprus, Cytherean, weaver of deceptions, (1) what is this
>   extraordinary gift that Zeus, showing you honour, (2) has bestowed
>   upon you?
> You overwhelm the high-mindedness (3) of mankind and there is no one
>   in existence who has the strength or wisdom (4) enough to elude you.

Notes

1 Note the combination of epithets with which Aphrodite is addressed: *Cyprogene* (bred on Cyprus); *Cytherea*; and *doloplokos* (weaving deceptions, wiles). On the epithet *Cytherea*, cf. Morgan.

2 Cf. 3 n. 8. The *doron* (gift; cf. 4 n. 6) Zeus has granted by way of showing Aphrodite *time* (honour) is the power to control the minds of men at the expense of their wisdom and self-control.

3 *phrenes* (pl.): lit. 'the heart, centre of the breast'. The focus is on courage and high-mindedness, the essentials of manliness, which Aphrodite has the power to overwhelm.

4 *sophos*: wisdom is the skilfulness that comes from experience.

6 Euripides *Hippolytus* 1–50: Aphrodite, Pitiless in her Anger

Euripides portrays Aphrodite, and the force that she wields and embodies, as 'powerful and pitiless' (Barrett 155); on her capacity to inspire awe from the time of her birth, cf. 3 n. 3. The laughter-loving divinity of Homer is nowhere to be seen when faced with the folly and arrogance of Hippolytus. Spurning her in favour of Artemis is not the issue, rather the insulting manner in which he justifies his decision. Her response is a stark warning to humankind. The forces she embodies are as old as creation and are beyond the capacity of mere mortals either to control or resist, let alone defy.

Powerful and not without renown among mortals,
and in heaven as well, I am called Cypris. (1)
Of all those, who reside within the boundaries of Pontus
and of Atlas, (2) looking upon the light of the sun,
I grant precedence to those honouring my power,   5
but I cast down all who are arrogant towards me.
For the race of the gods possesses this in common:
they enjoy being honoured by humankind.
Soon will I demonstrate the truth of these words,
for Theseus' son, the Amazon's child, (3)   10
Hippolytus, foster-son of holy Pittheus, (4)
alone of the citizens of this land of Troizen, (5)
says I am the vilest (6) of deities.
He rejects sexual-relations and does not touch marriage, (7)
he honours Phoebus' sister Artemis, daughter of Zeus,   15
thinking her the greatest of deities,
and in the green woods, always keeping company with the virgin, (8)
he exterminates from the land all wild beasts with his swift hounds,
having fallen into an association beyond the mere mortal.
I bear them no grudge – for why should I care?   20
But for the offences he has committed against me, I will punish
Hippolytus this very day. Most (of what needs to be done)
I have proceeded with long since; I do not need to do much (more).
For when he came one time from Pittheus' house
to Pandion's land (9) for the purpose of witnessing the rites   25
at the holy mysteries, (10) his father's noble wife
Phaedra, (11) upon seeing him, was seized in heart
by a terrible passion (12) – through my plans.
Before she came to this land of Troizen,
adjacent to Pallas' rock itself, (13) to look out over this land,   30
she founded a temple of Cypris,
out of her love for a love overseas, and in future men will see the
goddess' precinct (14) as being established on account of Hippolytus.
But now Theseus has left the Cecropian land,
fleeing the pollution of the blood of Pallas' sons (15)   35
and sailed to this country with his wife,
consenting to a year's exile from his home; (16)
now, groaning and maddened with the
goads of passion, the poor woman perishes without
speaking of it – and no member of the household knows her disease.   40

But this passion of hers is not to end in such a manner,
for I will expose the affair to Theseus and all will clearly be
    revealed.
As for the young man who is so inimical to me,
his father will kill him with curses which the lord of the sea
Poseidon gave to Theseus as a privilege,   45
the right to call upon the god three times, never without effect.
Albeit honoured, she will still perish,
Phaedra. For I do not think her misfortune (17) more important
than that my enemies render me
justice (18) sufficient enough to satisfy me.   50

Notes

1 Because she was born on Cyprus.
2 Pontus (the Black Sea) represented the easternmost extent of the Greek world and Atlas its westernmost extremity, beyond the Pillars of Heracles.
3 Hippolytus was the son of Theseus and an Amazon, Hippolyte. On the occasion of Theseus' wedding to Phaedra, Hippolyte and her warriors arrived and were killed in the subsequent violence (Apollod., *Epit.* 1.16–17).
4 Pittheus was the father of Aethra, Theseus' mother (therefore, Hippolytus' great-grandfather).
5 Located in the Argolis in North-Eastern Peloponnese where Theseus spent time in exile; cf. n. 15.
6 *kakiste* (the worst, vilest) is the superl. of *kakos* (evil); note how Hippolytus deems Artemis *megiste* (the greatest) at *l.* 16.
7 *gamos*: a wedding or the state of wedlock. Hippolytus shuns both casual and socially sanctioned sexual unions.
8 *parthenos* refers to Artemis.
9 Pandion was a legendary king of Athens and synonymous with the land of Attica. There were two of them: Pandion I was the father of Procne and Philomela (cf. 104); Pandion II was the father of the Pandionidai – Aegeus, Pallas, Nisus and Lycus; the first of whom was the father of Theseus (cf. n. 15).
10 The Mysteries celebrated at Eleusis in Attica.
11 Phaedra, daughter of Minos and Pasiphae, sister of Ariadne (abandoned on Naxos by Theseus after his defeat of the Minotaur). Now married to Theseus, she bore him two sons, Acamas and Demophoon.
12 *eros*: also at *l.* 39, 41.
13 The Acropolis of Athens. The site of the temple of Aphrodite is not known.
14 Lit. 'the goddess', but here the precinct associated with her. Once the tragedy had unfolded, the people learned of her motive in dedicating the temple.
15 Pandion II had divided Attica between his sons. The sons of Pallas (the Pallantidai) opposed Theseus receiving his father's portion, during which conflict Theseus slew them. Polluted by this shedding of kindred blood, he consented to go into exile to be cleansed.
16 In this version, the exile is spent in Troizen, scene of the tragedy of Phaedra and Hippolytus.
17 *kakon*: an evil, misfortune; something of a contradiction in view of the honour that will accompany Phaedra in her destruction.
18 *dike*: not only 'justice', but the penalty entailed in its breach. E. highlights how relentless and devoid of pity Aphrodite is, but at the same time does not question the inherent justice of her position.

7 Nossis *Greek Anthology* 5.170: Nothing is Sweeter than Love

Nossis is one of the few female voices from antiquity. This poem is noteworthy for its contradiction of Sappho's view (12) of desire as a combination of sweetness and bitterness. (1) It reflects the naivety of a relatively inexperienced young woman, one who has tasted the joys but not yet the reversals that Aphrodite brings to the lover. Like Sappho (4), however, she acknowledges that the lover needs the patronage of Aphrodite in order to achieve those joys.

'Than love (2) nothing whatsoever is sweeter. All forms of happiness (3)
    rank second. Even from my mouth, I spit out honey.' (4)
Nossis makes this statement. But anyone whom the Cyprian does not
    love, (5) that girl does not know what blossoms roses are. (6)

Notes

1 Cf. Barnard; Skinner 1989, 1991a, 1991b.
2 *eros* here is gentle, albeit erotic, love rather than uncontrollable passion.
3 It is the notion of prosperity and the happiness emanating from being blessed with riches. Nossis is echoing the sentiments expressed by Sapph. in *Fr.* 16 (18).
4 Even the taste of honey cannot compare with *eros* for sweetness.
5 Aphrodite. The verb *ephilasein* conveys connotations of affection combined with love, rather than just the intensity of raw passion.
6 The rose is supreme among the flowers due to its beauty and its scent. A girl untouched by Aphrodite's favour has no experience or sense of appreciation of such beauty and delicacy: on roses and their association with beauty and beautiful girls, cf. Irwin. The allusion could be to the verses of the poet and refer to the quality of sensitivity required both of a lover and a reader (cf. Skinner 1989: 6–11; 1991a: 33).

8 Lucretius *On the Nature of Things* Book One Extracts: Invocation of Venus

Written in the Late Republic, this epic poem is an explication and eulogy of the teachings of the Greek philosopher Epicurus (341–270 BC). Lucretius calls upon Venus as his Muse. In view of the many attacks on Epicurus for allegedly describing the gods as inactive, devoted to pleasure and indifferent to the human condition, this invocation may seem surprising. As the deity who inspires sexual activity and procreation, Venus is vital to the process of creation; consequently her depiction is akin to a universal life force rather than as an anthropomorphic being dallying in love affairs. (1)

Begetter of the race of Aeneas, of both humankind and gods the
    delight, (2)
nurturing Venus, beneath the smooth signs of heaven, you who fill by
your presence the sea with ships, who fill the lands
with fruits, since through you every species of animate beings
is generated and, having grown, looks upon the light of the sun: 5
you, goddess, you the winds flee from, you the clouds of heaven
    flee from

and from your approach; for you the earth, manifold in its works,
sends up sweet flowers; for you the expanses of the sea laugh
and the peaceful heavens shine with widely diffused light.
From the moment the springtime features of the day are made
    manifest   10
and the fruitful breeze of the south, once liberated, blows strongly,
you, first of all, goddess, and your imminent entry, the birds of
    the air
signify, stricken to their very core by your power.
Next, maddened herds beat down the rich pasturelands,
and swim through swift-flowing streams for, captured by your
    charm,   15
each follows you eagerly, wherever you go to lead them.
In short, across seas and mountains and rapacious torrents
and the leaf-bearing homes of birds and green plains,
inflicting coaxing love (3) right through the breasts of every creature,
you bring it about that they eagerly beget generations, species by
    species.   20
Since you are she who alone governs the nature of things (4)
and since without you nothing is born into the bright regions of
    daylight
nor is made anything joyful and lovable,
I am keen to have you as my ally in the writing of my poem,
which I am striving to pen concerning the nature of things. . . .   25

In particular, grant my words, goddess, eternal charm.   28
See to it, in the meantime, that the fierce works of war
throughout every sea and land grow quiet and still. (5)   30
For you alone are able, with tranquil peace, to give delight
to mortal beings, since the fierce works of war are presided over
by Mars, powerful in arms, he who on your lap often
lays himself down, overwhelmed by the never-ending wound of love;
and so, looking upwards with smooth neck thrown back, he
    feasts   35
his eyes, avid with love, gaping open-mouthed at you, goddess,
and from your mouth hangs his breath as he reclines.
You, goddess, wrapping him from above with your holy body
as he reclines, pour forth sweet murmurings from your mouth,
glorious one, seeking peaceful calm for your Romans. (6)   40

Notes

1 Cf. R. D. Brown; Duff.
2 Note the two achievements with which she is credited: the begetting of the race that founded
  Rome and being the source of delight (*voluptas*) in mortals and immortals alike. To Lucr.,

the function of Rome, therefore, should be to ensure the attainment of the second. The concept of pleasure (*hedone*/*voluptas*) is at the heart of Epicurean teaching. One of the main areas of attack against the Epicureans was their espousal of *voluptas* as the ultimate 'good', that the happiness of humankind depended on it. Their view was not of a pleasure based on personal indulgence or gratification of the senses, but mental excellence and the pursuit of virtue as the only source of true happiness.

3 *amor*: love, especially carnal love (also at *l*. 34, 36). One would expect such a term, indicated by the adj. *blandus* (coaxing, using endearments), to be applied to humans not animals, but via this image Lucr. defines the urge towards procreation in all life forms as the work of Venus.

4 *De Rerum Natura* (*On the Nature of Things*) is the title of the overall poem (again at *l*. 25); it is pointedly linked in this line with the governance of Venus.

5 War is the enemy of pleasure. The poet hankers after tranquil peace and peaceful calm at a time when war, most likely civil, threatened the very continuance of the Roman state. One of the main war-makers of the era was Gaius Julius Caesar, a 'descendant' of Venus (cf. Suet., *Caes* 6).

6 Lucr. presents Venus and Mars as intimate and complementary: Venus, the goddess of love and beauty, soothes the violent war god. Lucr. establishes the linkage between love and war and the prosperity of Rome through the symbolism of Venus and Mars: the former is the mother of the Roman line, the latter the father of the first king of Rome, Romulus.

9 Tibullus 1.2.15–32: Venus Helps and Protects Lovers

Tibullus begins the poem with a call for more wine in order to alleviate his anguish and bring sleep. This is followed by a rage against the door that separates him from the object of desire, Delia, and in the lines quoted below he appeals to her for a meeting. Part of this appeal is an evocation of Venus as goddess of love and desire and the assistance she brings to one dedicated to the cause of love. (1)

You, too, without faint-heartedness, Delia, (2) deceive the guards.   15
There must be daring: to the brave, Venus herself lends aid.
She shows favour whether some youth attempts to storm a new
     threshold
or a girl (3) unlocks the door from its fixed pin;
she teaches how to creep furtively down from the soft bed,
she teaches how to be able to place a foot without making a sound,   20
how in the presence of a husband to exchange nods that 'speak'
and how to conceal seductive words beneath carefully prepared
     signals. (4)
She does not teach everyone this, but only those whom neither
     inertia holds back
nor fear restrains from rising during the murky night.
See! When, in a state of anxiety, I wander through the whole city
     in the shadows,   25
[in the shadows Venus makes me safe], (5)
nor is anyone allowed to encounter me who might wound my
     body   25a
with steel or, having seized my clothing, seek a reward.

33

Whoever is in the grip of love (6) can go safely with heavenly
    protection (7)
wherever he wants; he need have no fear of ambush.
Not for me do the numbing chills of a winter night render harm,
not on me does the rain fall with heavy downpour.   30
Hard work brings no pain, provided Delia unlocks the door
and wordlessly calls me with a click of her finger.

Notes

1 Cf. Putnam (61–73); Bright (133–49, 167–75); Murgatroyd (70–98); R. J. Ball (36–49).
2 On Delia, cf. Bright (99–183); Cairns (176–81); Lyne 1980 (159–63); Booth (xxxi).
3 *puella*: girl, a standard word in the verbal repertoire of the elegiac poet. In *l.* 17–18 Venus
   is linked with young lovers who especially need her aid: note how both youth and girl are
   eager for a successful outcome.
4 Note *l.* 18–22 and the emphasis on stealth. As goddess of love, desire and lust in all its
   manifestations, Venus will help in unions that are not socially sanctioned. She will assist in
   adultery and its concealment from a husband (*vir*) as referred to at *l.* 21. On the use of signals
   between lovers at social functions, compare with Ov., *Am.* 1.4.
5 A line is missing and the usual understanding is that Tib. would have written something
   close to what is suggested here.
6 *amor*: love, here an intense, passionate and irresistible desire or lust.
7 The patronage of Venus allows one to campaign and travel in safety. Furthermore, the lover
   is *sacer*, endowed with heavenly protection, one who is sacred 'because [he is] a devotee of
   Venus' (Putnam 65).

Eros and Amor

10 Hesiod *Theogony* 116–22: The Birth of Eros

This is the earliest account of the birth of Eros and the god himself is far removed from
his later depiction as a cute cherub with bow and arrow. Eros' birth from Chaos
emphasises his dark, primitive essence and he is presented as a powerful force of nature.
Hesiod's view of Eros is ambiguous; while extremely beautiful, he wreaks havoc on
the limbs (synonymous with manliness) and the mental resolve of men. (1)

In truth, the very first to come into being was Chaos, then afterwards
broad-breasted Gaia, (2) the unshakable abode of all the
[immortals who possess the peak of snowy Olympus,]
and murky Tartarus (3) in the depth of the wide-wayed earth,
and Eros came into existence, who is the fairest (4) among the
    immortal gods,
Eros the limb-relaxing. (5) He overpowers the mental strength of all
    gods and
all humankind, as well as the thoughtful counsel in their breasts. (6)

Notes

1 Cf. West 1966 (192–97); Vernant; Cyrino 1995 (45–49).
2 Gaia (or Ge) is the entity called Earth, depicted as female, floating upon vast waters and surrounded by Ocean. All living creatures, including the gods, are supported by her.
3 Tartarus is a personified figure here, although later becomes synonymous with the deep recesses of the Earth, a place of suffering; cf. Gantz (3–4).
4 *kallistos*: superl. of the adj. *kalos* (beautiful).
5 The epithet *lusimeles* (limb-relaxing, limb-loosening) is used here for the first time in extant Greek poetry in connection with Eros.
6 The impact of primal Eros is both physical and mental and the effect is irrational behaviour.

11 Alcman *Fragment* 59a: The Impact of Eros

Alcman, writing in Sparta in the Seventh Century BC, is one of the oldest surviving composers of choral lyric for public performance as well as private reading. Athenaeus (600f) notes a tradition that his lifestyle was devoted to the pursuit of women and the composition of erotic poetry. In this piece it is clear that the impact of Eros is welcome to the poet. (1)

Eros – once again! – for the Cyprian's sake (2)
the sweet one dripping down makes my heart get warm. (3)

Notes

1 Cf. Campbell (2: 435); Robbins 1997 (223–31).
2 Aphrodite.
3 For a comparable, albeit less positive view, cf. Sapph., *Fr.* 36: 'and I crave and I yearn for', and *Fr.* 37: 'in my dripping pain'.

12 Sappho *Fragment* 130: The Impact of Eros

Sappho acknowledges the potential for the god to inflict both pleasure and pain. While she regards Aphrodite as a goddess who can and does respond favourably to her supplication (4), she perceives Eros as a force, a beast, that she cannot resist, conquer or supplicate.

Eros the limb-loosener (1) yet again shakes me to the core,
the sweetly-bitter, (2) utterly irresistible little beast. (3)

Notes

1 *lusimeles*, the epithet for Eros used by Hes. (10) and Arch. (*Fr.* 193W).
2 She employs a powerful, descriptive epithet, *glukupikros*, combining the contrasting sensations of the sweet (*glukus*) and the bitter (*pikros*). This is the ultimate description of Eros as the bearer of pleasure and pain, joy and sorrow; cf. 7 for Nossis' view of the duality of Eros.
3 The term *orpeton* (*erpeton*) connotes unpleasant images of a beast that crawls on all fours, that creeps, something reptilian.

13 Ibycus *Fragment* 287C: The Impact of Eros

In this piece by Ibycus of Rhegium, Eros engages in a process of seduction, namely inducing the poet to be drawn to the god and to the snares set by his mother, rather than into a state of desire for another. Note the elements of enchantment (*l.* 3), nets and hunting (*l.* 4), fear (*l.* 5), reluctance (*l.* 7) and an overall feeling of helplessness that pervades the poem. Ibycus stresses the theme, which is continued into the age of the Augustan poets, of love and lust as being comparable to a hunt or chase, a 'game' that involves carefully planned strategies, nets, snares, deceptive ambushes and, ultimately, a victor and a victim. (1)

> Eros once again from beneath dark
>> eyelids darting me a melting glance
> with spells of all sorts cast me
>> into the inextricable nets of the Cyprian. (2)
> How I tremble at his onslaught,
>> just as the yoke-bearing horse, contest winner,
> near old age, (3) unwillingly goes with swift
>> chariot back into the race.

Notes

1 The poem is cited by Pl. (*Parm.* 137a), who equated himself with Ibycus' aged racehorse, unable to resist the desire to participate in the chase (Campbell 3: 256–57); cf. MacLachlan 1997 (87–97). The poet was famed for his passionate attachments to boys.
2 Aphrodite. The seduction and ensnarement of the poet is a team effort between son and mother. The play on her own entrapment in the nets forged by her husband Hephaestus suggests that she has learned much from experience.
3 The comparison between the ageing poet, forced against his will to fall in love, and the champion racehorse, now close to old age (*geras*), once again entering a contest of speed and stamina – against rivals who remain ever-young – demonstrates that the force of *eros* is not confined to the young. Cf. also 35; Houdijk and Vanderbroeck.

14 Anacreon *Fragment* 413: The Impact of Eros

Anacreon was described by the *Suda* as a poet whose life was 'entirely devoted to erotic encounters (*erotai*) with boys (*paides*) and women (*gunaikai*), along with song' (cf. Campbell 2: 25). Here he compares the impact of Eros with the violent workings of a blacksmith. (1)

> Again Eros struck me like a blacksmith wielding an enormous
> hammer (2) and bathed me in an ice cold torrent. (3)

Notes

1 Cf. MacLachlan 1997 (198–212).
2 The poet is contrasted with the fiery hot metal, passively lying on the anvil, and struck by the hammer of the blacksmith/Eros.
3 After hammering hot metal into shape, the blacksmith/Eros plunges it into cold water; the shock renders the poet, like the metal, hardened by the experience.

15 Catullus 85: Agony

As a recipient of the mixed sensations caused by the forces of Amor, Catullus analyses his condition. While lacking answers, he acknowledges the reality and pain of his situation. Particularly noticeable is the forcefulness of the poet's experience of simultaneous hatred and love (in that order).

> I hate and I love. (1) How can I do this, perhaps you ask?
>   I don't know, but I sense it happening and I'm in agony.

Note

1 *amare*: to love.

16 Propertius 2.12: Depiction of Amor

Depictions of Eros range from Hesiod's cosmic, primeval force that can overpower humanity (10), to Sappho's creeping, reptilian beast (12). In later representations, the god of love and desire becomes a winged creature, the first extant reference being in Eubulus, a Third Century BC comic playwright. (1) Plato (*Phaedrus* 250c) makes reference to the 'wings of love' but doesn't describe the god as a creature per se. The poets of the *Greek Anthology* frequently represent him as such (e.g. Meleager, *AP* 5.57; Archias *AP* 5.59). Here the Augustan age poet, Propertius, continues the later Greek tradition, treating the Roman equivalent of Eros – Amor – as a winged being whose nature can be determined by careful examination of his physical appearance.

> Whoever that man was, who painted Amor as a boy,
>   do you not think he was possessed of remarkable skill?
> He was the first to see that lovers devoid of sense
>   and great estates perish on account of frivolous anxieties. (2)
> The same man not without reason added wings swift-as-the-wind   5
>   and made it so the god can fly from heart to human heart:
> indeed, we are tossed on alternating waves,
>   and our breeze does not settle for long in any particular quarter.
> Deservedly is his hand armed with barbed arrows,
>   and a Cretan quiver hangs upright between each of his shoulders;   10
> he strikes once we feel safe and before we are aware of the enemy,
>   and no one goes away from that wound unharmed.
> In my case his barbs remain, his boyish behaviour also remains: (3)
>   but in my case he has assuredly lost his wings,
> ah, since he never flies away from my breast   15
>   and, ever present in my bloodstream, he wages war. (4)
> What pleasure is there for you to take up residence in my drained
>   marrows?
>   If there is a sense of shame in you, (5) direct your missiles somewhere
>   else!

It is better that you make an attempt on those untouched by
    that poison:
    it is not I, but a frail shadow of myself you are flogging.   20
If you were to destroy this shadow, who will there be to sing such
    things,
    (this foolish Muse of mine is your great source of glory),
who will sing of the head and the fingers and the dark eyes of my
    girl
    and who will sing of how softly her feet are accustomed to slip
along? (6)

Notes

1 Ath. 562c (cited by Camps 2: 112).

2 Amor is represented as a boy in Greek and Roman art. Prop. believes that such a portrayal is appropriate because the child-like recklessness inspired by the god – usually with unforeseen and disastrous consequences – originates, in part, from his boyish impetuosity and insensitivity.

3 *l*. 5–13 continue along similar and traditional themes. Love is appropriately depicted with wings, bow and arrow. Cf. **Illustration 1**.

4 At this point Prop. diverges from traditional views – including his own as expressed in *l*. 5–6 – and argues that for him personally Love has 'lost his wings'; for once the poet fell in love, the god never left his heart. *l*. 17–19 introduce disease imagery; for love as depicted by Prop. is an illness he cannot shake. The lines also combine such imagery with that of warfare (beginning at *l*. 16).

5 *pudor* is a sense of shame, an awareness of what is right and wrong. One MS reads *puer* (boy) for *pudor*, which would reinforce the picture of Amor in previous lines (esp. *puerilis*, boyish, childish, in *l*. 13).

6 The girl (*puella*) is possibly Cynthia, the central female figure in Prop.'s works. Note the qualities that constitute her desirability: her physical beauty, the sound of her voice and the movement of her body; compare Sapph. (18; 29) and Cat. (30).

II

BEAUTY

> . . . the most beautiful
> sight on the dark earth . . . is
> whatever an individual loves
> Sappho, *Fr.* 16.2–4

Although a significant proportion of pieces cited in this chapter are taken from writers whose chosen genre allows for personal expression, at a more universal level one can also identify criteria that influenced Greek and Roman definitions and contemplations of beauty. Public or civic literature is particularly insightful as are the widely distributed personal approaches of the lyricists and epigrammatists.

Ancient definitions of beauty tended to reflect on and incorporate more than appearance. This is not to argue, however, that physicality was not enough to designate beauty, but to suggest that among the artistic and intellectual elite (whose material is the very essence of this collection) there was regularly a search for an individual's innate qualities as a complement to their exterior merits. Hesiod's description of the first woman, Pandora (17), is illustrative of the dangers inherent in the combination of external beauty and the consequent desire it arouses. Such warnings are also found in tales concerning Helen (28), whose beauty set in chain the most destructive war of Greek legend.

Connected to these mythical stories are the concerns among both Greek and Roman men of the precarious consequences of becoming ensnared by the outward charms of beautiful people – those who too closely resemble the gods. Sappho wrote of the loss of self-control at the sight and sound of a beautiful woman worthy of the attention of the gods (29), a reaction revisited by Catullus several hundred years later (30).

Images of females in their natural state (naked, bathing, preparing for love-making) abound in amatory literature from Sappho through to Apuleius (18–23). In contrast, Sappho (24) and Demosthenes (25) provide examples of more idealistic explorations of ethical and spiritual beauty, which may be read as having been partially composed in contemplative response to the culturally embedded suspicion – at least in some literature – of exceptional outward splendour. In a similar vein, Catullus extols the inner charms of beautiful women (27).

In respect of beauty there are gender specificities, as well as sexual specifications. In both societies it remained a constant that adult males were idealised as beautiful in accordance with their embodiment of an intense masculinity, as in the description of heroes in epic and the martial poetry of Tyrtaeus (31). In same-sex love scenarios, the adult male was aroused primarily by youthful beauty, revealed in the multiple references to smoothness of skin and beardlessness (32–34). The specifications outlined by Aristophanes (32) are reflected elsewhere in literature and art from Classical Greece, with great stress placed upon an air of modesty on the part of the beautiful junior partner, the *eromenos*.

Potential wives (cf. **Chapter III**) were prized and praised for their temperament, chastity and general goodness as well as outward beauty. Prostitutes (cf. **Chapter IV**) were regarded as additionally attractive if they possessed musical abilities, intellect and other qualifications of a more cultured nature. By the Late Republic and Early Empire we witness the emergence of the 'elegiac woman' who embodies all these qualities, combined with sensuality, sexual freedom and sophistication, epitomised by Ovid's Corinna (20).

As today, antiquity also lauded beauty for beauty's sake. There are numerous texts that do little else but eulogise gorgeous bodies, natural sensuality, musculature, derrieres and great legs. There are also recognisable issues such as age – its positives and negatives in relation to beauty and attraction (35) – with praise of an ageing person usually being an exception (36–37).

Beauty was not solely a matter of individual appreciation. References to beauty competitions range from the Judgement of Paris (38) to private comparisons (39–40) and public contests for males and females (41–42). And while the ancients were particularly unforgiving when it came to bodily imperfections and deformities, there are significant exceptions (26; also 156–157; 160).

The creation of women

17 Hesiod *Works and Days* 59–89: Pandora

Hesiod describes the creation of the first woman, Pandora. The titan Prometheus had granted men the gift of fire, an action that led Zeus to punish him and, at the same time, punish man as compensation for possessing a commodity belonging to the gods. This story, also narrated in the *Theogony* (43), centres around the related themes of punishment and hardship, both of which are attributed to the female, and the demands of irresistible sexual desire. The duplicity of women and their dangerous sexual appeal – a *kakon* that is welcome in the heart (*thumos*) of a man – are also implicit in this cautionary myth. (1)

So Zeus spoke, and the father of men and gods laughed. (2)
He commanded famous Hephaestus as quickly as possible   60
to mix earth with water, to put in it human speech
and strength, and to make similar to immortal goddesses in face,
the beautiful, lovely shape of a girl. (3) And Zeus commanded
   Athena (4)
to teach her handicraft, to weave the cunning web.
And Zeus commanded golden Aphrodite to pour charm on her head   65
and cruel longing and cares that gnaw the limbs; (5)
and to put in her a dog's mind and a thievish disposition
Zeus commanded Hermes, (6) the messenger, the slayer of Argus.

So he spoke, and they obeyed lord Zeus, son of Cronus.
Immediately the famous lame god made from earth   70
something like a modest girl (7) through the counsels of Cronus' son.
The flashing-eyed goddess Athena girded and adorned her.
The divine Graces and Lady Persuasion
bedecked her body with golden necklaces.
The beautiful-haired Seasons wreathed her with Spring flowers.
 (8)   75
[Pallas Athena fitted all the adornments on her flesh.]
The messenger, the slayer of Argus, (9) placed in her breast
lies and wily words and a deceitful disposition in accordance with
the counsels of Zeus the thunderer. In her, the herald of the gods
placed the power of speech, and called this woman   80
Pandora, because all who have houses on Olympus gave her as
a gift, (10) a plague to men who eat bread.
But when he had completed the incurable sheer deceit,
the father dispatched the famous slayer of Argus, swift messenger
 of the gods,
to Epimetheus, leading to him the gift. Epimetheus did not   85
consider how Prometheus had told him never to accept a gift
from Olympian Zeus but to send it back,
lest it become an evil (11) to mortals.
But once he had accepted it, when he had the evil, he realised
 (his error). (12)

Notes

1 Cf. Brenk; Berg; Glenn; Marquardt; Zeitlin 1995a, 1995b.
2 Upon the revelation of his plan to punish mankind, it is noteworthy that Zeus finds it a source of merriment.
3 Pandora is described as having the beautiful (*kalon*) shape of a *parthenike* (cf. Sissa 1990b: 342–43).
4 In the account in the *Th.*, only Athena and Hephaestus fashion Pandora: Hephaestus moulds her as well as her gold headband, and Athena clothes and adorns her; cf. 43.
5 Aphrodite enhances the desirability and intense sexuality of Pandora with a mixture of charm and grace (*charis*), which generates a longing (*pothos*) in man; cf. Friedrich (106–107); MacLachlan 1993 (3–12).
6 At Zeus' command, Hermes endows her with the mind (*nous*) of a dog, a natural scavenger with the appearance of loyalty, and the nature (*ethos*) of a thief. In this sense, she is symbolic of the Greek male's fear of woman; cf. Arthur 1982; Sullivan 1984.
7 *aidoie*; *parthenos*.
8 The presence of the Charites and Persuasion (Peitho) contribute to the sensuality of the adornment scene and its end product: the Graces are associated with love and beauty, while Persuasion is a goddess of erotic pleasure. Likewise, the Seasons (Horai) are not only connected with beauty, as symbolised here by their gift of flowers, but also with the fruits of the earth and fertility. Pandora's attire is reminiscent of bridal costume. On the Graces in relation to Pandora, cf. MacLachlan 1993 (36–37, 56–57). Some scholars regard *l.* 76 as an interpolation.

9 Hermes is often called Argeiphontes (also at *l.* 84).

10 The name Pandora literally means 'All Gifts'.

11 *kakon*, also at *l.* 89. For Pandora as the 'beautiful evil' (*kalon kakon*); cf. 43.

12 The fate of Epimetheus (Afterthought), Pandora's husband, exemplifies the dangers posed by the first woman and her female descendants. Unfortunately for Epimetheus, he only realises the evil nature of Pandora after he has embraced her. The verb *echein* (to have) specifies the act of holding, embracing, possessing or taking as one's wife.

Natural beauty

18 Sappho *Fragment* 16.1–20: Beauty Defined

To Sappho, beauty is that which a person loves, thus stressing the importance of what matters to the person, hence individual diversity as distinct from the shared values of the wider community. In this definition of beauty in the eyes of the individual, Sappho argues it is not so much the loveliness of Helen herself that is at issue as the impact Paris had upon her in inducing her to abandon all she possessed for love. The beauty of Anactoria has inspired a similar reaction in Sappho. (1)

Some people believe a squadron of cavalry, others infantry,
and still others a fleet of ships, to be the most beautiful
sight (2) on the dark earth, but I believe it is
whatever an individual loves.   4

It is quite easy to make this
comprehensible to everyone: the one who by far
outshone all mankind in respect of beauty, (3)
Helen, abandoned her high-born husband   8

and sailed away to Troy with no thought whatever
for her beloved child or beloved parents,
but led astray [by love?] . . . (4)
lightly . . .   12

for [this]
has reminded me
now of Anactoria who is
no longer here; (5)   16

I would prefer to gaze upon her
delightful walk (6) and the shining sparkle of her
face than all the chariots of the Lydians and their
armies. . . .   20

Notes

1 Cf. Most; Burnett; duBois 1984; Race.

2 *kalliston*: superl. adj. used as substantive, lit. 'the most beautiful thing'.

3 *kallos*: beauty.

4 Sapph. does not condemn Helen's actions or the disastrous consequences of her departure but does indicate what she left behind on account of love. The verb *paragein* (to lead astray) is used in this context to suggest a non-rational force (most editors insert '*eros*') that interferes with one's mind (cf. *l.* 4).

5 The comparison is twofold: Anactoria with Helen as the beauty no longer present (and led astray?), Sapph. with Menelaus as the lover left behind.

6 Sapph. concentrates on physical details of the beloved, which conjure up images of subtle sexuality, the sway of Anactoria's hips and the radiance of her face.

19 Philodemus *Greek Anthology* 5.132: Beauty Inspires Carnal Desire

As with Sappho, several Greek and Roman male authors define female beauty in conjunction with inner qualities and various refinements. Philodemus, however, dispels the ideal by praising Flora for itemised physical qualities and external beauty alone. (1)

> Oh feet, Oh calves, Oh – and I am justly brought to ruin –
>> the thighs, Oh bum-cheeks, Oh pubic mound, (2) Oh hollow, (3)
> Oh upper arms, Oh breasts, Oh the tapering neck,
>> Oh hands, Oh – and I'm going mad – the eyes,
> Oh delicious sway of the hip, Oh passionate
>> tongue-kisses, Oh – may I die – the lilting-voice.
> What if she is of Oscan origin, a flower who does not sing Sappho, (4)
>> still Perseus fell head over heels in love with Andromeda, she an
>> Indian. (5)

Notes

1 On the various parts of her body, intermingled with movement and the build up of erotic tension, cf. Sider 1997 (103–108); Gow and Page 1968 (2: 381–82).

2 The word *kteis* can mean 'comb'. Here the pubic mound with its covering of hair.

3 The *lagon* is either the hollow below the ribcage (that is, the flank) or the hollow between her legs.

4 It is possible that her name is Flora, but Phld. could simply be calling her a 'flower'. From Campania in Central Italy, she speaks Oscan and appears to lack the literary refinements of girls from Rome, perhaps not speaking Latin let alone Greek. These inadequacies do not impede appreciation of her physical appeal and love of sex.

5 Andromeda was dark-skinned, coming from India (or Ethiopia); for the story of her being saved from a sea monster by Perseus, cf. Gantz (307–309).

20 Ovid *Amores* 1.5: Corinna

Corinna is very much an object of desire. Like the Oscan girl in 19, she is one who is gazed upon, her body described as if a work of art. For Ovid an appreciation of beauty is one thing, consummation of one's desire another: to have both is the perfect experience. (1)

It had been steamy, and the day had passed the middle hour;
    I spread my limbs in need of refreshment over the centre of the bed.
Part of the window was opened, the other part shut,
    such light as woods nearly always are accustomed to provide,
the kind of twilights that glow when Phoebus is on the point of flight   5
    or when night departs and the day is not yet risen.
That is the light that must be provided for shy girls,
    in which a timid sense of shame might hope to find concealment. (2)

Behold, Corinna comes, veiled in an unbelted tunic,
    with parted hair covering her shining neck, (3)   10
just as beautiful Sameramis (4) is said to have entered the
    bedchamber, and Lais, (5) loved by many men.

I tore away the tunic, not that the 'flimsy' suffered any great harm,
    but still she struggled to be covered by it;
she – since she was struggling like one who did not wish to prevail – 15
    was without difficulty vanquished by self-betrayal. (6)
As she stood before my eyes with raiment cast aside,
    nowhere over her entire body was there a single blemish:
what shoulders, such arms I saw and touched!
    How fit for pinching was the beauty of her nipples!   20
How flat the belly beneath firm breast!
    How fulsome and what a mound! (7) How youthful the thigh!
Why should I relate her features one-by-one? Nothing not laudable
    did I see,
    and I pressed her naked body against the full length of mine.
Who does not know the rest? Utterly worn out, we both took our rest. 25
    May the middles of the day often turn out so well for me.

Notes

1 Cf. Barsby; Elliott; Papanghelis.
2 Ov. describes the light as appropriate for 'shy girls' (*verecundae puellae, l.* 7) and those who possess 'a sense of shame' *pudor* (*l.* 8). Corinna's entrance at *l.* 9 shatters any illusions that she is such a woman, although she 'plays the part'.
3 Corinna enters the bedroom in scanty attire with hair let down. On her appearance and the behaviour of a 'proper' Roman lady, cf. Elliott (351 n. 5).
4 Sameramis was a famous Assyrian queen, builder of Babylon and leader of men. She is described as *formosa*, a term that usually specifies outward beauty and shape (*forma*), hence sexual appeal.
5 Lais was the name of two Corinthian *hetairai* of particular beauty. The first lived in the Fifth Century BC, while the second, from the Fourth Century BC, was the companion of the orator Demosthenes and the philosopher Diogenes. The verb *amare*, here in the passive, can mean: (i) to be loved or (ii) to be made love to.
6 Indicative of the Roman male psyche as represented by Ov., the woman who says 'no' really means 'yes'; at 114 he goes so far as to advocate the use of force should she persevere.

7 *latus* can mean flank, the region between hip and ribcage, or the groin area; cf. Adams 1982: 90. In view of the downward listing of her parts, the pubic mound is more likely here than her side.

21 Rufinus *Greek Anthology* 5.15: Melite

Rufinus' adoration of the physical charms of Melite is expressed in both a unique and traditional way. Page comments that the poem has 'no precedent in the Anthology' (1978: 75). (1)

> Where now is Praxiteles? (2) Where the creative hands of Polyclitus, (3)
> who bestowed the breath of life into artistic works of the past?
> Who will fashion the sweet scented curls of Melite,
> her fiery eyes and her lustrous neck?
> Where are the mould makers? Where are the stonecutters? The nature
> of such
> a beautiful body (4) as hers, just like a statue of the gods, warrants a
> temple.

Notes

1 On the poet, his date and the nature of his poetry, cf. Page 1978; Cameron 1981b, 1982.
2 Athenian sculptor (fl. *c.* 375–330 BC). His most heralded work, the Aphrodite of Cnidus, was supposedly based on his mistress, Phryne.
3 Argive sculptor (fl. *c.* 460–410 BC). Quint. (12.10.9) regarded his statues of mortals as without equal.
4 *morphe*: here, 'beautiful shape'.

22 Rufinus *Greek Anthology* 5.60: A Girl Bathing

The novel approach in his poem on Melite (21) is matched by this piece with its description of a girl bathing and the eroticism it engenders. (1) As with *AP* 5.48 (37), he places emphasis on natural imagery and fairness of skin.

> A virgin silver-footed was bathing, the apples of her breasts (2)
> dripping water, bright, with skin milk-white.
> Rounded buttocks rolled against each other, (3)
> rippling with flesh more fluid than any liquid.
> Her spreading hand covered not all of her swelling
> Eurotas, (4) but as much as it could.

Notes

1 Cf. Page 1978; Baldwin; Cameron 1981b.
2 On the apple and breast imagery cf. Foster; McCartney; Littlewood; Gerber 1978. The silver-footed epithet echoes Homeric descriptions of the goddess Thetis.
3 One cheek is rolling in opposition to the movement of its twin. The rippling effect of the muscular movement is intensified in the following line where the buttocks (*pugai*) of the girl, wet from her bathing, move more fluidly than the waters running over them.

4 Eurotas is the river that runs through the valley of Laconia, the site of Sparta. The reference is probably to the girl's pubic mound; the poet's gaze moves from her breasts to her buttocks to her pubis. Her feeble attempt at modesty increases the erotic impact of her charms; cf. 20, *l.* 14–16 where Corinna clings to her flimsy tunic in a similarly futile effort to cover her nakedness.

23 Apuleius *Metamorphoses* 4.28: Psyche

The tale of Cupid and Psyche depicts a recurring theme in Greek and Roman literature, namely, divine jealousy that could and did lead to divine wrath and its consequent misery for mortals. Psyche is the victim of such a scenario. So beautiful was she that she became more adored than Venus herself: the goddess, out of resentment, sent Cupid to trick her into falling in love with a loathsome, hideous creature. Unfortunately for Venus, Cupid himself became enamoured with Psyche. The passage places great emphasis upon female physical beauty, *forma.*

In a certain city there were a king and a queen. They had, in all, three daughters who were conspicuous for beauty, (1) but while the elder two were especially pleasing to look at, their features were considered sufficiently celebrated by human praise alone. [2] But the beauty (2) of the youngest girl (3) was so remarkable and so utterly unique that the poverty of human speech is such as not even to be able to describe it let alone give it adequate praise. [3] Indeed, many of her fellow citizens and an abundant number of foreigners, whom rumour of the extraordinary spectacle had brought together in eager throngs, were rendered dumbfounded with admiration for her unparalleled beauty (4) and were drawing the right hand to their mouths, with the forefinger pressed against the upright thumb, (5) so that they could <come> in devoted religious observance, as if to pay homage to the goddess Venus herself. [4] In the meantime the rumour had spread throughout nearby cities and neighbouring regions that the goddess, whom the blue depths of the sea had born and the moisture of the foaming waves nurtured, was now at random bestowing the favour of her divine presence (6) at gatherings of mortal beings; or, at the very least, that once again by a new germination of heavenly seed, not the sea but the land had brought forth another Venus, this time endowed with virginal flower. (7)

Notes

1 *forma.*
2 *pulchritudo*: another term for physical beauty. Apul. attaches two very emphatic adjs., which mean essentially the same: *praecipua* (special, remarkable) and *praeclara* (unique, distinctively famous).
3 Psyche is a *puella* in the bloom of her maidenhood. That so many gaze upon her spectacular beauty indicates that she is of an age ripe for marriage.
4 *formonsitas* (the essence of being *formosa*) is yet another term for beauty. It is an unusual word, but common in Apul.
5 On the significance of this ritual, with the forefinger pressed to the lips alongside the upright thumb, as a mark of reverence, cf. Kenney 117–18; Purser 1–2.

6 *numen*: not so much 'divinity' but the presence, the power of a divinity.
7 *virginalis flos*: virginal flower, 'and therefore one up on Venus' (Kenney 118).

Beyond the physical

24 Sappho *Fragment* 50: Beauty and Goodness

Sappho looks beyond the physical to the inner beauty of the soul and the spirit, urging her reader to see that the inner transcends and then transforms the external, which, by its nature, is transient. This phenomenon, in subsequent literature, leads the admirer to overlook physical blemishes and see only beauty in the beloved.

> For one who is beautiful (1) to look at is <beautiful> as far as that goes, but one who is noble in spirit (2) will become beautiful as a result.

Notes

1 While the masc. is retained throughout, the adj. *kalos* (repeated three times, provided it is adopted in the second instance) should be read as applying to an individual regardless of gender.
2 *kagathos* (= *agathos*): noble, well bred, excellent; endowed with the highest qualities; cf. Adkins.

25 Demosthenes 1410.30 [*Erotic Essay*]: The Ideal Qualities of the *Eromenos*

The subject is, as the title suggests, male–male attraction. The purpose of the work is to praise Epicrates, a beautiful youth with whom Demosthenes is clearly captivated.

For though it is a beautiful thing to be distinguished for one form of excellence, it is more beautiful (1) to combine all the excellences for which a sensible man would wish to be honoured. That is clear from this fact: we shall find that Aeacus and Rhadamanthys were loved by the gods for their prudent wisdom, (2) Heracles and Castor and Pollux were loved by the gods for their courage, (3) Ganymede and Adonis and others like them were loved by the gods for their beauty. (4) While I do not wonder at those who desire your friendship, (5) I do at those not feeling this way. Although some men, sharing in one of the aforementioned excellences, are deemed worthy of the company of the gods, for a man born mortal it is best to become the friend of one possessed of all these excellences.

Notes

1 *kalon* (a beautiful thing); *kallion* (more beautiful).
2 Aeacus, son of Zeus and Aegina, was renowned for piety; Rhadamanthys, son of Zeus and Europa, was renowned for wise decision-making and justice, and was made one of the judges of the dead in Hades.

3 Heracles, the mortal son of Zeus (or Amphitryon) and Alcmene, was known for bravery and strength. The twins, Castor and Pollux, are known for bravery and skill on the battlefield.

4 Ganymede, son of Tros, the epitome of youthful, masculine beauty (cf. 25). Adonis was son of Theias and his daughter Smyrna (cf. Gantz 730 with variants). This incestuous union was Aphrodite's punishment of Smyrna for her failure to pay the goddess due respect. When Theias discovered the identity of his partner, he pursued Smyrna with a knife, but the gods saved her by turning her into a tree. Adonis, born from the tree, was beautiful and subsequently the subject of Aphrodite's love (cf. Reed).

5 *philia*: friendship, friendly affection. The word does not specify an explicitly erotic element, although it can in the appropriate context. It is consistently used in connection with male–male relations (cf. Konstan 1996, 1997).

26 Anonymous *Greek Anthology* 12.96: A Blemish on Beauty

This is an unusual epigram written about a young man who is beautiful in all respects but for a deformity of foot. The poet invites the reader to address the issue of the superficiality of beauty, laying greater stress on the inner qualities that enhance the young man's external appearance. Even so, the need to conceal the blemish is a subtle reflection on the shallow values of society and the need for the individual to conform. The poem may well have been attached to the gift of the boot that will help correct the problem. (1)

> Not in vain among mortals this saying is shouted:
>> "The gods did not grant to all mankind to have all things."
> Your form is blameless, in your eyes is a distinctive
>> bashfulness, and around your breast flourishes grace, (2)
> and with these gifts you excel other young men. But in fact (the gods) did
>> not grant your foot the same grace.
> But this boot will hide your misshapen step, good Pyrrhus, (3)
>> and with its beauty (4) will cause you delight in your enjoyment of it.

Notes

1 Cf. Garland 1994; Edwards.
2 The youth possesses many praiseworthy features: an attractive physique, modesty reflected through the eyes, and a form of *charis* around his breast (and heart, synonymous with his personality and character). The poet notes (*l.*6) that the youth, because of his foot, has not received the totality of grace and external beauty: the gift of the beautiful boot will conceal the blemish and the foot, externally, will appear to be perfect.
3 The name means 'Ruddy' or 'Blushing' and emphasises his modesty as well as beauty.
4 *kallos*.

27 Catullus 86: Quintia and Lesbia Compared

The poet's beloved, Lesbia, (1) is compared to another contemporary beauty and is consequently depicted as the epitome of desirability. Lesbia's appeal, unlike Quintia's, includes but transcends mere physicality.

Quintia is beautiful (2) to many. To me she is fair, (3) tall,
  erect. These individual attributes, I concede.
The overall description 'beautiful', I reject. She lacks sensuality. (4)
  In so statuesque a body there is not an ounce of wit. (5)
Lesbia is beautiful, for she is not only extremely attractive, (6)
  but she has stolen all the gifts of Venus (7) from all women.

Notes

1 On the identity of Lesbia, cf. Neudling (97–98); Levens (362–65); Rankin 1969; Wiseman
   1969 (42–60), 1985; Skinner 1983. For those who equate her with Clodia Metelli, the superl.
   form of her family name – Pulcer – in *l.*5 is used as an argument (along with even more overt
   punning on the name in *Cat.* 79). On this poem, cf. Rankin 1976.
2 *formosa*: again at *l.*3, 5. It lit. refers to her shape (*forma*).
3 *candida* (lit. 'shining') denotes complexion as well as general grace, delight, beauty, aura
   (similar to *dia*; cf. 1 n. 2).
4 *venustas*: lit. 'the essence of Venus'. It evokes a combination of physical beauty, inner charm
   and grace. On Cat.'s use of derivatives of the name 'Venus' and related concepts, cf. Seager;
   Wiltshire.
5 *sal*: wit, also salt. A woman needs wit, erudition and personality in addition to physical
   appeal.
6 *pulcerrima*: superl. adj., lit. 'prettiest', therefore 'most attractive' (derived from *pulchritudo*).
7 *veneres*: the gifts of Venus. As with *venustas*, the expression is suggestive of charm and
   sensuality, but with overtly sexual connotations.

The powerful effects of beauty

28 Homer *Iliad* 3.154–60: Reaction to Helen

Homer's avoidance of any detailed description of Helen's physical beauty became a
conventional literary device in subsequent generations of Greek and Roman poetry.
By concentrating on the effects of Helen's presence, Homer allows his readers to create
their own image of this most beautiful of women. Here the Trojan elders, on seeing
her, liken her face to that of the goddesses, yet they still want to be rid of her,
recognising that her beauty has brought travail and disaster upon them.

When therefore they saw Helen going to the tower,
they softly spoke winged words to each other: 155
"Is it not a cause for anger that the Trojans and well-greaved Achaeans
should suffer woes for a long time over such a woman?
She is terribly like the immortal goddesses in the face.
But even so, though she is like that, let her go home in the ships,
and let not trouble be left for us and our children hereafter."   160

29 Sappho *Fragment* 31.1–16: The Sight of the Beloved

Divine imagery and the evocation of physical reaction at the sight of a girl are used by Sappho to define the impact of beauty on the beholder. Sappho sees the girl's male companion as equal to the gods in respect of good fortune at being able to sit with her and drink in her conversation and laughter. Sappho's subsequent response is described in terms of a seizure, in which all her senses are subjected to a powerful erotic and emotional crisis. This testimony to the potent effects of beauty is to become, like her other responses, a metaphorical commonplace in the erotic repertoire of antiquity, particularly among the Roman poets of the Late Republic and Early Empire. (1)

He seems to me equal in good fortune to the gods,
that man, who sits on the opposite side of you
and near you listens to your
sweet responses   4

and desire inducing (2) laughter: indeed that
gets my heart pounding in my breast.
For just looking at you for a moment, it is impossible
for me even to talk;   8

my tongue has splintered, all at once a delicate
flame has stolen underneath my skin,
my eyes can see nothing at all,
my ears are ringing,   12

perspiration pours down me, a tremor
shakes me, I am more greenish than
grass, and I think that I am on
the very point of dying. (3)   16

Notes

1 Cf. Koniaris; Devereux 1970; Marcovich; McEvilley 1978; Tsagarakis 1979; Robbins 1980; Tsagarakis 1986; Winkler 1990a (178–80); duBois 1995 (64–75).
2 A derivative of *himeros*; the laughter is not simply lovely or beguiling, it arouses the listener.
3 Her physical symptoms represent or symbolise her emotional turmoil. The series of images culminates with Sapph. on the brink of death.

30 Catullus 51: The Sight of Lesbia

This poem was written as an imitation of and compliment to *Fragment* 31 of Sappho (29). The durability of her intense and erotic sentiments is utilised by Catullus to express a male reaction to female beauty. As with the depictions of beautiful women in Homer and Sappho, Catullus does not attempt to describe in detail the appearance of Lesbia, but concentrates on evoking the effects of her beauty on the observer. The poem has a distinctly Roman quality, particularly its final stanza. (1)

That man seems to me to be equal to a god,
that man, if it is permitted, seems to surpass the gods,
he who, sitting opposite you, again and again
    watches and hears you

sweetly laughing, which snatches all the   5
senses from wretched me. For, as soon as I gaze at you
Lesbia, there is nothing more for me.
    . . . (2)

But the tongue is numb, a subtle flame
spreads down through the limbs, with their own din   10
the ears ring, the eyes are covered with a
    double night. (3)

Idleness, (4) Catullus, is bad for you.
In idleness you exult and participate too much.
Idleness, previously, has ruined kings and   15
    prosperous cities. (5)

Notes

1 *imitatio* is a standard Roman literary device. It is more than slavish translation: at its best it captures the essence of the original and personalises it with an individual touch that pays homage to the source while creating something new. On the poet's translations of Sapph., cf. Wormell; Greene.
2 There is a line missing from the text.
3 Cat. experiences some but not all of the symptoms of Sapph. Note the omission of the reflexive 'my'. What is common to both is the emphasis on the impact of the sight and sound of the object of desire. The final image refers to each eye having its own darkness descend upon it.
4 At a personal level *otium* can mean idleness or leisure time; at the public level it denotes periods of tranquillity in political life. Depending on context this can be perceived as being either positive or negative. For Cat. it is the time he spends with friends and writes poetry; cf. Frank; Segal 1970.
5 This stanza has been the focus of debate as to whether it was a part of the original poem: in favour, cf. Kidd; Fredricksmeyer; Vine; contra, cf. Jensen; Wilkinson; Copley.

Male beauty and adornment

31 Tyrtaeus *Fragment* 10 Extracts: The Beauty of Youth

The setting for the poetry of Tyrtaeus was a prolonged period of warfare in the Archaic age between Sparta and Messenia. Tyrtaeus places manly courage and behaviour in battle, in essence the qualities of a Homeric *agathos*, at the forefront of his poetry. He moves beyond Homer, however, in that for him these are qualities visibly displayed by the individual on behalf of society. The successful individual stands to gain considerable esteem and tangible reward for selfless sacrifice in the eyes of the community. (1)

1–2

It is a beautiful thing (2) to perish, having fallen in the front line,
  a brave (3) man, fighting for the sake of his fatherland.

27–30

. . . for the young man, however, it is seemly,
  so long as the splendid flower of lovely youthfulness (4) remains,
while he lives, men marvel at him, and desire fills women
  at the sight of him; he is beautiful (5) still, even had he fallen in the
  frontline.

Notes

1 On the values of Tyrt. and his age, cf. Fuqua. On the first piece, cf. Verdenius (where 6–7 D = *Fr.* 10).
2 *kalon* here is a thing of beauty, a thing that is admirable. In *l.*30 it is used as an adj. in its regular sense of beautiful to behold.
3 The Homeric term for a successful aristocrat and hero, *agathos*, is used here in the strict sense of brave or courageous. It also conveys the notion of 'success' despite having fallen in battle; cf. Verdenius (338–39).
4 *hebe*: the prime of youthful beauty.
5 Tyrt. adds another dimension to being *kalos*: the beauty of a youth who dies bravely in battle never fades.

32 Aristophanes *Clouds* 1010–1019: Youthful Beauty

The *Clouds*, produced in 423 BC (and later partially revised), deals with the misfortunes of a farmer, Strepsiades, who married a woman from a higher social class and whose son, Pheidippides, has driven him into debt. The *agon* or contest takes the form of a debate between Fair (Argument) and Foul (Argument). Fair represents the traditional mores of Athenian society and is highly suspicious of contemporary youth, while Foul personifies the new lifestyle of the exuberant young men inspired by the teaching of the Sophists.

If you listen and do what I say,   1010
  you'll eternally have:
a radiant chest, skin that is bright,
shoulders quite grand, but just a wee tongue, (1)
a sturdy great bum, and a miniscule dick. (2)
If you practise the present youth's way,   1015
  to begin with you'll have:
anaemic white skin, (3) shoulders too light,
a chest that's too thin with a tongue that's too l-o-n-g,
a lean upper thigh, and a long thing to tweak. (4)

1 Less a sign of sexual restraint than of failure to learn the art of clever speaking that is associated with the new amorality. Over-exercise of the tongue is widely associated with the new fashion, cf. *N.* 931; *Ran.* 91.
2 *posthe*: the foreskin in medical literature, but less technical otherwise. This is the preferred proportion, as suggested in vase paintings.
3 The colour that is acquired by too much indoor activity, including extended study of fancy new subjects.
4 The manuscripts here have 'a long decree' (*psephisma macron*). As Dover notes, 'we miss either a reference to the penis or a surprise substitute for it' (1964: 223). But 'decree' or 'proposal to be put to the vote' does not seem the right substitute, and we look for a word that is not usually used for the penis but is, nevertheless, sufficiently suggestive to be understood as referring to it. Harold Tarrant (University of Newcastle, NSW) reads *plektisma*, which could easily be coined from the verb *plektizesthai* (to toy amorously with), first attested in this sense in *Ec.* 964.

33 Straton *Greek Anthology* 12.5: Preferences

Straton, a writer of erotic epigrams mostly on pederastic themes, sings the praises of boys between the ages of 12 and 17 when they are at the height of their beauty and physical appeal (cf. 92). (1)

> I really like (boys) pale, and at the same time I love (2) them honey-
> coloured and golden as well; on the other hand, I am content with
> ebony ones. (3)
> Nor do I overlook hazel eyes. (4) But I exceedingly
> love (boys) with lustrous dark eyes.

Notes

1 On the poet, his date and poetic content, cf. Maxwell-Stuart 1972, 1975; Cameron 1982.
2 *philein* (to love); also in *l.*4; compare with the less sensual *stergein* (to be content with; love of parent towards a child) in *l.*2. The gender of the objects of desire is determined by the masc. pronoun, here and in *l.*4.
3 The physical qualities most sought after are pale, honey-coloured and golden skin colouring, an effeminate look, but Strat. also likes dark-skinned beauties.
4 The word *korai* (pl.) can mean 'girls' or 'pupils' (of the eye); were the former meaning to be adopted it would create a diversion from the essential theme of the poem.

34 Straton *Greek Anthology* 12.192: Unadorned Beauty

Straton, who claims to have been commissioned to write poems about boys and therefore to cater for all tastes, alludes to the gymnasium as a potential venue for those who appreciate a more vigorous and manly form of beauty.

> Long locks do not provide me with delight, nor an over-abundance
> of ringlets,
> taught as works (1) of craft, not nature.

But the dusty filth of a gymnasium boy does,
   and the anointed skin on the flesh of his limbs.
My desire (2) is sweet when it is unadorned, but a beguiling
   appearance (3) conveys the work of the more feminine Paphian. (4)

Notes

1 The term *erga* (works) here and in *l*.6 (sing.) is suggestive of artifice and deception. Throughout the poem, natural beauty is preferred to that which is contrived.
2 Strat. refers to his *pothos*, 'desire' or 'longing', which is also sweeter when unadorned.
3 *morphe*: both facial appearance and bodily shape (cf. 21 n. 4), here in the case of a girlish boy.
4 Aphrodite.

The issue of age

35 Mimnermus *Poem* 5: Youth is Fleeting, Old Age Looms

While Sappho laments the loss of the company of those she has desired, Mimnermus writes of isolation due to the onset of old age (*geras*), something implicit but not stressed in Sappho. Eros is not sparing of the old and their pain is even greater due to the indifference (and ignorance) of the young; both poets, however, are affected by the power of youthful beauty. (1)

The sweat pours down me, and my heart is filled with trembling,
   when I gaze upon (2) my generation in full flower of
pleasure (3) and what is beautiful. (4) If only it would last much longer!
   But as transient as a mere dream is
precious youth; (5) soon ugly, dire, loathsome
   old age looms above us,
disgusting and without honour, (6) that renders a man
   unrecognisable, and overwhelms both his eyes and his mind. (7)

Notes

1 Cf. Gerber 1997 (108–09) and 1999a (85); Edmonds (1: 93 n. 1). Prop. says of him: 'In respect of love (*amor*) a verse of Mimnermus is of greater value than one of Homer's' (1.9.11). The text adopted is that of West 1971–72 (2: 84).
2 Compare the sentiments and the images with the experience of Sapph. (29).
3 *terpnon*: adj., delightful, pleasurable.
4 *kalon*.
5 Youth (*hebe*, *l*.5) and *geras* (*l*.6) provide the central contrast within the poem. Note the respective imagery of flowers and beauty (exhilarating but transient) as opposed to harshness and ugliness (prolonged and lingering).
6 *atimon*: devoid of worth or status, valueless.
7 Cf. Edmonds 'or when it is poured over eyes and wits' (1: 93 n. 3); Miller 'and ruins his eyes and mind as it pours about him' (28).

36 Philodemus *Greek Anthology* 5.13: Charito, Ageless Beauty

Many poets in the *Greek Anthology* treat age in a negative fashion, especially the effect its onset has upon youthful beauty. A rare exception is Philodemus, follower of the Epicurean School, who is, with Catullus, the outstanding epigrammatist of the First Century BC. Philodemus does not see age as equating with decline in beauty. (1)

> Having completed a full cycle of sixty years, Charito (2)
>   still retains her long, flowing dark hair,
> and those well-known breasts, with their white marble smooth (3) cones,
>   stand erect without the aid of an encircling breast-band,
> and her skin, devoid of wrinkles, is redolent of ambrosia, (4) the very
>   essence of enticement, (5) and the distillation of multiple graces. (6)
> Thus all lovers, (7) who are not afraid of wild, sexual desires, (8)
>   come this way, and give no thought to her number of decades.

Notes

1 On the poem and others on the theme of the older woman, cf. Sider 1997 (95–98); the theme of repugnance felt towards old women is raised in 121–124.
2 Her name means 'Grace' and the poet plays on this meaning in *l*.6.
3 Both the qualities of whiteness and smoothness are in the poet's mind as he praises her breasts (Sider 1997: 96; Gerber 1978: 203–04); note the emphasis on their firmness and the pertness of her nipples.
4 While *ambrosia* is technically the food of the gods, it also exudes a wonderful scent.
5 *peitho*: usually persuasion, here enticement.
6 *charites*: not only all of the graces, but her name as well, which Sider defines as distillation 'into an ambrosial desire' (1997: 97).
7 While technically meaning lovers, *erastai* here can simply indicate those who enjoy sex.
8 *pothoi* (pl.).

37 Rufinus *Greek Anthology* 5.48: An Ageing Beauty

In discussing an ageing beauty, the focus of Rufinus is largely on light or pale complexion, a standard feature of Greek and Roman erotic attraction from the time of Homer. (1)

> Eyes shining like gold, and cheek translucent as glass,
>   and mouth more delightful than a purple bud.
> Neck of white marble, breasts gleaming,
>   and feet whiter than those of silvery Thetis. (2)
> If there is thistledown, just a little, gleaming in her hair,
>   I pay no attention to the white thread.

Notes

1 Page 1978 notes that this (and *AP* 5.62) 'are variations on a common theme' (90), and he includes the preceding poem of Phld. (36). It should, however, be noted that in *AP* 5.21, 5.28 and 5.76 (123) Rufin. presents a negative interpretation of ageing beauty.

2   Thetis was a sea nymph and mother of Achilles and her most common epithet is Thetis 'of the silver feet'.

Beauty contests

38   Euripides *Trojan Women* 924–44: The Judgement of Paris

There was a strong competitive element in both Greek and Roman society and it extended to the judgement of beauty – both in myth and in real life. One of the earliest examples of this mentality is the story of the Judgement of Paris. Here the inherent danger of beauty, a recurrent theme within Greek literature, is also represented. Helen, the prize offered by the winner of the contest to Paris Alexander, speaks the following lines to her former husband, Menelaus.

[Paris Alexander] . . . judged the threefold group of goddesses.
The gift Pallas offered to Alexander was   925
that as general of the Phrygians he would destroy Greece.
Hera promised that he would have Asia and the frontiers of Europe
as his kingdom, if Paris picked her.
But Cypris, admiring my beauty,
promised me, if she triumphed over the goddesses   930
in beauty. (1) Consider how the following story goes: (2)
Cypris defeated the goddesses and I was given in marriage
for the benefit of the Greeks. Because of this barbarians do not rule you,
either as the result of a battle, or through a tyranny.
Greece's fortune was my sorrow.   935
I, sold for my beauty, am reproached
for what I should be crowned.
You will say that I do not speak of the point in question,
and that I secretly departed from your house,
and that he came without a goddess,   940
he, this avenging spirit, whether you wish
to call him by the name Alexander or Paris,
he whom you, cursed man, left in your home
while you sailed away from Sparta to Crete. (3)

Notes

1   The gifts offered by Athena and Hera, military glory and the headship of an empire, pale in comparison to the promise of Aphrodite: possession of beauty in the form of Helen. Noteworthy is the fact that Helen does not interpret the gifts as bribes, which is perhaps an indication of the Homeric value of reciprocal giving (for the gift of being judged the most beautiful, each goddess will offer a gift in return). The topos of gift-exchange (or, to the modern reader, bribery) does not, however, appear in the Homeric version (*Il.* 24.27–30), and seems to have been a later addition.
2   The story Helen tells is the traditional, mythical account of the origins of the Trojan War. Herein she presents herself as an unwilling and thereby blameless pawn, a victim of her beauty and the goddess, Aphrodite.

3 Helen reminds Menelaus that of his volition he left Sparta to go to Crete, leaving her alone
to entertain their Trojan guest.

39 Rufinus *Greek Anthology* 5.35: Matters for Judgement
– The Back View

The Judgement of Paris provided a literary motif that became traditional in erotic
epigram. This poem by Rufinus should be read in conjunction with the following one
(40). They constitute a delicious parody of the famous contest. Since the goddesses
appeared naked before Paris, so, too, do these three contenders. In a series of frank
admissions, Rufinus defines what are the criteria determining female desirability, and
his focus is clearly on those parts of the anatomy usually kept hidden. (1)

> I judged the derrieres of three women. (2) They themselves picked me
>   so they could put on show the starry splendour of their naked
>   limbs. (3)
> One, marked by rounded dimples blossomed
>   with bum-cheeks both gleaming and soft. (4)
> However, the snowy flesh of the second blushed crimson   5
>   in the parted cleft, redder than the purest rose. (5)
> The third, like a tranquil sea, was split by silent waves,
>   rippling over her soft skin of their own accord. (6)
> If the Arbiter of the Goddesses had gazed upon these three derrieres,
>   he would no longer have wanted to look upon the three originals.   10

Notes

1 Cf. Page 1978 (82–84), who notes that this and the following poem are 'unique in the
  Anthology' (82); Richlin 1992a (48–49).
2 Rufin. casts himself as the new Paris. The joke is centred on the fact that, unlike Paris, Rufin.
  judges each woman's *puge* (backside); cf. J. Henderson 1991 (201–02) who notes that the
  term is not necessarily vulgar.
3 To capture the impact of the splendour of their limbs (*mela*), Rufin. uses the word *asterope*
  (lit. 'lightning').
4 The term *gloutoi* (bum-cheeks) is more specific than *puge*.
5 The flesh around the area is snowy white, but that within the cleft, as the woman spreads
  her legs, takes on a crimson hue.
6 The image is of a smooth, continuously moving swell, which ripples over the entire expanse
  of her derriere.

40 Rufinus *Greek Anthology* 5.36: Matters for Judgement
– The Front View

Having started with the back view (39), Rufinus moves around to inspect the front of
the three competing beauties. (1)

> In competition with each other were Rhodope, Melite, and Rhodocleia (2)
>   to determine which of the three had the best groin. (3)

They picked me to be judge. Just like goddesses these naked women
    stood there on display, dripping with nectar. (4)
And the midpoint between Rhodope's thighs (5) gleamed, richly,   5
    like a bed of roses ruffled by the gentle west wind.

....

.... (6)

That of Rhodocleia was transparent alabaster, with a melting brow, (7)
    like a freshly sculpted statue in a temple.
Because I knew only too well how much Paris suffered for his
    judgement, to these three 'immortals' I awarded a joint prize.   10

Notes

1 Cf. Page 1978 (84–85); Richlin 1992a (48–49).
2 The names Rhodope and Rhodocleia are derivatives of rose / rosy, while Melite is derived
    from honey.
3 *meriones* (pl.), often means 'thighs', but here indicates the area in between; cf. Page 1978 (84).
4 On the image (and some possible readings), cf. Page 1978 (84); Rufin. most likely is referring
    to their state of excitement.
5 This line provides the clearest indication that the area for judgement is that which lies
    between the thighs. Rhodope's loins not only shine, but exude the scent (and moisture) of
    expensive perfume.
6 Melite's couplet is missing.
7 Her pubis is as smooth as an alabaster statue. Page argues that the crest is likely to be 'soft'
    (1978: 85), rather than 'moist' (Paton 1: 147); 'melting' captures the essence of each.

41 Athenaeus 565f–566a: Male Contests in Sparta and Elis

Beauty and physical fitness were highly valued in the Greek world. Male beauty was
judged in competitions known as *kallisteia* throughout Hellas. Crowther notes that
these competitions 'were connected with cults' and that the winners 'performed a ritual
for the deity' (285). Other competitions, focusing more on physical prowess and fitness,
were called *euandria* and *euexia*; these were 'athletic in that they required training and
performance and were found at local agonistic festivals alongside the more traditional
events' (Crowther 286). In the following passage, there is mention of both *euandria*
and *kallisteia*. Interestingly, in the brief reference to the former, it is suggested that
beauty is the prime criterion for victory. Thus it seems that the boundaries between
beauty, manliness and physical prowess or strength were blurred, even at contests that
appeared to mark distinctions between such criteria. (1)

But I myself also praise beauty. (2) For in contests of manliness (3) they select
the most beautiful boys (4) and order them to be the 'first-carriers'. (5) But in
Elis there is even a beauty contest, (6) and to the victor is granted the privilege
of carrying the vessels of the goddess, second is granted the right to lead the
ox, [566a] and third places the sacrificial offering onto the fire. (7) Heraclides
Lembus records that in Sparta the most beautiful man and the most beautiful
woman are admired above all else, with the most beautiful woman in the world
having been born in Sparta.

Notes

1 Cf. Crowther; Golden 1998; Scanlon. Of the terms, *euandria* entails a supply of good men, manliness, the essence or display of manly spirit and courage; while *euexia* places emphasis on good health and bodily fitness. The *euandria*, according to Crowther, 'was . . . a team event which incorporated elements of beauty, size and strength, perhaps as a celebration of manhood' (288). Golden speculates that at the Athenian Panathenaea it was 'a test of physical fitness and fortitude that may have included a tug of war or shield manoeuvres and mock combat' (1998: 37). As there are surviving victory lists for the *euexia*, it would appear that it was for individual competitors and divided into contests for men and for boys. Scanlon, commenting on major festivals at Athens, argues that 'not only bodily size and strength, but also mental and moral qualities and some demonstration of physical prowess were taken into account' (205, cf. also 404 n. 24). The *kallisteia* were not sporting or athletic in nature, but were judged solely on the basis of male beauty.

2 *kallos*.

3 *euandria*.

4 *kallistoi*: superl. of *kalos*; also used in the final sentence.

5 The reference to the 'first-carriers' is obscure. Agonistic contests throughout Greece – ranging from the major Games at Olympia, Delphi, Isthmia and Nemea (the *periodos*), through to other festivals both large (like the Panathenaea) and small – have cultic significance, be it Pan Hellenic or local; cf. Golden 1998.

6 As the competition at Elis focused on beauty (*kallos*) it was a *kallisteia*.

7 On the competition at Elis, cf. Robertson (250–51). The goddess is probably Hera (Gulick 6: 57 n.b; Golden 1998: 129).

42   Athenaeus 609e–610b: Male and Female Contests

Athenaeus discusses beauty competitions for females as well as males in a variety of centres.

I also know of a contest for beautiful women, which was established at one point in time. According to Nicias, in the *History of Arcadia*, (1) Cypselus instigated it after the founding of a city on the plain of the river Alpheius. Here he settled [609f] some Parrhasians and dedicated a precinct and altar to Demeter of Eleusis in whose honour he held the beauty contest. At the inaugural event Herodice, his wife, was awarded the prize. The competition is still conducted in our day and the female contestants are called Chrysophoroe. (2) According to Theophrastus, there is also a beauty contest for men in Elis that is held with much ritual and weapons are the prizes for the victors. Dionysius of Leuctra states that these weapons are dedicated to Athena [610a] and the winner, adorned with ribbons by his friends, leads a procession to her temple. Myrsilus, in *Historical Paradoxes*, notes that the winners are given myrtle crowns. (3) Theophrastus also records that in some places there were female contests for good character and governance of the house, (4) as is also the case among some barbarians. Elsewhere there are contests for beauty alone, (5) as if this too merited a reward of honour, such as those on Tenedos and Lesbos. He goes on to say, however, that this honour is a matter of chance or nature, (6) whereas a special prize for good character should be awarded. [610b]

For only so is beauty honourable for there is always a risk that it could lead to licentious behaviour.

Notes

1 Possibly the philosophical writer, Nicias of Nicaea: cf. Gulick (6: 285 n.g).
2 Cypselus, Seventh Century tyrant of Corinth, inaugurated this competition in the Arcadian town of Basilis, on the river Alpheius. The name Chrysophoroe means 'Wearers of Gold' (Gulick 6: 286 n.a), so adornment must have played a key part. The establishment of major cultural competitions was a feature of Seventh and Sixth Century tyrants: Cleisthenes at Sicyon, Peisistratus at Athens and Polycrates of Samos made use of such events to promote their *poleis* as well as to establish a cultural identity for their respective citizenry.
3 Crowther regards this as a reference to a second beauty contest at Elis (285), in honour of Athena, while it has been suggested that the first was in honour of Hera (41 n. 7). Hera was involved in the female beauty contests held in Lesbos (cf. Page 1955: 168) as well as the athletic contest for girls at Olympia called the Heraea (cf. Golden 1998: 127–32).
4 The criteria for judgement were *sophrosyne* (self-control, discretion, modesty) and *oikonomia* (good management of the household).
5 *kallos*.
6 Beauty is an accident of chance (*tyche*) or nature (*physis*) and therefore not worthy of special honour (*time*).

III

MARRIAGE

Marriage is the principal vehicle for exploration of male–female relationships in antiquity. The opening passages from Archaic Greece (43–45) portray marriage as a necessary evil, a state-of-mind that reflects a view of women as a troublesome sex. Ancient Greece and Rome were public societies in terms of the emphasis placed on reputation and the strongly felt element of shame that underpinned decisions and actions. The choice of a partner, therefore, was of paramount significance to a man's standing in the community. Inappropriate unions, even among the middle and lower classes, were a potential source of public scrutiny and criticism, as Hesiod reminds his audience (44). The misogyny inherent in Hesiod's viewpoint (43) is developed to extremes by Semonides (45), while the matter of appropriate age of a prospective partner (44) is taken up in the salutary advice of Honestus (46).

In contrast to the Archaic male tradition, in Sappho's *epithalamia* or marriage hymns (47) we see the idealisation of marriage as an institution to be aspired to by both bride and groom, and as the beginning of a fruitful union that promises love, devotion and desire. Greek vase paintings of the Classical age also evoke such romanticism. In **Illustration 2** the groom leads his bride to the marriage-bed while two Erotes hover over her as symbols of her impending expression of sexuality; the implications of the anticipated desire on the part of the bride astounds a bystander or attendant, who holds up her hands in surprise (cf. **Illustration 3**). The epithalamic tradition presenting marriage as romantic and personally fulfilling finds its culmination in Catullus' Poem 61 (49). Additional insights into pre-marital tradition and the anxieties of both bride and groom are conveyed in 50–54.

The idealised expectations espoused in the *epithalamium* are further developed in the many texts that extol the institution of marriage: a married couple must present a cohesive and disciplined image to the public, that of the obedient wife and responsible, authoritative husband. In view of such social restraints and the customary dictates that established the public image of marriage, there are few texts that delve into the emotional bonds between husband and wife. Marital tenderness is illustrated publicly, via inscription (55–57), and privately, in poetry and correspondence (58–60).

Wives

43 Hesiod *Theogony* Extracts: Irresistible 'Evils'

According to Hesiod, the first woman was created at the instigation of Zeus to punish men for the crime of receiving fire from Prometheus. She is depicted as being utterly irresistible on account of her beauty and the response it generates. Man will have an overwhelming urge to mate with her and keep her locked unto himself in marriage (*gamos*). To Hesiod both woman and the institution of marriage are irresistible evils. The choice is clear. The one who avoids marriage will live comfortably, lacking nothing, until the arrival of old age when there will be no one to care for him. His relatives will divide his wealth. Marriage, even if his wife is suited to his temperament, brings on constant 'evil' (*kakon*) and conflict with the 'good' (*esthlon*). (1)

> But when he had made a beautiful evil instead of a good thing, (2)   585
> he led her out to where the other gods and men were . . .
> Wonder seized the immortal gods and mortal men as well   588
> when they saw the sheer deceit irresistible to men.
>
> [For from her (3) originates the race of female women,]   590
> from her originates the deadly race and tribe of women, (4)
> a great plague dwelling among mortal men;
> women are not suited to baleful poverty but only to surfeit.
> Women are no help to men in dreadful poverty but only in wealth.
>
> And a second evil thing he gave instead of a good thing: 602
> he who attempts to avoid marriage and the troublesome works
>   (5) of women
> and opts not to marry, arrives at destructive old age (6) with no one
> to care for him. Even though he lacks nothing while he is still alive,   605
> when he does come to die his relatives will arrive to divide up
> his wealth. But the man who does opt for marriage,
> and takes as his wife one who is both good and suited to his
>   temperament,
> lives with evil contending with good on a
> constant basis. (7) The man who gets the dreadful kind (of wife),   610
> exists with never ending grief in his mind and
> his heart, and this is an evil beyond any curative. (8)

Notes

1 For the bibliography on the passage, cf. 17 n. 1.
2 *kalon kakon*: beautiful evil; repeated at *l*. 602. There is an ambiguity in the reading, for 'instead of/in place of' can be read as 'in return for' the *agathoion* (good thing, i.e. the gift of fire to mankind): either makes sense.
3 I.e. Pandora. Note that she is not named in this version (compare 17).

4 On the unlikely placement of these two lines together, cf. West 1966 (329–30).
5 The *erga* (works) of 'painfulness' (*l.* 601–02) and those of 'women' are inseparable.
6 *geras*: old age.
7 *kakon* and *esthlon* are two diametrically opposed alternatives: note there does not appear to be any other possibility – it is one or the other.
8 There are gradations of the 'evil', and this kind of wife will make his life an utter misery; on the many evil forms a wife can take, cf. 45.

44 Hesiod *Works and Days* 695–705: Choosing a Wife

Hesiod's advice on choosing a wife reflects the community-based ideas of Archaic Greek society. A wife must be young, virginal and trainable. Neither love nor even physical attraction is the primary consideration in the selection process.

Bring a wife to your house when you are of the right age,	695
not far short of thirty years nor much above. (1)	
This is the right age for marriage.	
Your wife should have been an adolescent for four years, and	
married to you in the fifth. (2)	
Marry a virgin so that you may teach her good ways. (3)	
Especially marry one who lives near you and be observant about	
everything	700
around you. See that your marriage is not a joke to your neighbours,	
for a man wins nothing better than a good wife;	
and again he wins nothing worse than a bad wife, (4)	
greedy for food, who roasts her man without fire,	
strong though he is, and brings him to a premature old age.	705

Notes

1 Hes.'s suggestion as to the appropriate age for a man to marry seems to be in keeping with some modern statistical studies, which give the average of 33.
2 The bride was much younger than the groom. As Hes.'s advice attests, the right age for a young woman to marry is between 16 and 20, although there are accounts of younger brides. On the issue of age, cf. Garland 1990 (210–13).
3 The young wife can be trained by her older husband whose role was that of *kyrios* or guardian. As the Greeks believed that pubescent girls were full of sexual curiosity as well as lust, it was also important for them to be married as soon as possible so as to prevent any blemish on the girl's name or that of her family.
4 *agathe* (*l.* 703) and *kake* (*l.* 704).

45 Semonides *Poem* 7: Varieties of Wives

Semonides of Amorgos (Seventh Century BC), author of the beast fable on women, was, not surprisingly, a writer of imabic verse. This poetic genre, popular at the symposium, was connected with the word *iapto*, '"meaning to hurl"; it had connotations of "pelting with abuse"' (Lloyd-Jones 13–14). Indeed, in the tradition of Hesiod, Semonides does pelt his women with the cruellest abuse – so intense its hyperbolic quality becomes funny (at least to some). His affirmation that nature has differentiated the sexes, making the mind of women different (*l.* 1), establishes the premise and poetic approach of his diatribe; namely, that women are faulty in design, inferior to men and, by means of explication, synonymous with certain animal species. Except for bee-woman (*l.* 83–93) who is the epitome of the perfect wife – the wife all men should strive to attain – the others are nothing but grief to their spouses. (1)

At the beginning the God (2) made the mind of woman different. (3)

One kind he fashioned out of a bristled sow,
throughout whose household is a pile of filth;
she, messy with muck, rolling about on the floor,
unwashed, in dirty clothes,   5
squats in shit, growing fat.

Another kind he fashioned out of a wicked vixen,
a woman expert in everything. No form of evil
eludes her notice, nor that which is good,
for she more often calls the good bad and the   10
bad good (4). Her moods swing from moment to moment.

Another kind comes from a bitch, filthy tempered, mother
revisited; (5) she has to listen in on everything, know everything,
snoop everywhere, and bark for the sake
of it regardless if anyone's there.   15
No man can shut her up with threats,
not even if in the grip of anger he smashes her teeth
with a rock, nor even by speaking in a sweet manner;
even if by chance she is sitting among guests, (6)
she will keep on barking and nothing can stop her.   20

Another kind the Olympians (7) fashioned of the earth
and gave her, flawed, to man: for this woman neither
knows what is evil nor what is good.
Of work the only thing she knows is eating.
And when the god sends an evil winter, she is too inert   25
to pull her chair near to the fire. (8)

Another kind is of the sea, and she has two moods.
One day she is all sparkle and smiles.
A guest in the household will be full of praise:
"There is no other woman superior to this one   30
in all of humankind, and none more beautiful." (9)
Another day she is intolerable even to look upon
or to come near to; then she raves like a maenad,

she is like a bitch around pups,
relentless and confronting with everyone   35
be they enemies or friends. (10)
Just as the sea frequently is without so much as
a ripple, unthreatening, a great delight for sailors
in the season of summer, but then just as often
rages and tosses with pounding waves,   40
so this type of woman is very much like the sea in respect of
temperament. Like it, she has a character unlike anything else. (11)

Another kind comes from an ashen coloured ass, conditioned to
   the whip,
so that when coerced and abused she
grudgingly yields to do the barest amount   45
of work. In the meantime, withdrawn from sight,
day and night she eats at the hearth.
She is just the same with the task of lovemaking
and welcomes any companion who happens to come along. (12)

Another kind comes from the weasel, a wretched breed,   50
for there is nothing beautiful in her appearance nor desirable,
nor even a source of pleasure nor an incentive to love.
She is a 'thrasher' (13) when it comes to the bed of sex,
and renders seasick the man who 'boards' her. (14)
She perpetrates many evils against her neighbours through   55
thievery and frequently devours unburned sacrificial offerings.

Another kind was bred from a long-maned, fancy mare: (15)
she turns up her nose at servile work and anything hard
and will not endure the millstone, or lift up a
sieve, or clean the shit from the house,   60
or attend the oven being fearful of
soot. Yet she forces a man to be her lover. (16)
On a daily basis, twice, sometimes three times,
she washes her body clean and massages perfume into her skin,
she combs out her thick long hair,   65
intertwined with the shadows of flowers.
A beautiful thing is a woman such as this for others
to see, but an evil thing for the one to whom she belongs,
unless he happens to be a tyrant or bearer of a sceptre,
whose heart revels in things of this sort. (17)   70

Another kind is that of an ape. Above all others, this one is
the very worst evil that Zeus has bestowed upon mankind.

Her face is the epitome of ugliness; such a woman is
an object of derision as she walks around the town.
Her neck is stunted, she moves stiffly, skinny legged,   75
and has a withered bum. (18) Wretched is the man,
who holds in his arms such an evil as this.
She knows all the lurks and the tricks,
just like an ape, but has no sense of humour,
and does not care if everyone laughs at her in mockery;   80
she never thinks of doing something nice for somebody else,
but devotes her entire attention to doing the utmost evil.

Another kind is that of a bee. The one who gets her is most fortunate:
for it is only on her that no blame alights;
the course of life prospers and increases;   85
loving, she grows old with her beloved spouse,
the bearer of beautiful offspring with an honourable name. (19)
She shines among all other women
and a grace worthy of the gods encircles her. (20)
And she gets no pleasure sitting among other women,   90
when all they do is gossip about sex. (21)
Wives such as these does Zeus bestow upon mankind,
and they are the best and the most sagacious.

But the other kinds, due to the contrivance of the God,
exist as a misery and will remain as such for mankind.   95

Zeus indeed made this the greatest evil –
women. And even when she seems to be a helper,
that is when she does her possessor the greatest harm;
for he who spends his life alongside a woman,
will never survive a single day in a state of good cheer;   100
and from his household he will not easily drive away Hunger, (22)
a despised lodger within a household, an inimical deity.
Whenever a man in his mind feels particularly glad in spirit
in his household, by the gift of god or the kindness of men, (23)
that is when she will carp and ready herself for battle.   105
For wherever a woman is in residence, the household
will never be able to extend a welcome to a guest.
And the one who appears to be most endowed with self-restraint (24)
is constantly one who does the greatest harm:
for while her man is mooning over her, her neighbours are   110
delighted at another one being conned.
And everyone who calls his woman to mind will praise
her, and will pass all blame onto the wives of others:

and yet we know well that it is the same in every case.
Zeus indeed made this the greatest evil (25)   115
and put us in chains that cannot be broken,
ever since the time that Hades greeted those
who fought in that war over a woman. (26)

Notes

1 On the poem, cf. Lloyd-Jones; North; Gerber 1978, 1999b; Svarlien; Osborne.
2 Zeus rather than Hephaestus. Note the pl. at *l.* 21 for the other deities who assisted the manufacture of the first woman.
3 The mind (*nous*) of women is either diverse (in respect of each other) or different from that of men (Gerber 1999b: 305 n. 2). Lloyd-Jones suggests 'from us', indicating the poem may have been written for men at a symposium (63); cf. also Osborne (55).
4 The poet employs a series of negative images for the vixen: she is wicked (*l.* 7), revels in evil/s (*l.* 8, 10, 11) and confuses evil with good (*l.* 11); compare with the woman of earth at *l.* 22–23, who is ignorant of the difference. Evil (*kakon*) is all-pervading in the poem (also cf. *l.* 55, 68, 72, 77, 82, 96, 98, 115).
5 *autometora*: 'her mother's own child' (Lloyd-Jones 68); 'a mother through and through' (Svarlien 6); 'her mother all over again' (Gerber 1999b: 305).
6 The entertainment of guests (*xenoi*) was a key role for women of the household. It recurs through the poem, culminating in the ultimate betrayal by wife and guest, Helen and Paris; cf. also *l.* 29, 107.
7 Here the poet acknowledges the part played by other Olympians (Athena and Hephaestus) in the creation of woman: note that she is flawed (crippled; incomplete) and of little use to a husband due to her inertia.
8 Or 'she shivers and draws her chair nearer the fire' (Gerber 1999b: 307). The image of her being too lazy to move even when freezing with cold is the stronger.
9 Possibly a comparison with Helen. On the surface she is the most desirable of women, but her other side renders her utterly unbearable. Note the comparative of *kalos*, and the implied echo of the *kalon kakon* of Hes. (43 n. 2).
10 *philoi*: 'friends', used in the sense of 'lover' at *l.* 62.
11 The reading of Lloyd-Jones (73); cf. Svarlien 6–7 for a full review of the options.
12 Just as she compulsively eats anything on offer, so she also indulges her lust for sex (*aphrodision*, also at *l.* 53, 91) with any male companion (*hetairos*) who comes along.
13 Most offer a variant on 'mad', 'sex-crazed' for *alenes*. Echoes of modern colloquialisms come to mind, hence 'thrasher', one who engages in vigorous, noisy and insatiable coupling.
14 The nautical image of Svarlien (7) has been adopted. She thrashes about so much in the act that her 'boarder' is rendered seasick. For an alternative reading, 'the man who is present with her', cf. Lloyd-Jones (78) and Gerber 1999b (309).
15 The mare-woman is described as 'proud, luxurious, delicate' (Lloyd-Jones 79).
16 Cf. Lloyd-Jones (80); Svarlien (8). Gerber 1978 (20) notes the story of Neaera's seduction of her husband's friend Promedon by locking him in a bedchamber and forcing him to surrender to her enticements (Parth. 18.2).
17 Tyrants were invariably big spenders. Only tyrants or kings could afford the high maintenance of mare-woman.
18 Lloyd-Jones notes that '[t]he *puge* was a mark of female beauty in ancient Greece', and cites examples (83); there is a famous statue of Aphrodite called the Aphrodite Callipyrgus (Aphrodite of the Beautiful Bum).
19 The ideal woman is the one who marries only the once, who lives blamelessly and lovingly to old age having produced illustrious offspring.
20 *charis*.

21 Other women have a propensity for gossip, especially about sex (cf. *l*. 48, 53): her avoidance of them indicates good judgement and wisdom (*sophrosyne*).

22 Hunger is personified as a deity (*Aipsa*).

23 A man wants a generous serve of fate or favour (*moira*) from the gods and the kindness (*charis*) of other men. 'When a god does one a kindness, it is a [*moira*]: when a man does it, it is a [*charis*]' (Lloyd-Jones 89). Wives, as a rule, spoil what joy he receives from their reception.

24 To practise self-restraint (*sophronein*) also implies chastity and respectability, cf. Lloyd-Jones (90).

25 A verbatim re-rendering of *l*. 96.

26 Helen is the ultimate manifestation of the *kalon kakon*. The image incorporates and concludes previous allusions to the treatment of guests (*xeneia*), which have permeated the poem.

46 Honestus *Greek Anthology* 5.20: Neither Too Young Nor Too Old

Of uncertain date (possibly First Century AD), Honestus argues for a sensible approach to choosing a bride. An adverse view of older women is expected but he is also averse to choosing a young girl as a bride. His preference is for a woman who is ripe for the demands of the conjugal couch. (1)

> With neither a young girl do I want to take delight in marriage, nor an old woman: (2)
> for the one I feel compassion, for the other I stand in awe.
> Neither an unripe grape nor a dried grape do I want: but a ripe one, (3)
> a beauty in season (4) for the bedchamber of the Cyprian.

Notes

1 On the dating of Honestus, cf. Gow and Page 1968 (2: 301), who conclude that he 'was active during the reign of Tiberius, and that he was one of those who sought or enjoyed patronage in the imperial court'; *LSJ* hesitantly suggests First Century BC.

2 While his rejection of an old woman (*geraia*) as a marriage partner is to be expected on several grounds, it is surprising to hear him dismissive of a *parthenike*, especially in light of his declaration of being in awe of such a girl. The verb (*terpein*, to take delight in) is the key to his sentiments, as revealed in the final line.

3 The metaphor of the grape is clever: the girl is unripe (*omphax*, also 'sour') for sex; cf. *LSJ* 1229, *omphaka mazdou*, the unripe breasts of a young girl. The old woman is *astaphis*, collective for 'dried grapes', therefore wrinkled, devoid of juice. The ripe one (*pepeiros*, used of fruit and girls) is both juicy and ready for bed, as well as possessing a mild personality.

4 The ideal 'grape' is beautiful (*kallosune*), and ready (*horia*, in season) for sexual intercourse.

Marriage songs

47 Sappho *Fragments*: Epithalamia – Marriage Hymns

Sappho's *epithalamia* provide a rare glimpse into some of the rituals and attitudes associated with aristocratic wedding ceremonies of the Archaic age. These songs, sung by individuals (possibly Sappho herself on some occasions) and choirs at the wedding banquet, vary in subject matter with the tone ranging from gentle sensuality, to didacticism and playful ribaldry. (1)

103B
. . . chamber . . .
. . . a bride with beautiful feet . . . (2)

105(a)
As the sweet apple reddens on the very end of the bough,
on the very end of the furthest bough; the apple-pickers have
   forgotten it.
No, they have not really forgotten it, they could not reach it. (3)

105(c)
Like the hyacinth that shepherds in the mountains
trample upon with their feet, and on the ground the purple
bloom . . . (4)

107
Do I still yearn for virginity? (5)

110(a)
The doorkeeper's feet are humungous,
five oxen provided material for his sandals;
ten shoemakers toiled in their making! (6)

111
Up high with the roof,
Hymenaios! (7)
Hoist it up, workmen,
Hymenaios!
The bridegroom is
approaching, a match for Ares,
the largest of large men. (8)

112
Joyous bridegroom, your marriage has reached the fruition
for which you prayed, you possess the girl for whom you prayed . . .
Your body is graceful, gentle your eyes . . .
and love (9) pours over your beautiful features
. . . Aphrodite bestowed great honour upon you.

113
Bridegroom, there has never been a girl like her.

114

"Virginity, virginity, where have you gone? Have you abandoned me?"
"I will never come to you again, I will never come again." (10)

115

To what may I best compare you, beloved bridegroom?
To a slender sapling, more than anything else, will I compare you. (11)

116

Salutations bride, salutations groom!

Notes

1 Cf. Page 1955 (119–26); Hallett 1979 (455–57); Wilson (142–57); Stehle (266–70, 274–82); on the public performance, cf. Lardinois.
2 Goddesses and heroines in Greek literature are regularly described as having beautiful ankles and feet. The refinement of a young woman's feet indicates a life of ease and leisure.
3 These lines and *Fr.* 105(c) may well have been connected (although not preserved together) and may have served the function of giving advice to unmarried girls at the ceremony. The didactic aspect of the song may have involved praise of the girl who preserves her virginity for marriage (rendered symbolically by the apple out of reach) and the lament for the girl who loses her virginity before marriage (symbolised by the trampled flower). Cf. Davison; Stigers (90–98); Griffith; duBois 1995 (40–54). On apple imagery, cf. Foster; McCartney; Littlewood; Gerber 1978.
4 Stigers: '[the] hyacinth on the hillside . . . is a beautiful girl in a vulnerable position, harmed, presumably raped or seduced, by careless, wandering men.' (90). Alternatively, the warning may well have been to the girl who willingly indulges a mutual desire and so renders herself stained and therefore unsuited to marriage. On the fate of girls caught alone in the wilderness without the protection of their male kin, cf. 113.
5 The ancients valued virginity (*parthenia*) as arguably the most desirable feature of the bride. Most editors interpret the fragment as a question (contra West 1994: 45).
6 Ribald fun was part of some marriage songs. Sapph., in words that may have been sung by the bride's attendants to the doorkeeper of the bedroom, could be euphemistically equating his long feet with the size of his penis.
7 Hymenaios is both wedding god and wedding song. He instructs young men to hoist a lofty canopy over the nuptial proceedings.
8 Contains similar innuendo to *Fr.* 110(a), here with respect to the 'size' of the groom. Page suggests that this extract may well be from 'a song presumably recited by the assembly which went in procession from the bride's house to the bridegroom's after the ceremonial banquet' (1955: 120). The comparison of the groom with Ares evokes an equation of the bride with Aphrodite (cf. 3).
9 *eros*, here the capacity to evoke love.
10 Here the bride addresses her *parthenia* and it replies (cf. n. 5).
11 The comparison evokes mild eroticism with its image of supple, youthful vigour (as in 18) and a hint of phallic suggestiveness. For the idealism of love and eroticism on behalf of both the bride and the groom, cf. **Illustration 2.**

48 Theocritus *Idyll* 18: Epithalamium for Helen and Menelaus

This piece by the Hellenistic inventor of pastoral poetry is the first complete extant
epithalamium, and appears to have been composed as a literary exercise. Theocritus
utilises the earlier conventions of traditional wedding song. Firstly, he has a chorus of
virgins who have been selected to sing and dance to the song. He also situates the
performance outside the bridal chamber and employs standard themes such as their
beauty, good omens for their life together, the birth of a child. Finally, he ends the
work with a farewell to the couple and an appeal to Hymenaios. (1)

Once upon a time at Sparta in the palace of fair-haired Menelaus,
virginal girls with blooming hyacinth in their tresses
set up the dance before the newly painted bridal chamber,
twelve of them, the pick of the community, the flower of Laconian
 girlhood. (2)
Then he shut the doors on the beloved daughter of Tyndareus,   5
Helen, after he had wooed her, he, the younger son of Atreus. (3)
They all sang, dancing to the same music
with feet in time, and the house echoed with the wedding song. (4)

"Have you fallen asleep so early, dear bridegroom? (5)
Are you too heavy limbed? Are you too fond of sleep?   10
Had you been drinking a long time when you threw yourself down
 on the bed?
Wanting to sleep early, you ought to have slept by yourself,
and let the girl child, (6) along with other girls at the side of their
 loving mother,
play late until dawn – for the day after tomorrow and the day after
 that
and year after year, Menelaus, she is your wife.   15

Happy bridegroom, some good man sneezed on your behalf when
 you came
to Sparta, just as the other princes came, in order that you might
 prevail. (7)
You alone among demigods will have Zeus son of Cronus as your
 father-in-law.
The daughter of Zeus lies underneath the same blanket as you,
an Achaean woman such as none other walks the earth;   20
the child she bears will be remarkable if it is the same as its
 mother. (8)
We are girls of her age and we all run as a group together,
after anointing ourselves as men do at the bathing pools of Eurotas;
we are four by sixty girls, (9) a group of young females
of whom not one is faultless when compared with Helen.   25

Upon rising, Dawn reveals her fair face,
oh Lady Night, and when Winter ends, Spring reveals hers;
and so in the same way among us golden Helen revealed herself.
As a cypress grows so high to adorn a fertile field
or garden, or as a Thessalian horse adorns a chariot,   30
so rosy Helen is an ornament to Lacedaemon.
No one from her spinning-basket winds such yarn onto the shuttle
   as she does,
nor at her patterned loom, having woven with the shuttle, does
any woman cut from the great loom-beams a closer web.
Nor is anyone as skilled as Helen in playing the lyre,   35
singing of Artemis and broad-bosomed Athena, (10)
as Helen does, in whose eyes are all desires. (11)

Beautiful, gracious girl, you are now a housewife. (12)
Off to the running track are we, early tomorrow,
and to flowery meadows to gather sweet smelling garlands,   40
remembering you, Helen, as suckling
lambs who long for the teat of the mother ewe. (13)
Once we have woven for you a wreath from lotus growing on the
   ground,
once we have woven it, then we will place it on a shady plane-tree;
once we have drawn smooth oil from a silver flask,   45
once we have drawn it, then we will let it drip beneath a shady
   plane-tree.
On its bark this will be inscribed, in order that anyone passing by
may read in Doric, 'Worship me; I am Helen's tree.' (14)

Hail, bride. (15) Hail, bridegroom with a noble father-in-law.
May Leto, nurse of children, (16) grant to both of you   50
fertility. May the goddess Cypris grant you equal love
for each other. (17) May Zeus son of Cronus grant lasting prosperity,
and have it pass down forever from noble ancestors to noble
   descendants.
Go to sleep, breathing love and longing (18)
into each other's breasts.
Don't forget to wake at dawn.   55
We, too, will come at first dawn when the cockerel
crows after raising his well-feathered neck from sleep.
Hymen, O Hymenaios, in this wedding rejoice!"

Notes

1 Cf. Gow (2: 348–61); Stern; Hunter (149–66).

2 Wellborn, aristocratic girls, social equals and companions of the bride, were selected for the composition of the choir.

3 Tyndareus was Helen's earthly father (cf. *l.* 18–19 where Zeus is noted as her real father); Menelaus was the younger brother of Agamemnon, sons of Atreus.

4 *hymenaios* is the wedding/bridal song performed by the bride's attendants who escorted her to the house of the groom. In the final line, the term is used to address the god of marriage (first mentioned at *Il.* 18.491–96).

5 The hymenaeal begins with a mildly mocking and suggestive address to the *gambros* (bridegroom; also at *l.* 16, 49).

6 *pais*: child, here a girl. The presentation of the bride as a child or girl is a recurrent image in *epithalamia*. On the age of Greek brides at marriage, cf. Garland 1990 (210–13).

7 Sneezing is regarded as a good omen among the Greeks (cf. *Od.* 17.541) and is represented as the sign of divine approval given to lovers by Amor himself in Cat. 45. Many suitors came seeking Helen's hand (cf. Apoll., *Lib.* 3.10.8; Hygin. 81).

8 Helen's daughter Hermione was renowned for her beauty (cf. Sapph. *Fr.* 23).

9 The reference to the size of this group has caused scholarly dispute. The group singing the *epithalamium* is specifically numbered at 12 in *l.* 4; Gow (2: 354) notes that the number 240 possibly refers to organisation of all girls of this age in Archaic Sparta corresponding to the known group divisions of young boys.

10 She sings of virgin goddesses, both of whom have major cults at Sparta. Athena presides over the education of girls in the skills required of a wife and mother while Artemis plays an important role in childbirth; cf. Gow (2: 357).

11 *himeroi* (pl.): desires. Helen's eyes inspire desire, in both would-be suitors and her maiden friends.

12 The girl is both *kala* (beautiful) and *chariessa* (gracious, graceful). As an *oiketis* (housewife) Helen is 'no longer free to join in the pursuits of the unmarried girls' (Gow 2: 358).

13 The girls will continue their usual pursuits (athletics, picking flowers). The image of the ewe and her lambs indicates Helen's leadership of the group and their affection for her rather than any age difference.

14 *l.* 43–48 'account aetiologically for a cult of Helen at Sparta in which she is associated or identified with a plane-tree. The maidens will be the first celebrants . . . of the rites, and founders of the cult' (Gow 2: 358).

15 The verb can be used as a welcoming salutation or one of farewell, and may simply be rendered as 'rejoice!' as at *l.* 58. The term for a bride (*nymphe*) could continue to be used of Helen after the wedding, up until she gave birth.

16 Leto does figure as a goddess of childbirth (equated with Eileithyia), although not as frequently as Artemis; cf. Gow (2: 360).

17 Note the role granted to Aphrodite to promote an equal love between them, a theme taken up by Cat. and other amatory poets.

18 Sleep will bring shared love (*philotes*) and mutual desire (*pothos*).

49 Catullus 61: The Epithalamium for Junia and Manlius

While Catullus provides an idealised presentation of marriage among the Roman aristocracy of the Late Republic, it is set within the context of a real marriage in that the names of the bride and groom can be assigned to contemporary figures, Junia and Manlius Torquatus. Poem 61 contains detailed descriptions of the marriage traditions and conveys important insights into the social and psychological issues of marriage. (1)

Invocation of the God of Marriage
O dweller of the Heliconian
mountain, offspring of Urania, (2)
you who carry off (3) to the man the tender
maiden, O Hymenaeus Hymen,
   O Hymen Hymenaeus: 5

bind up your brows with flowers
of sweetly fragrant red marjoram,
take up the bridal veil with joy, here,
come here, wearing the yellow slipper (4)
   on snow white foot; . . .   10

For Junia comes to Manlius, (5)
such as, dwelling in Idalium, (6)
Venus came before the Phrygian
judge, (7) a good maiden with
   a good omen will be married, . . .   20

To the house summon the mistress,
filled with desire for her new spouse,
binding fast her mind with love,
just as clinging ivy, straying here
   and here, envelops a tree. . . . (8)   35

A Hymn of Praise to Hymen
What god ought to be more sought out
by lovers who are already loved?
Whom of the heaven-dwellers ought mankind
cultivate more, O Hymenaeus Hymen,
   O Hymen Hymenaeus?   50

You, on behalf of his dependants, the trembling parent
invokes, for you maidens
loosen the folds from their virgin belt, (9)
you the apprehensive new bridegroom
   listens out for with eager ear.   55

To the fierce youth, into his hands you,
you yourself, give the flowering little
girl from the bosom of her
mother, O Hymenaeus Hymen,
   O Hymen Hymenaeus.   60

Without you Venus can partake of no
pleasure which good fame
would condone. Ah, but she can
when you are willing. Who would dare to be
  compared to this god? 65

Without you no house can
provide children, and a parent cannot
depend upon offspring. Ah, but he can
when you are willing. Who would dare to be
  compared to this god? 70

Address to the Bride
Cease to weep. Not for you,
Aurunculeia, is there danger,
that any woman more beautiful
has looked upon the shining day 85
  rising up from Ocean.

Such a hyacinth flower usually
stands in the multifarious ornamental
garden of a wealthy lord. (10)
But you are delaying, the day is passing. 90
  <Let you come forth new bride.>

Your man will not – given over
lightly to an evil adulteress,
chasing after shameful acts of dishonour –
wish to bed down away from 100
  your tender breasts,

but just as the pliant vine
envelops the trees planted nearby,
he will be enveloped in your
embrace. But the day is passing: 105
  let you come forth new bride.

Address to the Boy-Attendants
Raise up, <O> boys, the torches:
I see the bridal veil coming. 115
Go, sing in harmony the measure
'Yo, Hymen Hymenaeus, Yo,
  Yo Hymen Hymenaeus.'

Let not the impertinent Fescennine (11)
jesting be silent for very long,   120
and let not the bed-boy (12) deny nuts
to the boys, hearing that the love of
    his lord is lost.

Address to the Bed-Boy
Give nuts to the boys, lazy
bed-boy! You have sported with nuts   125
sufficiently long enough: now it is time
to render service to Talasius. (13)
    Bed-boy, give out the nuts.

Address to the Bridegroom
You are said to be abstaining with
difficulty from your beardless bed-pets,   135
perfumed bridegroom, but abstain.
Yo, Hymen Hymenaeus, Yo,
    <Yo, Hymen Hymenaeus.>

We know that you are aware of the things that
are permitted to a bachelor, but to a bridegroom   140
those same things are not permissible.
Yo, Hymen Hymenaeus, Yo,
    Yo, Hymen Hymenaeus.

Address to the Bride
Bride, you too beware lest you deny
things which your husband asks for,   145
lest he go seeking them elsewhere.
Yo, Hymen Hymenaeus, Yo,
    Yo, Hymen Hymenaeus.

See how potent and blessed for you
is the house of your man.   150
Permit it to render service to you –
<Yo, Hymen Hymenaeus, Yo,
    Yo, Hymen Hymenaeus > –

With a good omen, take across
the threshold your golden little feet,   160
and pass through the polished doorway. (14)
Yo, Hymen Hymenaeus, Yo,
    Yo, Hymen Hymenaeus.

See how, as he reclines inside
upon a Tyrian couch, your man   165
is wholly intent upon you.
Yo, Hymen Hymenaeus, Yo,
    Yo, Hymen Hymenaeus.

For him – no less also for you –
in his inmost heart burns   170
the flame, but see, he dies with love even more.
Yo, Hymen Hymenaeus, Yo,
    Yo, Hymen Hymenaeus.

A Call to the Bridegroom
Now it is permissible for you to come, bridegroom:
a wife is in the bridal chamber for you,   185
with flower-like features she shines,
just like white chamomile
    or yellow poppy.

Ah, bridegroom, so may the heavenly ones
help me, you are by no means less   190
beautiful, nor does Venus
neglect you. But the day is passing:
    proceed, do not delay.

You have not delayed for long:
now you come. May good Venus   195
assist you, since quite openly you
desire what you desire, and do not hide
    a good love.

An Address to the Bride and the Groom
Let that man first calculate the
number of African sands   200
and of the glittering stars,
who wishes to enumerate the many
    thousands of your delights. (15)

Take delight as you like, and in a short time
bring forth children. It is not fitting that   205
so old a name be without
children, but that it constantly be
    reproduced from the same line.

A Prayer for a Son
I would that a tiny Torquatus,
from the bosom of his mother,   210
reaching out his tender hands
should laugh sweetly to his father
    with semi-parted liplet.

Final Instructions
Close the front doors, maidens:
we have sported enough. Ah, good   225
spouses, live well and, by means of
continuous giving, exercise your
    healthy youth.

Notes

1 Cf. Fedeli; Thomsen; Godwin; Wheeler; Treggiari. For a complete version of the poem,
   with more detailed geographical and mythical references, cf. Johnson and Ryan.
2 Urania, daughter of Zeus and Mnemosyne, was the muse of astronomy and astrology.
   Hymenaeus, the wedding god, was her son by Dionysus.
3 *rapere*: to carry off, to seize by force; rape. Festus (364L) states that the pretence of forcible
   removal of the virgin from her mother was an imitative re-enactment of the rape of the
   Sabine women.
4 On bridal costume, cf. La Follette.
5 The bride is also called Aurunculeia (*l.* 83), while the groom is identified as Torquatus (*l.*
   209–16), member of a noble family in Republican Rome. Cf. Neudling; Mitchell.
6 Site of a temple sacred to Venus on Cyprus.
7 Paris; cf. 38.
8 Key images in *l.* 31–35: *domina* in this context is the woman who manages the *domus* (the
   house/household of her husband); *coniunx* (lit. 'a conjoined one' or 'spouse') applies to both
   husband and wife; at *l.* 33 *amor* binds their minds, as the garland of marjoram binds the
   brow of Hymenaeus at *l.* 6–7, and the ivy binds the tree at *l.* 34–35.
9 The *zona* was a belt worn around the breasts or hips by unmarried girls. The first to untie
   the belt was the groom at the time of consummation.
10 Note that here the hyacinth is protected and nurtured as opposed to growing wild, being
    vulnerable, and trampled upon in Sapph. *Fr.* 105(c) (cf. 47).
11 Festus (76L): 'Fescennine verses, which were sung at weddings, were said to have been called
    thus from the city of Fescennina [= Fescennium], or because they were thought to have
    provided a defence against witchcraft [*fascinum*: the evil eye].' They were designed to inject
    laughter and fun into the proceedings and frequently adopted an impertinent and risqué
    tone, as can be seen by the sexual allusions that follow.
12 Opinion on the *concubinus* (bed-boy) ranges from a personal valet, to someone who acts as a
    bodyguard, to a younger boy who provides sexual relief for an older youth. He refers to such
    boys as *glabri* (pl.) at *l.* 135, boys who are smooth skinned and clearly *delicati*.
13 Ancient opinion was divided on the origin of this term and the transformation of it into a
    divinity associated with marriage.
14 'The reference is to the Roman ceremony of conducting the bride across the threshold of
    her new home' (Quinn 1973: 272).
15 *ludi*: (pl.) sport, game, here referring to delights of a sexual nature.

Traditions and customs

50 Euripides *Iphigenia in Aulis* Extracts: Marriage Traditions

This tragedy, left unfinished by the playwright and possibly completed by his son, was produced in *c.* 406 BC. Here the strong connection between marriage and death is a major theme, as Iphigenia is prepared as a bride only to be offered as a sacrifice to Artemis. The following excerpts have been selected to illustrate wedding rituals in Classical Athens. (1)

430–39
Messenger

They are saying: "Is it a wedding? (2) What is going on?	430
Has king Agamemnon, experiencing a longing for his daughter, (3)	
brought the child here?" (4) From others you would have heard:	
"They are preparing the girl for Artemis, (5)	
queen of Aulis. Who is going to marry her?"	
But come, begin the rites, get the baskets ready,	435
crown your heads and you, king Menelaus,	
prepare the wedding song and throughout the pavilion	
let the flute resound and let there be the noise of dancers' feet;	
for this is a happy day for the maiden.	

607–22
Clytemnestra

I regard as a good omen	
your kindness and auspicious words,	
and I hope that it is to a glorious marriage	
that I am going as leader of the bride. (6)	610
[To the servants]	
Take from the chariot the dowry I am bringing for my daughter,	
and carry it inside with care.	
And you, my offspring, leave the horse-drawn chariot,	
setting down gently your tender feet.	
And you, young maids, take her in your arms	615
and help her from the chariot.	
And let one of you give me the support of her hand	
that I may leave my seat in graceful style.	
Some of you stand in front of the horses' yoke,	
for a horse's eye is easily frightened and can not be soothed	
with words.	620
And take this child, (7) offspring of Agamemnon,	
Orestes.	

716–22

Clytemnestra
Let them prosper! On what day will she be married?

Agamemnon
When the full moon comes with her blessing. (8)

Clytemnestra
Have you already offered a sacrifice to the goddess for the child's marriage?

Agamemnon
I am about to do so. I have begun the preparation.

Clytemnestra
And then will you celebrate the marriage feast afterwards?   720

Agamemnon
Yes, when I have offered a sacrifice required by the gods.

Clytemnestra
But where am I to prepare the women's feast? (9)

Notes

1 Cf. Foley; Seaford; Rehm.
2 *hymenaios*: wedding; also used for the wedding-song at *l.* 437.
3 *pothos* can mean love, desire or longing. The reference could mean Agamemnon misses his daughter or it could even be an implied suggestion of incestuous desire. This line increases the tone of apprehension and impending doom that characterises the scene.
4 Images accentuating the youthfulness of the bride permeate the passages: on *pais* as bride, cf. *l.* 621, 718; Iphigenia is also called *neanis* (girl, *l.* 433; used in the pl. at *l.* 615); and *parthenos* (virgin, *l.* 439).
5 As goddess of virginity, youthful creatures, especially girls and young women, Artemis is honoured and invoked as part of the marriage procedure.
6 *nymphagogos*: the one (usually a male) who takes the bride from the home of her father to that of her husband.
7 The presence of the young Orestes is a symbol of good omen (cf. Golden 1990: 30).
8 Athenians regarded the full moon as a positive time of the month, particularly favourable for conception.
9 A reference to the women's feast (*l.* 722), indicative of the separation (within the one room) of males and females; cf. Oakley and Sinos (22–24).

51 Plutarch *Moralia* 138.1 [*Advice to the Bride and Groom*]: Marriage Customs

Plutarch's advice to newly-weds extends to the occasional digression on marriage customs. Here he provides information on practices that seem to be connected with the promotion of sexual attraction on the part of the bride as well as fertility.

Solon (1) commanded the bride to lie with the bridegroom after eating a small amount of quince, (2) suggesting, so it seems, that the charm (3) from mouth and voice ought on the first occasion to be well balanced and sweet. In Boeotia, after they have veiled the bride, they crown her with asparagus. (4) This plant sends up the sweetest fruit from the roughest thorny plant, just as a bride will provide a tame and sweet life together with a man who does not flee from nor find objectionable any ill temper or unpleasantness of hers from the very first.

Notes

1 Solon was a famous lawgiver at Athens in 594 BC. Over time, practices and conventions were attributed to him in order to achieve a measure of authority.
2 '[B]y accepting food in her husband's home, the bride is united with her husband, as . . . Persephone was bound to Hades after she ate the pomegranate seeds he offered.' (Pomeroy 1999: 47). The fruit may have been part of a love spell to encourage the development of feelings and increase her attraction for the husband (Faraone 1999: 95).
3 The reference to the *charis* of her mouth could well be a practical one in that the quince ensured fresh breath on the occasion of consummation.
4 'The wild asparagus has sharp pointed leaves and small cream-colored flowers' (Pomeroy 1999: 47).

52 Athenaeus 602d–e: Pre-Marital Practice at Sparta

Athenaeus describes pre-marital practice at Sparta in which maidens, presumably those betrothed, were 'dealt with as boys', that is taken anally by their intended partners.

Among the Spartiates, as Hagnon, a philosopher of the Academic School, (1) states, [e] it was the norm (2) for maiden girls, prior to their weddings, (3) to be dealt with as if they were boys. (4)

Notes

1 Hagnon of Tarsus was a student of the Academic philosopher, Carneades of Cyrene (214–129 BC).
2 *nomos*: law or, more generally, custom, practice.
3 This phrase, following 'maiden girls' (*parthenoi*), suggests sexual relations between engaged partners. On Spartan wedding practice, cf. A.-J. Ball; Pomeroy 2002 (39–44). Cf. also Cartledge 2001.
4 *homilein*: here in the sense 'to share intimacy with'. Anal sex preserved virginity as well as acting as a contraceptive. On the practice and the sexual connotations of 'lakonizing', cf. Dover 1978 (188–89).

Pre-marital anxiety

53 Seneca the Elder *Controversies* 1.2.22: The Bride

A method of dealing with the fears a bride had about the act of defloration is addressed in this extract from Seneca. In the light of this passage, 54 and 49 (*l.* 144–56), it is possible that the practice of anal sex on the first night was common.

"We know," he said, "about the abstinence on the part of newly married men,
(1) who, although granting a remission of the first night to fearful virgins, still
take their pleasure (2) in nearby locations." (3)

Notes

1 The question of 'abstinence' on the part of newly married men (*mariti*) appears odd since it
   is clear that deferral of the perforation of the hymen is at issue, not restraint from sexual
   activity.
2 *ludere* (to sport, play) may seem slightly inappropriate here, but for the fact that the speaker
   adopts the viewpoint of the new husband.
3 A euphemism for the bride's anus. It is difficult to determine if this practice arose solely
   from genuine consideration for a bride's first night anxieties: it may have had a symbolic
   purpose (the husband abandoning his *concubinus*; cf. 49 n. 12); and it may also have introduced
   her to an ongoing method of contraception.

54 Martial 11.78: The Groom

While advice to the bride occurs in a number of writers, there is a paucity of similar
material for the groom. It is assumed that, unlike the bride, the man will enter the
relationship with at least some basic experience. Here Martial addresses a groom who
apparently has no experience of women, hence the need to offer some helpful hints.

> Experience feminine embraces, enjoy them, Victor, (1)
>   and let your cock (2) learn something as yet unknown to it.
> Red veils (3) are being woven for the betrothed, now the virgin
>   is being prepared,
>   the new bride (4) already will be giving your boys a haircut. (5)
> Just the once will she give her lustful husband a bum-fuck, (6)   5
>   while she is still fearful of the initial 'wounds' of that new
>   weapon: (7)
> her nurse and her mother will veto this happening more frequently
>   and will say: "That girl is a wife to you, not a boy."
> Alas! What great anxieties, what great troubles for you to endure,
>   if a cunt will prove to be a matter totally alien to you!   10
> So, hand the apprentice over to a Mistress in the Subura. (8)
>   She will make a man out of him: a virgin is not a good teacher.

Notes

1 On the name 'Victor' ('Winner'), cf. Kay (233).
2 Mart. employs blunt terminology, *mentula* (cock, prick) and *cunnus* (cunt) in *l*. 10.
3 The bridal veil (*flammea*) was red; cf. La Follette.
4 Note the sequence: at first she is called *sponsa* (betrothed), then *virgo*, and finally *nupta* (bride).
5 The groom's boys, being long-haired, are likely to have been *delicati* or bed companions; the
   cutting of their hair indicates their arrival at manhood. Cf. 49 n. 12; Kay (233–34).
6 Since the husband is on fire with lust (*cupidus*), the bride will allow him the right to sodomise
   her (*pedicare*).

7 As Kay notes (234), conceding her rectum out of fear of pain in her vagina appears odd. Victor does, however, have experience of anal sex and thus will be less nervous and more considerate if that is what is offered.

8 A pun on *magistra* (brothel keeper and teacher). The Subura was located between the Viminal and Esquiline hills at Rome and 'was a busy shopping area as well as a red-light district' (Kay 205).

The pain of separation

55 *EG* 44.2–3: Epitaph for Chaerestrate

This inscription from the Piraeus (Fourth Century BC) is short but emotive. While it could be argued that in a public monument the bereaved may present an overly positive view of the prior relationship, the reference combining love and grief suggests genuine sentiment.

> In this tomb lies Chaerestrate. Her husband loved her
> as long as she lived. When she died he grieved for her.

56 *CIL* I.2 1211: Epitaph for Claudia

This inscription was set up by a husband in honour of his wife, Claudia (*c.* 150 BC). While the sentiments are controlled, as one would expect in a testimonial by a Roman noble, they are also quite tender and provide some insight into the private world of a good marriage.

> Stranger, (1) what I ask is but a little thing: stand close and read carefully.
> This is the not so beautiful sepulchre of a beautiful woman:
> the name her parents gave her was Claudia. (2)
> Her husband she cherished (3) from the depths of her heart.
> She gave birth to two children – one of these she left
> on the earth – the other she placed beneath it.
> She was possessed of charming speech, and moreover a pleasing gait. (4)
> She maintained the household. She made wool. I have spoken. Go
> forward.

Notes

1 The speaker is the tombstone, formally addressing passers-by. The use of a conversational form on an inscription was widely practised throughout the ancient world.

2 The stone has a wry sense of humour: the tomb itself is not beautiful compared to its occupant, the beautiful Claudia. The pun is clever in view of *pulcer* (beautiful) being the cognomen (or family name) of a famous branch of the patrician *gens Claudia*.

3 Note the verb *diligere* meaning to cherish, to esteem highly, to love. It does not convey the passionate or erotic connotations of *amare*.

4 In a domestic context the reference to Claudia's gait seems to be the to-ing and fro-ing about the house rather than the way she walked (compare to that of Anactoria at 18).

57 *ILS* 7472: Epitaph for Aurelia

This epitaph, from *c.* 80 BC, was inscribed on a statue that depicted a couple with the woman holding the man's right hand with both her hands. As with 56, this inscription erected by the husband of the deceased reflects a harmonious union with a strong element of mutual love (cf. also **Illustration 4**).

> Lucius Aurelius Hermia, freedman of Lucius, a butcher
> from the Viminal Hill. (1)
> She who has gone before me by reason of fate, with chaste body,
> a unique spouse, loving, was possessed of my heart. (2)
> She lived faithful to a faithful husband with equal application. (3)
> Without bitterness, she departed from her duty.
> Aurelia, freedwoman of Lucius. (4)

Notes

1 The stone speaks in the persona of its inscriber, the husband of the deceased. The format imitates the much grander style of the nobility, who recited their immediate ancestry and their achievements. As a freedman (he has taken the name of his former master, Lucius Aurelius), Lucius has subsequently had a successful trade as a butcher.
2 The qualities of the deceased are to be expected but are not simply conventional: she was chaste, she was *una* (unique, indicating that she knew no other partner), she was loving (*amans*), and she was cherished in return.
3 The focus here is on faithfulness (*fides*) and a union that was equal (*par*).
4 As with her husband, the deceased had formerly been a slave of Lucius Aurelius and she took his name upon being freed.

58 Ovid *Tristia* 1.6 Extracts: To His Wife from Exile

Ovid's poetry is known for its playful, amatory nature and questioning of conventional sexual and social mores. In the *Tristia*, a collection of poems written while he was in exile in Tomis, (1) the tone is understandably subdued and serious. In this extract, Ovid writes to his third wife and the intensity of feeling is testimony that love and romanticism were possible in Roman marriage.

> Lyde was not so cherished in the eyes of the Clarian poet, (2)
> nor was Bittis (3) so beloved by her own Coan bard,
> so much as you, wife, cling fast to my emotions,
> a woman worthy of a less wretched, not better husband.
> Upon you my state of ruin is propped up as if by an underpinned
> beam: 5
> if I am as yet anything at all, it is entirely of your gift. (4)
> You bring it about that I am not made 'spoil', nor am I stripped bare
> by those
> who sought the very timbers of my shipwreck.

In the next six lines he draws comparisons with ravenous wild creatures preying upon his resources

'That man' (5) was removed by your courage, along with that of
    brave hearted friends,   15
    for whom no appropriate thanks can be returned.
Wherefore, you have found approval from a witness as wretched as
    he is truthful,
    if only this witness possesses any authority.
In respect of your upright character, neither the wife of Hector (6)
    is superior, nor Laodamia, companion to a deceased husband. (7)   20
If fate had allocated you the Maeonian bard, (8)
    the fame of Penelope would have been second to yours:
for one you would hold a place among the revered list of heroines,   33
    for one you would be looked upon for the good qualities of
    your spirit. (9)   34
It may be that this is due to yourself, made loyal by no teacher,   23
    that patterns of behaviour were granted you at your very first
    dawn,
or perhaps the leader of women, (10) cultivated by you all these years, 25
    taught you to be the epitome of the good spouse,
and by long association rendered you similar to herself –
    if it is permissible to compare great things to small.
Ah me, that my songs do not possess much power
    and my utterances are lesser than your merits!   30
If in the past there ever was any living creativity in me,
    it is long extinct from longstanding misfortune!
Yet in so far as my commendations have any effect at all,   35
    you will live forever by reason of my songs.

Notes

1 For Ov.'s exile or *relegatio*, cf. Norwood; Rogers; Goold 1983.
2 Antimachus (Fifth Century), better known as a resident of Colophon, a city in Lydia near Claros. He wrote an elegiac work to a woman called Lyde, whose death rendered him inconsolable. He is seemingly admired at Rome where his work is referred to in positive terms; contra Cat., who described him as *tumidus* (overblown, 95b.2).
3 The beloved of the late Fourth Century Alexandrian poet, Philetas of Cos.
4 Ov.'s wife remained at Rome to defend his interests, protect his property and work towards his recall.
5 In the preceding lines, Ov. comments on an unnamed individual who was working against his interests in order to acquire his property.
6 The upright character (*probitas*) of Hector's wife Andromache was proverbial after Homer's treatment of her (*Il.* 6). Such loyal and chaste wives will receive *fama* (fame, *l.* 22).
7 Laodamia was married for barely a day when her husband Protesilaus joined the expedition to Troy, was the first of the Argives to leap ashore, and the first to die. Homer (*Il.* 2.701) writes 'leaving behind a wife, her cheeks torn with grieving, and a household half-complete'; Cat. (68.74–75) describes it as a 'house commenced in vain'.

8   Homer. Penelope's fame as a chaste wife was proverbial; note also the story of Hermesianax
    of Colophon (Third Century BC) that Homer was enamoured of Penelope (cf. Ath. 597e).
9   *l.* 33–34 placed between *l.* 22–23 follow Green 1994.
10 Livia, wife of Augustus. Note the language associated with Livia and Ov.'s wife: loyal (*pia*,
    l. 23) and good spouse (*bona coniunx*, *l.* 26).

59 Martial 10.38: To Calenus, on Sulpicia

Sulpicia and her husband, Calenus, were among the patrons of Martial, which may
account for his idealised portrayals of them. Addressed to Calenus, this poem appears
to have been written at the time of Sulpicia's death (*c.* AD 94–98). Such unions, based
on emotional equality and harmony, are regularly depicted in Italian artwork, such as
the Etrurian sarcophagus lid showing an intimate scene of a somewhat mature married
couple embracing each other in bed (cf. **Illustration 4**).

Sweet for you, (1) Calenus, are the fifteen
wedded years which, with your Sulpicia,
the god bestowed and accomplished!
Every night and every hour were ones marked
with darling little pearls of the Indian shoreline! (2)   5
What 'battles,' what 'struggles' for each of you (3)
did the lucky little bed and the lamp gaze upon,
drunk with Nicerotian outpourings! (4)
You have lived, Calenus, through three lustrations: (5)
this is the totality of life by your calculations   10
as you count only the days when you have been a husband. (6)
Were Atropos (7) to restore to you a single one
of these days, just one much longed for,
you would opt for it rather than four spans of Pylian old age. (8)

Notes

1   *molles* (pl.): soft, luxurious; here in the positive sense of sweetness and delight. The adj. should
    also be applied to the 'night' and the 'hour' in *l.* 4.
2   Cf. Cat. 107.6 for an allusion to marking special days with a bright stone.
3   Note the parody of the military imagery: well-matched lovers engage in full-scale battles
    and struggles on their bed (cf. also Cat. 6.7–11; 66.13–14 with reference to 'virginal spoils').
4   Reference to a well-known brand of heavy perfume.
5   *lustra*: the five-year terms of the Censors, whose task it was to cleanse society of impure
    elements through a redrafting of the citizen, senatorial and equestrian lists combined with
    the power to introduce moral reform.
6   *maritus*: although translatable as 'husband', it has connotations of being new to that status;
    Calenus still acts and feels like a bridegroom after 15 years.
7   Atropos was one of the Parcae, the Fates who spun the lifespans of mortals. Her name means
    'Non-changing', therefore inexorable, immovable, her primary task being the cutting of the
    life-thread.
8   Nestor, King of Pylos, outlived his own peers and their offspring, surviving into a third
    mortal generation.

60 Pliny the Younger *Epistle* 7.5: To His Third Wife

Pliny's letters to his third wife, a young woman by the name of Calpurnia, (1) clearly reveal his devotion to her. In the following piece, Pliny writes of his distress about their separation.

It is incredible by how much longing for you I am gripped. In relation to the cause, firstly there is love, next because we are not accustomed to being apart. Then there is the fact that I spend the great portion of nights awake with your image. (2) Then because during the day, at the hours I was in the habit of seeing you, my very feet lead me to your room (I speak the truth) and at last, sick and as wretched as a man locked out from an empty threshold, I depart. (3) The only time I am free from this torment is in the forum when I am being exhausted by the demands of friends. Judge for yourself what my life is like when I find rest in work and solace in misfortunes and anxieties.

Notes

1 There is scant information about Plin.'s former wives; we know that his second wife died some time before AD 97. Cf. Shelton; de Verger. This letter was written to Calpurnia while she was in the country, resting after an illness: cf. *Ep.* 4.19; 8.10.
2 The term *imago* can mean an image or likeness (a bust, for example); a ghost or phantom; an image conjured up in one's thoughts. The erotic vocabulary (*desiderium*, longing, and *amor*) is reminiscent of elegiac poetry.
3 The image of the lover locked out (*exclusus amator*) is a strong motif in New Comedy and Latin elegiac poetry.

IV

PROSTITUTION

The lives of both female and male prostitutes in the Greek and Roman worlds were, on the whole, miserable. The large majority came from the slave class and were bought and sold as their owners saw fit. Wealthy *hetairai* such as Aspasia (62) lived fortunate lives but such women were a rarity. While Neaera (61) is often seen as living a relatively opportune existence, having finally settled with an Athenian man of not immodest means, her childhood years, comprised of brothel life and training in the arts of pleasing clients, suggest another side to her story.

Prostitutes were despised then just as the lifestyle is generally denigrated today. At Athens, for example, adultery was illegal, and freeborn youths were legally protected from violation, so an Athenian citizen had to relieve his extra-marital desires among prostitutes. Socrates observes that the streets of Athens offer numerous legal opportunities for citizens to 'release the compulsions of lust' (Xenophon, *Memorabilia* 2.2.4). From the time of Solon, in the early Sixth Century BC, women engaged in prostitution and their clients had not been subject to financial penalty (Plutarch *Solon* 23) and, as a result, brothels came to acquire legal status. Investment in such establishments was deemed an ordinary business outlet (albeit a disreputable one) two centuries later by the philosopher, Theophrastus (*Characters* 6.5). The conditions of the brothels are impossible to describe as they varied in relation to the physical environment, state of hygiene (or absence thereof) and the expectations of the workers. One may assume, however, that the *ergasterion* (workshop) and the *porneion* (brothel) at the bottom end of the market were a dismal environment for the *porne* (harlot) and *pornos* (rent-boy) alike.

In the multi-cultural centres Corinth and Eryx (in Sicily), temple prostitution in honour of Aphrodite survived into the Augustan age as a remnant of an antique cultic tradition (72–73). In purchasing one of the temple slaves, the client is presumably making a donation to the goddess and experiencing a religious act, as opposed to paying for a girl from downtown Athens or Pompeii.

In the Roman world, the legal practice of prostitution was placed under the jurisdiction of the Curule Aediles; prostitutes were required to register and, during the reign of Caligula, to pay tax. The profession was linked with *infamia* (ill-repute), most notably in relation to the work of a *leno* or *lena*, respectively a male and female pimp. The clients, however, did not (on the whole) suffer from censure, as evident in the comment by Cato the Censor (66), where the timeless necessity for prostitution is based on the argument that the existence of brothels ensured there would be less likelihood of adultery. In other words, prostitution ensured that wives were safe from other men. The perceived role of the prostitute as some kind of societal safety valve, as a requirement for the maintenance of a calm home environment, may also be witnessed in the more graphic sources, those that refer to sexual acts not publicly associated with connubial relations (64; 65). It is evident that in some, if not many, circumstances, prostitutes of both sexes (74–76; 82) were there to provide services one would not ask of a wife.

The lifestyle of the *hetaira*

61 Demosthenes 59.18–19 [*Against Neaera*]: Training Little Girls

In this speech attributed to Demosthenes, the courtesan Neaera is prosecuted for posing as an Athenian and as the wife of an Athenian citizen by the name of Stephanus. Neaera is accused of a number of reprehensible acts, including prostitution. Although we do not know the verdict or what happened to her, it is likely that, had she been found guilty, she would have been sold into slavery. This extract details her past and explains how, as a child, she was trained for the profession of a *hetaira*. Apollodorus, as co-prosecutor, addresses the court. (1)

There were seven young girls (2) who were purchased when they were small children by Nicarete, the freedwoman of Charusius of Elis, and the wife of his cook, Hippias. She had the talent to recognise the potential beauty (3) of little girls and knew how to raise them and educate them with expertise – for it was from this that she had made a profession (4) and from this came her livelihood. [19] She called them 'daughters' so that, by displaying them as freeborn, (5) she could obtain the highest prices from the men wishing to have intercourse (6) with them. After that, when she had enjoyed the profit from their youth, she sold every single one of them: Anteia, Stratola, Aristocleia, Metaneira, Phila, Isthmias and this particular one, Neaera. (7)

Notes

1 Cf. Keuls 156–57; Just 140–42; Omitowoju; also Calame (111–12), who discusses the speech in terms of the light it sheds on the avenues for social mobility achievable by successful *hetairai*.

2 The age of the girls is stressed by the adj. *mikra* (small, little) used in conjunction with the term for girl children, *paidiska*. As Keuls writes: 'Neaera was "working with her body" [22], although she had not yet reached the proper age; in other words, she became what Aristophanes [*Fr.* 141] calls a "not-yet-maiden-harlot" [*hypoparthenos hetaera*]. The fact that there was a term for this category of prostitute shows that the practice was not uncommon' (157).

3 The adj. *euprepes* combines notions of attractive appearance, comeliness.

4 *techne*: skill; a means of making a living.

5 *eleutherai* (pl.): freeborn females. Note, however, one aspect of Solon's law on prostitution that 'made it illegal for a man to put up either his daughters or his sisters for sale, unless he had discovered that she, not as yet married, had had intercourse with a man' (Plut., *Sol.* 23).

6 *plesiazein*: to have intercourse.

7 Anteia, 'Answer-to-your-Prayers'; Stratola, 'The Campaigner'; Aristocleia, 'The Thorough-bred'; Metaneira, 'The Accommodator' (lit. behind/between the abdomen); Phila, 'Loveable'; Isthmias, 'Both Ways' (The Corinthian?); Neaera, 'The Fresh One'.

62 Plutarch *Pericles* 24.5–11: Aspasia

Born in Miletus and later residing in Athens, Aspasia ('Gladly Welcomed'), technically a resident alien or metic, lived with Pericles from approximately 440 BC to the time of his death in 429 BC. Plutarch's portrait sketch reveals some of the positive qualities associated with *hetairai*, namely their educational and social skills, as well as criticism of Aspasia on the basis of her profession. (1)

Some sources claim that Aspasia was highly esteemed by Pericles on account of her political wisdom. Socrates occasionally visited her with his pupils and his close friends brought their wives to listen to her, (2) despite the fact that she presided over a business that was neither respectable nor honourable, but one in which she trained young girls (3) to become prostitutes. [6] Aeschines claims that Lysicles, the sheep-dealer, a man of low-birth and low nature, came to be the foremost Athenian on account of the fact that he lived with Aspasia after the death of Pericles. (4) [7] In the *Menexenus* of Plato, despite its playful beginning, there is a good deal of insight in its assertion that this woman had a reputation for consorting with many Athenians as a teacher of rhetoric. (5) Nevertheless, the affection Pericles had for Aspasia was essentially of an amatory (6) nature. [8] The wife of Pericles was a relative of his and had previously been married to Hipponicus to whom she bore Callias; to Pericles she bore Xanthippus and Paralus. Later on, as their marriage deteriorated, Pericles legally gave her to another man, (7) and took Aspasia, whom he loved above all else. [9] They say that twice a day, going to and from the marketplace, he would greet her with a tender kiss. But now in comedies she is addressed as the new Omphale, Deianira, and Hera. (8) Cratinus blatantly calls her a whore in the following lines:

As his Hera, Aspasia was born, the offspring of Katapugosune,
a dog-eyed whore. (9)

[10] Furthermore it seems that from her Pericles had a bastard, referred to by Eupolis in *The Demes* when Pericles inquires thus:

Is my bastard alive?

To which Myronides responds:

Yes, and he would have been a man long ago,
had he not feared the evil associated with a whore. (10)

They say Aspasia became so renowned and famous that even Cyrus, [11] the leader who went to war with the Persian king for the sake of his throne, (11) gave the name 'Aspasia' to his favourite concubine, previously known as Milto. (12)

Notes

1 Cf. Podlecki 1987; Stadter; Henry; Podlecki 1998 (109–17).
2 On Aspasia's reputation as a woman of wisdom and learning among contemporary and subsequent writers, cf. Podlecki 1987 (58–59).
3 *paidiskai* (pl.): young girls or young female slaves, here trained to become *hetairai* (cf. also 61 n. 2).
4 Aeschin., *Aspasia* Fr. 8 (cited Stadter 237). Lysicles, like his controversial contemporary Cleon, made his fortune through trade, became politically important, and as a result a popular target for comic playwrights.
5 'The *Menexenus* consists almost entirely of the text of a funeral speech for the dead of the Corinthian War composed by Aspasia and recited by Socrates' (Stadter 237). On the work, cf. Podlecki 1987 (58) for the allegation that she also wrote the famous Funeral Oration of 430 BC; cf. also Stadter 237–38.
6 *agapesis*: a respectable term for a higher form of affection and love, commonly employed by philosophers. It may have been used by Pericles himself of his relationship with Aspasia; Plut. asserts it was in reality *erotikos*.
7 Pericles, as a relative, acted as her *kyrios* (legal guardian). On her first husband, cf. Podlecki 1987 (59–60); Stadter 238–39.
8 Three women from mythology who rendered miserable the men in their lives. Omphale was Queen of Lydia who reduced the hero Heracles to the status of an indentured bond slave for a period of three years; Deianira caused the death of Heracles by giving him a poisoned robe; Hera constantly nagged Zeus on account of his infidelities. Aspasia is thus accused of a combination of enforced servitude, metaphorical (or actual?) death, and a lifetime of nagging in her relations with Pericles, frequently called 'The Olympian' in comedy; cf. Podlecki 1987 (60); Stadter 240–41.
9 *Katapugosune*: personification of lust for anal sex, here suggesting this was the means by which she was conceived; the adj. *kunopis* (dog-eyed) is used of Helen (*Il.* 3.180; *Od.* 4.145) and Aphrodite (*Od.* 8.319); *pallake* means both whore and concubine.
10 *nothos*: bastard; i.e. Pericles the Younger. On the need for special arrangements for his enfranchisement, cf. Plut., *Per.* 37. Eupolis declares the misfortune (*kakon*) of the youth as due to Aspasia being a *porne*.
11 Cyrus, son of Darius II, waged war against his brother Artaxerxes for the Persian throne; it was the subject of X.'s *An*.
12 A *pallake* (cf. n. 9, here concubine); her story is told at Ath. 576d where she is described as a *hetaira* renowned for being both very wise (*sophotate*) and extremely beautiful (*kalliste*).

Female prostitutes and their clients

63 Plautus *Pseudolus* Extracts: A Comic Pimp Rules His Women

The earliest extant Roman literature on prostitutes of both sexes comes from the comedies of Plautus in the Third and Second Centuries BC. The following speech by Ballio, the pimp, demonstrates the authority such a man has over the prostitutes in his brothel.

172–93

For you women (1) I have this declaration.

You who pass your tender years in elegance, softness, delights, (2)

you famous 'girlfriends', (3) with men of the highest rank, now I'll
  find out and today I'll test,

which of you pays attention to her head, which to her stomach,
  which to her personal interests, which to sleep.   175

Today I'll test which of you I'm able to credit as my freedwoman
  and which to put on sale.

See to it that today many gifts come to me from your lovers. (4)

For unless annual provisions come to me today, tomorrow I'll
  prostitute you to the common herd.

You know today is my birthday. Where are those men to whom you
  are 'eyes', as well as 'lives', 'delights', 'kisses', 'sweet boobs',
  'honey pots'? (5)   180

See to it that right here at my house 'gift-bearers' are drawn up in
  military formation.

Why do I provide you all with clothing, gold and the things you
  need? Or what has your effort brought home other than evil? You
  wretches are only greedy for wine: (6)

with that you drench yourselves inside and outside, (7) while I'm
  here parched.

Now this really is the best way to go, that I address each individual
  by her name,   185

lest any of you should then deny that what was said was meant for
  her:

so, pay attention all of you.

Firstly, Hedytium, (8) I deal with you, the 'girlfriend' to the
  corn-dealers, every one of whom has an enormous mountain of
  corn at home:

see to it, if you would, that corn is conveyed here to me, sufficient
  for this year,   190

for me and my entire household, (9) so that I'm so overflowing with
  corn

that the city will change my name and pronounce me

King Jason instead of Pimp Ballio. (10)

196–201

Aeschrodora (11) – you who have 'friends', (12) rivals of pimps, the
butchers, who by swearing just like us, seek gain in the worst
possible manner – listen up: unless three meat-frames are laden with
a rich burden of prime beef this day for me, tomorrow you, just like
Dirce once upon a time, as they record, the two sons of Jupiter bound
to a bull, (13) in like style will I string you up to a meat-frame;
that, for sure and certain, will become a bull for you. (14)

Notes

1 *mulieres* (pl.): respectable, neutral word for 'woman', also used as 'wife'.
2 Ballio conjures up a seemingly genteel lifestyle for these prostitutes: *munditiae* (pl. elegance; free from dirt, clean); *mollitiae* (pl. bodily softness; licentiousness, luxury); *deliciae* (pl. life of indulgence and luxury). The use of the dim. *aetatula* (tender years) suggests they commenced the trade when prepubescent.
3 *amicae* (pl.): mistress, girlfriend; also at *l*. 188; cf. Adams 1983 (348–50).
4 *amatores*: pl. of *amator*: lovers; here, regular clients.
5 Ballio mocks the nicknames given to the women by their regulars.
6 Like slaves, prostitutes had a reputation for love of wine.
7 The aforementioned propensity for over-indulgence in wine leads to the drunken women being drenched both inside and outside.
8 Probably a derivative of the Greek *hedone*, suggestive of pleasure, sweetness of smell and taste.
9 *familia*: a clever play on its range of meaning: (i) family; (ii) household; (iii) collection of household slaves.
10 The reference to Jason may be to the hero of the quest for the Golden Fleece or to the famous Fourth Century BC tyrant of Pherae in Thessaly. The title 'king' (*rex*) is certainly more impressive than 'pimp' (*leno*), but the treatment of his female 'subjects' as slaves is more appropriate to the behaviour of a tyrant.
11 Her name combines notions of 'shame' and 'gifts' (possibly also 'ruddiness').
12 *amici* (pl.): friends. As women do not have male friends any more than males have female ones, the term applies to their lovers.
13 Dirce, wife of Lycus of Thebes, was torn to pieces after being tied to a bull by the sons of Jupiter, Amphion and Zethus. The punishment was meted out for the cruelty she had inflicted on their mother, Antiope, Dirce's predecessor as Lycus' wife (cf. Hyg., *Fab*.7).
14 The meat-rack, which normally would hold a slaughtered bull, will be Aeschrodora's 'bull' if she fails to secure the required provisions.

64 Gallus *Greek Anthology* 5.49: Lyde's Sexual Services

The intense physical demands made on a prostitute are illustrated in this light-hearted portrait of Lyde who, from the fantasy account of a male poet, not only enjoys but also essentially demands penetration of all three orifices at once. Lyde may not be performing such exhausting activities because she is old and has no choice, but because she is out to provide as many services for as much as she can charge in the shortest space of time. (1)

> Lyde, who renders service to three men at one and the same time,
> one over her belly, the other below, another from above, said:
> "I let in arse-lover, (2) cunt-lover, (3) mouth-lover. (4)
> If you're urgent, even if you get in alongside two others, don't hold
> back!"

Notes

1 For visual representations and the question of age, cf. Kilmer 1993; cf. also **Illustrations 7–8.**
2 *philopais*: lit. loving boys, i.e. a preference for anal sex.
3 *gunaikomanes*: lit. mad for women, i.e. a preference for vaginal sex.

4 *philubristes*: lit. fond of wanton violence (*hubris*). Since her mouth is the only available orifice, it must be a reference to oral sex. So strong a term, however, suggests oral acts of even greater debauchery are provided by Lyde.

65 Nicarchus *Greek Anthology* 11.328: Group Sex

The poem is a parody of the division of the earth between Zeus (Sky), Poseidon (Sea) and Hades (Underworld), here, respectively, the woman's vagina (Nicarchus), anus (Hermogenes) and mouth (Cleoboulus). In view of her name and age, the poem may well be an allegory for contemporary treatment of traditional, if old fashioned, political values.

> Hermogenes, Cleoboulus and I once upon a time
> brought in Aristodike, (1) the one woman, for group sex. (2)
> By lot I got to dwell in the depths of her grey sea; (3)
> for we divided her up, one to one, all of us not getting all of
> her. (4)
> By lot Hermogenes got the dreaded dark haven,   5
> the last haven, Hermogenes going down into the place of
> darkness, (5)
> along which are banks of the dead, and wind blown 'figs'
> are rotated by the blast of roaring gusts. (6)
> Put Cleoboulus down as Zeus; by lot he got to rise up to heaven, (7)
> holding in his hand blazing fire.   10
> The earth stayed common to us all; for spreading over it a
> mat of rushes, thus we divided up the old woman. (8)

Notes

1 Her name combines high class, aristocratic values, justice and fairness; such concepts, in real life, were as long gone and as old as she was.
2 Group sex (*koine cupris*), lit. the activities of the Cyprian shared in common.
3 A euphemism for her vagina: 'grey' because of her pubic hair, 'sea' because of her loose and swampy orifice.
4 The men cast lots for her orifices and were confined to whichever one they drew.
5 A euphemism for her rectum.
6 Her bowel is a river, whose 'banks' are lined with the 'dead' (faeces). The windblown 'figs' are either her haemorrhoids or her partner's testicles set in motion by the old woman's violent, loud farts.
7 He is Zeus because he obtained the use of her upper orifice. Oral sex is usually seen as the least desirable form of sexual relief; in the case of Aristodike, Cleoboulous drew the lucky straw.
8 The action took place outdoors, on a mat of rushes laid upon the ground. Cf. **Illustrations 7–8**, representations of a symposiac scene illustrating insensitive treatment of aged prostitutes; compare with **Illustration 9**, in which younger prostitutes are treated in a more amenable manner.

66   Horace *Satires* 1.2.28–36: Endorsement from Cato

Horace suggests young men should frequent brothels for the purpose of gaining experience and release rather than committing adultery with respectable women. In support of his position he draws upon no less an authority than Cato the Censor.

There's no middle ground. There are men unwilling to touch a
woman except those whose hemlines cover their ankles with a
garment fringed to the bottom; on the other hand, another will not
unless she is standing in a stinking brothel.   30
When a certain well-known person was exiting a brothel, "Well done!
Keep it up!" (1) was the inspired utterance of Cato, (2)
"for as soon as vile lust (3) swells the veins,
it is right for young men to go down to such a place, and not be
grinding away (4) at the wives of others!" "I do not wish to have
    myself   35
praised for that," says Cupiennius, an admirer of any cunt robed
    in white. (5)

Notes

1   Lit. 'maintain your manliness (*virtus*)'. The concept embodies all aspects of manliness, courage, excellence, as well as the ability to be and act like a man.
2   Cato the Censor (234–149 BC).
3   *libido*: lust; unlawful desire and wantonness.
4   The verb *permolere* (to grind grain) is an agricultural term transferred to a sexual context; cf. Adams 1982 (152–53).
5   *cunnus*: cunt. Reference to the shade of clothing worn by a respectable Roman *matrona* makes Cupiennius a serial adulterer.

67   Martial 9.32: The Ideal Girl

To Martial the ideal girl is young, spirited, exhibitionist, adventurous and willing to undertake any form of sexual activity that realises the fantasies of the male. Since Martial clearly wants her to be very experienced and an adept, the girl most likely to fulfil his needs would be a professional. One important proviso is that she not be greedy for payment: a fair and agreed price (*l.* 3) and the pleasure of sex are reward enough.

The girl I want is one who is 'easy', who walks about in a 'mini', (1)
    the girl I want is one who has already given herself to my boy; (2)
the girl I want is one whom another *denarius* purchases in her entirety, (3)
    the girl I want is one who on her own takes care of three at once.
Let a girl demanding money and sounding off in hoity-toity language
    be filled by the cock (4) of a thick-head from Bordeaux. (5)

Notes

1 She is both readily accessible (*facilis*) and scantily clad (*palliolata*).
2 She employs his slave-boy as a *delicatus* to get herself 'warmed up' for the main event; cf. Watson.
3 This kind of girl is not greedy, the *denarius* being the equivalent of ten *asses*, 'an ordinary price for a prostitute' (Henriksén 170).
4 *mentula*: cock.
5 On the possible links to *Galli*, Gauls and/or the effeminate eunuch priests of Cybele, cf. Henriksén 170–71. The image bears out the poet's distaste for foreigners and the appeal they have for women of all classes at Rome. The play on 'thickness' is clever: the bigger the penis, the 'thicker' its owner.

68 Athenaeus 568a–d: Maid to Order

Woman as a body to be gazed upon by the male viewer is revealed in this depiction of the prostitutes who are prepared and adorned for the approval, purchase and pleasure of the male.

Alexis, in the play called *Isostasion* (1) thus sets out the preparation of prostitutes (2) and their contrived embellishments:

To start with, for the purpose of gain and robbing male neighbours,
everything becomes secondary to them; and they weave
plots against all men. When at some stage they become rich they take in
new prostitutes (3) who are taking their first steps in the trade. (4)
At once they refashion these girls, so that neither their behaviour
nor their appearance remains the same as before. (5)
One girl happens to be small? Cork is stitched to the sole of her   b
delicate shoes. One girl happens to be tall? She wears a flat slipper,
and goes out drooping her head on her shoulders, thus
taking away some of her height. One girl doesn't have hips?
She puts on a girdle with padded hips under her clothes so that
as a result men, on seeing her beautiful derriere, call out to her.
She has a pudgy stomach? For such a one they make 'falsies' out of the
materials that actors have on the comic stage. (6)
Once these are added and set straight, around to the front,
as if with support poles, they haul the clothing over the stomach. (7)   c
One girl has red eyebrows? They paint them with lamp soot.
One girl happens to be black? She anoints herself with white lead.
One girl is too white-skinned? She smears on rouge.
One part of her body is beautiful? (8) She shows it naked.
Her teeth are pretty? She must, of necessity, smile so that
the men present may see what an elegant mouth she has.
But if she does not enjoy smiling, she has to spend the day   d
indoors and, like something positioned by a butcher
when selling goats' heads, (9)

she must hold upright between her teeth a thin stick of myrtle;
that way, in time she will show off her teeth whether she likes to or not.
By these clever tactics they artfully prepare their faces.

Notes

1 The title could mean *Equal Measure* (Gulick 6: 67).
2 *hetairike*: adj., that which befits a companion or prostitute (*hetaira*).
3 *hetairai* (pl.).
4 The oldest profession is here referred to as a trade (*techne*); cf. 61 n. 4; 69 n. 5.
5 The training of young girls recalls Neaera's early life (cf. 61).
6 The breasts are false as men played women's roles in both tragic and comic productions.
7 Gulick notes the unsound nature of the text and suggests that the 'main idea is that much pulling and hauling were necessary to adjust the figure as the women desired' (6: 69 n.b).
8 *kalon*. The list of techniques, displaying the best features in the most appealing way, echoes the concluding advice in Ov., *AA*. 3.769–808 (158).
9 Note the equation of women with animals / meat.

69 Athenaeus 569a–d: Brothel Life

The depiction of Greek prostitutes in brothels is vividly captured in Athenaeus' quotation from Xenarchus, a comic playwright of the Fourth Century BC. As with the previous citation from Alexis (68), the male gaze is of significance: the women in question parade about in a brothel smorgasbord, enticing their customers, and making themselves readily available.

In The *Pentathlon* (1) Xenarchus denounces those who live like you and who are devoted to expensive prostitutes and freeborn (2) married women:

Shocking, shocking, and totally unbearable,
are the ways the young men (3) in our city conduct their lives.
For here there are very attractive young girls   b
practising prostitution, whom the young men may see
sun-bathing, breasts openly displayed,
naked (4) for action and lined up in rows.
From them you may select one for your pleasure:
thin, fat, round, tall, short,
youthful, antique, middle-aged, or overly ripe,
with no need to erect a ladder to gain secret access,
or get to via a hole under the roof,
or by a clever trick getting yourself 'in' under a pile of straw. (5)   c
The girls themselves make use of force and drag
their clients in, calling the old ones
'Daddy' and the younger ones 'Little Brother'. (6)
And every one of these 'types' is available without fear, easily paid for,
during the day, during the evening, adopting any position.
But other women are ones you cannot look at, at least

not directly, except in a state of terror and anguish . . . (7)
in fear, taking your life in your hands.
How then, Cypris, Mistress of the Sea, (8)
are men able to fuck, (9) when the laws of Dracon (10)　　　　　　　　　**d**
come to mind while they are thrusting away? (11)

Notes

1 As Gulick points out (6: 73 n.f) the title refers to the man who entered the athletic contest known as the Pentathlon.
2 Liaisons with *hetairai* and respectable freeborn women (*eleutherai*) are equally denounced.
3 The *neoteroi* are not simply young men but the avant-garde. Their behaviour is of a type to cause consternation among the respectable elite.
4 *gymnai*: stripped naked in readiness for athletic activity, as at the gymnasium.
5 These stratagems are all common features of comedy and amatory poetry: *techne* is used here in the sense of 'clever stratagem'; cf. **68** n. 4.
6 Note the use of family names 'daddy' and 'little brother' with incestuous overtones.
7 I.e. married or freeborn females; to mess with such women is to invite violent, even fatal, consequences for the would-be lothario. Note the lacuna.
8 Aphrodite. Gulick (6: 75 n.d) notes the reference to a line uttered by Phaedra about unfaithful wives at Eur., *Hipp*. 415.
9 On *binein*, cf. Bain 54–62.
10 Dracon was the first to codify Attic law (*c*. 621 BC); these laws, noted for their harshness, were still referenced in speeches and inscriptions during the Fourth Century BC.
11 *proskinein* means to thrust or screw. The recollection, during illicit sex, of the severity of the Draconian Code should be enough to have a man lose any hope of sustaining an erection. Their main purpose was to curb strife among the ruling elite (hence the laws dealing with homicide and blood price), so it is fair to assume they dealt with adultery, the cause of much dissension in aristocratic circles from earliest times.

The ageing prostitute

70 Martial 10.75: Galla

As beauty was most commonly equated with youth in antiquity – and age with abhorrence, particularly in relation to women – an old prostitute could generally expect little more than scorn. Such women would have experienced a significant reduction in the amount they could charge, in direct proportion to an increase in demands for additional services (again at a reduced cost).

There was a time when Galla demanded twenty thousand (1) from me
　　and I admit she was not excessive at that price.
A year passed: "You will give ten thousand sesterces," she said.
　　She seemed to be demanding more from me than before.
Six months later, when she was demanding two thousand,　　　　　　5
　　I was offering a thousand. She refused to accept.
Two, maybe three Calends passed by, (2) when
　　she, of her own accord, sought four gold pieces. (3)
I did not give them. She ordered me to send a hundred *sesterces*,

but to me this amount also seemed 'weighty'. (4)   10
A meagre dole handout joined to a hundred small coins;
     she wanted this: I said it had been given to a boy. (5)
Could she not go down somewhat lower? She did. (6)
     Galla offers it free of charge. Of her own accord she offers it to me.
     I say no.

Notes

1   The *sestertius* (between 2.5 and 4 *asses*) was the major unit of Roman currency; the sum being charged here was an extraordinarily high amount for sexual services.
2   The Calends were the first day of the month on which debts were settled. What is amusing here is the notion that prostitutes also settled on the same day as other creditors.
3   Approx. 400 *sesterces*; her price was dropping rapidly.
4   Initially coinage was based on the actual weight of the precious metal it contained, hence the pun.
5   *puer*: presumably a boy prostitute.
6   The joke is based on lowering oneself in terms of (i) reducing your price; (ii) 'going down' in our modern sense (i.e. giving 'head'); and (iii) self-abasement.

71   Athenaeus 570b–d: Lais

In one of the most poignant portraits of old age, Athenaeus quotes a play, *Anti-Lais*, by Epicrates (a Fourth Century BC comic playwright), which depicts the fate of this once beautiful *hetaira*.

But Lais (1) herself is lazy and a drunk,
seeing only to daily drinking and eating, (2)
and she seems to me to have shared the same life experiences
as eagles. For when these are young they   c
eat sheep and hares from the mountains,
using their strength to snatch them aloft,
but when they begin to age, then
they sit on the temples of the gods hungering miserably;
and this action is then considered a portent! (3)
Lais, therefore, should rightly be considered a portent.
This woman from when she was a mere chick, then young,
was rendered wild and wilful by coins of gold,
and you would more readily get an audience with Pharnabazus (4)
     than her;
but now that she has run the distance in respect of long years   d
and the harmonies of her body have become distended,
it is easier to get an audience with her than it is to spit,
and now she roams the streets, flitting about, as if on wings,
and accepts both a gold coin and a three *obol* coin,
taking on both the old and the young alike. (5)

Ah, dear friend, she has become so tame these days
that she takes the money out of your hand. (6)

Notes

1 Probably the Elder Lais who died in 392 BC (Gulick 6: 81 n.a).
2 Note the stereotype of the prostitute: love of wine and food, both of which equate with a life of indolence (cf. 63).
3 The ancients placed great stock on the actions of birds as omens. The eagle is the bird associated with Zeus.
4 A Persian satrap (Fifth–Fourth Century BC). The luxuriousness and elaborate protocols of the Persian court were as nothing compared to that of Lais. Pharnabazus is as much a stereotype of Persian opulence as she is of the *hetaira*.
5 Lais can no longer be discerning about clients and has had to adjust her prices. She can still extract a gold *stater* from her older customers due to her famous reputation, but the younger clientele see only an ageing *hetaira* and are prepared to pay far less: the *obol* was the basic coin in Attica.
6 The niceties of the high-priced *hetaira* have been dispensed with: she now demands the money up front and receives it directly in hand, rather than maintaining the pretence that she is the recipient of gifts and presents.

Temple prostitution and worship of Aphrodite

72 Strabo 6.2.6: Temple Prostitution at Eryx

Strabo's *Geography*, written in the First Century BC, presents important evidence for the existence of temple prostitution in the Greek, Italian and Near Eastern worlds. (1) In this piece he describes the temple prostitutes at Eryx in Western Sicily.

The lofty hill of Eryx is also populated. It has a temple of Aphrodite (2) that is particularly revered and was, in earlier times, inhabited by female temple-slaves, who had been dedicated in fulfilment of vows, (3) not only by the Sicilians but by many foreigners. At the present time, however, like the community itself, the temple is almost vacant, and the multitude of temple-slaves has dwindled.

Notes

1 Cf. Beard and Henderson; MacLachlan 1992; cf. also Str. 12.532.
2 The cult name for this incarnation of Aphrodite is Erycina. Like the temples of Aphrodite Urania (Heavenly), this temple to Erycina is located on a sheer precipice surmounting the ocean. For the association of Aphrodite Urania with the Phoenician Astarte, cf. MacLachlan 1992.
3 Cf. Price who observes: 'In all these cases, the adjective [sacred] denotes no more than manumission by fictive dedication' (1264). The fact that Sicilians and foreigners dedicate girls to this shrine is an indication of the extent of its earlier fame.

73 Strabo 8.6.20: Temple Prostitution at Corinth

Strabo draws attention to the practice of temple prostitution at Corinth during its heyday as one of the commercial centres of the Mediterranean.

The temple of Aphrodite (1) was so affluent that it housed more than one thousand temple-slaves, courtesans, (2) who had been set up as votive gifts to the goddess, by both men and women. It was actually on account of these women that the city was crowded and became wealthy, for the commanders of ships spent their money recklessly, and herein lies the anecdote: 'Not for all men is the journey to Corinth.' Moreover, it is recorded that one courtesan, in response to a woman who accused her of laziness and not working wool, replied: 'I, being who I am, in this short space of time, have completed three webs.' (3)

Notes

1 Aphrodite Urania.
2 *hetairai.*
3 The expression 'completed three webs' is in the context of the accusation of not working wool (on representations in art of *hetaira* weaving, cf. Davidson 86–87). There is an implicit pun for it can also mean 'lowered three masks'; in view of the reference to the commanders of ships, it means that she serviced three sea captains.

Pompeian graffiti: female prostitutes

Pompeii was, at the time of the eruption of Vesuvius in AD 79, a provincial city of modest size. Many erotic murals and inscriptions from Pompeii come from locations that served as *lupanaria* (brothels), such as *tabernae* (taverns), *cauponae* (inns) and *thermopolia* (lunch counters). On their walls are scrawled names, prices, acts and other information about the prostitutes and their clients. In these establishments the women worked in small, dark cells (*cellae meretriciae*) that were usually only large enough to house a bed. Women who worked the streets often waited around archways for their clients and other standard locations such as graveyards and public baths. (1)

74 Advice and Observations

CIL IV 794
Thrust slowly.

CIL IV 1830
A [hairy] cunt (1) is much better being fucked (2) than a hairless one. (3)
It retains the heat (4) and at the same time [crave]s cock. (5)

CIL IV 9847
Candida (6) instructed me to hate black
girls. I will hate (them) if I am able to: if not,
against my will, I will 'love' (them). (7)

Notes

1 *cunnus*: cunt. The adj. is in doubt: Varone (58) reads *{pil}ossus* (hairy, spiky); contra Zangemeister 116.
2 *futuere*: here in the passive, 'to be fucked'.
3 *glaber*: smooth, devoid of hair; shaved; more likely here a reference to depilation than to the age of the prostitute. Cf. 79 n. 6 (*glabraria*, a woman who has a passion for smooth skinned lovers).
4 *vapor*: steamy exhalations, heat, steam. Notions of moisture and humidity, as well as heat, are appropriate to female genitalia.
5 The verb is damaged in the inscription (cf. Zangemeister 116). It is clear, however, that her *cunnus* welcomes a *mentula*; Krenkel 1981 renders it 'makes the cock twitch' (53).
6 *Candida*: 'shining'. Corte (62) suggests 'blonde, fair-haired' as opposed to 'brunettes', but *nigrae* (pl. black women) indicates skin rather than hair colour.
7 *amare*: used in both the sense of 'make love to' and 'love, favour'.

75 Praise and Abuse

CIL IV 2273
Myrtis, (1) well
do you suck. (2)

CIL IV 4185
Sabina,
you suck –
you do not do it well.

CIL IV 10004
Euplia (is) slack (with) a big clitoris. (3)

Notes

1 An example of the exotic names of prostitutes, here possibly a reference to the myrtle, a plant sacred to Venus.
2 *fellare*: to take the penis in the mouth; also at *CIL* IV.4185; 5048 (76); 5408 (82, man–man). Myrtis is described as a *fellatrix* (female cock-sucker) at *CIL* IV.2292; at *CIL* IV.8185 she is said to charge two *asses*, as cited by Krenkel 1980 (86).
3 *laxa* (adj.): loose, slack; gaping wide, presumably referring to the opening of her vagina. *landicosa*: adj. 'endowed with a large clitoris (*landica*)'. Cf. Adams 1982 (96, 97–98), who notes the adj. is only used here (97). Her vagina gapes from over use and she has an overly large clitoris, which may have given her a masculine or hermaphroditic appearance. On Euplia, cf. *CIL* IV.2310b, 5048 (76).

76 Advertisements

CIL IV 7089
Cock (1)
you are
enormous.

CIL IV 2310b
Euplia here
with 'beautiful people'
two thousand. (2)

CIL IV 5048
Euplia sucks (3) for five *asses*.

CIL IV 5372
I am yours (4)
for an as. (5)

CIL IV 1751
If anyone is going to take up a seat here (6)
let him read this before all else:
if he wishes to fuck (7)
Attice, let him find sixteen *asses*. (8)

Notes

1   *mentula*: cock. The actual word order in the graffito is 'enormous/cock/you are'.
2   On Euplia, cf. *CIL* IV.10004 (75); *CIL* IV.5048. The *homines belli* are the 'beautiful or good'
     people, the sophisticates. The number refers to her clients rather than her fees, as the
     following inscription shows.
3   *fellare*. While she charges more than some she is not overly expensive.
4   The writer is female.
5   The reading adopted by Varone (139): the inscription could read 'I am yours / for two asses'
     (cf. Zangemeister 594).
6   The term *sedere* usually refers to the prostitute taking up a seat; here it seems to apply to the
     customer electing to sit outside her stall awaiting his turn.
7   *futuere*.
8   Sixteen *asses* represents a high price for a prostitute (cf. Duncan-Jones 246), borne out by the
     verb that could be rendered 'let him come up with'. Her name suggests she was Greek,
     perhaps indicating her speciality was anal sex.

Male prostitutes and their clients

77   Aeschines 1.21 [*Against Timarchus*]: The Law On Male
   Prostitution

In 346 BC Aeschines brought a prosecution against Timarchus, an Athenian politician,
based on the allegation that Timarchus had spent his youth as a prostitute, thereby
breaking the law that specified certain conditions for a man to be eligible to speak in
the Assembly. Aeschines won and Timarchus was disenfranchised. (1) Aeschines'
speech made reference to several of the laws (*nomoi*) attributed to Solon (594 BC). Here
the clerk reads the law concerning the punishments for an Athenian citizen who offers
himself for prostitution. The severity of Solon's long-standing penalties indicates the
outrageousness of Timarchus' actions. (2)

If any Athenian has prostituted himself, (3) he will not be permitted to become one of the nine archons, or to hold a priestly office, or to act as an advocate for the state. He will not occupy any office at all – at home or abroad – whether gained by lot or election. He cannot be sent as a herald or allowed to take part in any debate or be a participant in public sacrifices. When the citizens wear garlands he will not. Neither can he enter the purified area set aside for the People's Assembly. If a man convicted for prostitution acts contrary to these laws, he will be sentenced to death.

Notes

1 Dover 1978 analyses both the trial and all the related issues (19–109). His activities not only debased his own body but, as a citizen at the time, brought shame on the city itself. Omitowoju notes: 'It is *hubris* to use men as women. . . . [T]he points at issue must be passivity and penetrability, which normatively characterize the female in sexual relationships. . . . [B]ecause Timarchus has behaved, sexually, as a woman . . . as if he had the sexual honour of a woman, then his civic status should be changed and he should be denied the right to advise the city by speaking in the assembly' (5).
2 Cf. Dover 1978 (19–31); Davidson 252–53.
3 *hetairein*: to prostitute oneself; also repeated in the last line. On the word, Dover 1978 writes: 'In the classical period the verb *hetairein* and the abstract noun *hetairêsis* do not seem to have been used of a hetaira, but exclusively of a man or boy who played a homosexual role analogous to that of a hetaira' (21).

78 Plautus *Pseudolus* 767–88: A Pimp's Slave-Boy

A young slave-boy laments his lot in life at the hands of the crass Ballio, already introduced in 63, a pimp who owns both male and female prostitutes.

> Any boy to whom the gods grant servitude to a pimp,
> and to that same boy if they add ugliness, (1)
> then on that boy, inasmuch as I can sort it out in my heart,
> they are bestowing a great deal of trouble and monumental
>   tribulation.   770
> For instance, look at this servitude of mine, whereby I am hedged in
> by every conceivable kind of wretchedness, small and great alike:
> and I am unable to find anyone to be my lover, (2)
> one who will love me, so at last I might be looked after a little
>   more comfortably.
> Now, today is the pimp's birthday: 775
> threats have been issued, from the smallest to the greatest:
> should there be anyone who, today, does not send him a gift,
> that person, tomorrow, will perish in utmost agony.
> Now, by Hercules, I don't know what I can do in the midst of my
>   troubles;
> and I'm not able to do what others, who can, usually do. (3)   780
> Now, unless I send the pimp a gift today,

I'm going to have to drink 'fuller's fruit' tomorrow. (4)
O dear, how small (5) I am, even now, for that sort of activity,
and yet, by Pollux, wretch that I am, I'm so terribly afraid of him,
so that if someone were to offer anything heavier than my hand, (6)   785
even though they say it can be managed with a lot of groaning,
it seems I'll have to be able to control my teeth somehow. (7)
Right now, the need is far greater for me to control my voice and
    choice of words.

Notes

1 *turpitudo*: ugliness; also baseness, shamefulness.
2 *amator*: lover, here a regular. The boy wants someone to love him or make love to him (*amare*, *l.* 774).
3 Lacking a generous lover, the boy is short of the means by which he can purchase a gift for the pimp.
4 *L&S*: 'tomorrow I must swallow ink' (790). Ker (1: 417 n. 4) notes that fullers collected urine in pots at street corners for use in their trade; *fructus fullonius*, is either what fullers take pleasure in or the fruits, i.e. product, of their trade or their bodies. Some form of oral sex by way of punishment is at issue.
5 In view of the dominant oral emphasis throughout these lines he is probably alluding to his mouth and his inability to drink all the semen (or urine?) that will be coming his way.
6 This most likely refers to someone else's penis, something big enough to weigh down the boy's hand.
7 It makes sense if the sexual service is oral; due to his small mouth, he will have to ensure he can control his teeth while performing painful *fellatio*.

79 Martial 4.28: Chloe and her Expensive Toy-Boy

Unlike the case of the young but plain slave in the service of Ballio (78), the lifestyle of the handsome toy-boy of Chloe is a startling contrast. Martial outlines her monumental extravagance and warns that such indulgence will eventually leave her stripped of everything she owns. The topos of the handsome gigolo is a recurrent one in Roman satire of the Early Empire, a reflection of the financial and moral independence of wealthy women.

Chloe, you have bestowed on sweet young (1) Lupercus
scarlet coloured Spanish and Tyrian (2)
and a *toga* bathed by the warm Galaesus, (3)
precious stones from India, translucent greenstones from Scythia, (4)
along with a hundred 'masters' of freshly minted coinage, (5)
and, whatever else he asks for, again and again you hand out.
Alas, for you, lover of smooth skins. (6) Alas, for you, wretched poor girl:
that Lupercus of yours will leave you standing naked. (7)

Notes

1 The adj. *tener* connotes youth, delicacy, tenderness; the object of Chloe's desire is soft and pretty.

2 Presumably cloaks and outerwear imported from Spain and Tyre and, by dint of the dyes involved, expensive.

3 The *toga* indicates that Lupercus has recently reached manhood status. The reference to the river Galaesus points to Tarentum, an area renowned for producing prime quality wool.

4 *sardonyx* is a precious stone of yellow or orange cornelian (i.e. sard) intermingled with white-layered onyx. The *zmaragdus* is a translucent, bright greenstone 'including not only our emerald, but also the beryl, jasper, malachite, etc' (*L&S* 1714).

5 The image refers to the faces of rulers (*domini*) on gold coins.

6 *glabraria*: lit. 'a woman who loves smooth skin', i.e. very young boys or youths who have yet to develop body hair. There is also a play on the notion of a woman who has been 'skinned' (i.e. bankrupted) by dint of her passion for such young males (*L&S* 815). On the use of *glaber* (smooth), cf. 74 (*CIL* IV.1830). Since Lupercus has recently reached manhood he must be practising depilation.

7 The verb *statuere* (to stand, take a stance) is unusual in this context: (i) Chloe will be the one 'set up on public view'; or (ii) 'left standing' naked in the manner of a prostitute, a profession to which she may have to turn. The pun on Lupercus and the Luperci, the naked priests who conduct the festival of Lupercalia, is clever.

80 Petronius *Satyricon* 126: Different Tastes for Different Classes

In her address to the hero of the novel, Encolpius (pretending to be a slave), Chrysis, the handmaiden of a beautiful, but wanton, noblewoman called Circe, presents an unusual set of insights into the desires and tactics of women across the class divide in their pursuit of sexual gratification.

"Because you are completely aware of your own sex appeal, (1) you arrogantly grasp after <proof of> it and you sell your embraces, you do not give them away. (2) Why else have your tresses shine when shaped by the comb, why else your features rubbed with facial treatment, why else the alluring sauciness of your glances, why else your walk practised by means of art so that not even the traces of your feet stray beyond a measured tread – unless it is because you are putting your beauty on display (3) in order that you might sell it? Take a look at me: I know nothing about omens and I am not in the habit of paying attention to the astrological calculations of mathematicians, (4) yet I understand the habits of human beings from body language, and when I see one striding along, I know exactly what he is thinking. Therefore, if you undertake to sell to us what we are after, you have a buyer on hand, or, what is more generous, if you give it away, you see to it that we owe you a debt of gratitude. Due to your admission that you are a slave and lowly born, you fuel the desires of a woman already on fire. Some women glow with passion for sordid types, they can't get turned on with lust unless they're gazing at slaves or flunkeys showing off their thighs. (5) The arena gets some of them fired up, or a muleteer soaked in dust, or an actor playing the lead in a stage show. (6) From this particular class (7) comes my mistress: she springs away from the orchestra, all of fourteen front rows, (8) and in the furthest back seats among the common herd she hunts out what she wants." (9)

Filled with delight at such a charming speech, I said:
"May I ask whether the woman who is in love with me is . . . yourself?"

The maidservant laughed aloud after such a preposterous proposition and said:

"I am in no mood to have you quite so full of yourself. To this very day I have never lain beneath a slave, and may the gods never allow me to offer my embraces to someone fit to be crucified. Let respectable married women (10) take care of that lot, the types who press their lips to the trace-marks of floggings; even if I am a maidservant, still I never take up a seat (11) unless it is among the ranks of the Equites." (12)

Indeed I began to marvel at such discordant forms of lust (13) and to include these among the lists of portentous events: (14) that the maidservant was possessed of the arrogance of a respectable married woman and the respectable married woman the gutter taste of a maidservant. (15)

Notes

1 *venus* (sex), here the more modern concept of female sex appeal.
2 Chrysis is of the view that the trouble women go to in the attraction of lovers entitles them to recompense. She proceeds with a list of feminine tactics to achieve these ends; compare with those of Hera in 1.
3 *forma*: physical beauty. Chrysis believes that it must be flaunted, put on display (*prostituere*, in its literal sense).
4 The importance of omens and astrology, the mathematical calculation and measurement of the stars, cannot be over stressed in the world of prostitution and love magic.
5 The combination of being a slave and lowly born renders Chrysis' aristocratic mistress Circe sweaty, hot, passionate (*aestuans*) and fires her lust (*libido*).
6 The gladiator (here symbolised by the sand of the arena) and the muleteer are common characters who are the object of women's lust in satire (cf. Juv. 6.103–12 on the 'charms' of the gladiator Sergius; Barton 47–49). Actors are of long standing ill-repute.
7 Circe belongs to the nobility, those who are known by their position on the census lists.
8 The first fourteen rows at the theatre, behind the orchestra (where Senators sat), were filled by the Equites under a law passed by a Tribune of the Plebs, Lucius Roscius Otho, in 67 BC. Circe has no interest in men of her own class and prefers to 'slum it' in the back rows with the common throng.
9 At the end of her previous speech, Chrysis used the verb *diligere* (to care for, pay close attention to) to describe her mistress' passion for lower class lovers. In his response, Encolpius uses *amare*.
10 *matronae*.
11 A very precise choice of wording is her use of *sedere*: not only does it have a general meaning 'to sit, to take a seat' (as in the theatre) but it can also mean 'to take a seat in a public place', as a prostitute (cf. 76 n. 6).
12 The Equites were among the richest men in the Roman Empire. Unlike her mistress, Chrysis prefers to sit with them, for they are the ones most likely to be generous in return for sexual favours. In some respects, Circe is more natural and honest in that she follows her heart and her loins: Chrysis does it solely for the money.
13 *libido*.
14 *monstra* are unusual events or sights, things totally out of the ordinary.

15 The normal expectation is for high-born and wealthy women to display arrogance (*superbia*) and slaves to display low-born tastes and preferences (*humilitas*): in the case of Circe and Chrysis these roles and modes of behaviour are reversed, hence the resort to omens and portents to explain the abnormality.

81 *Oxyrhynchus Papyrus* 3070: A Proposition by Mail

This piece of papyrus from the First Century AD is a letter described as having been 'folded, and addressed on the back . . . shakily written and shakily spelt' (Parsons 163). The delivery of a letter suggests that the boy in question did not belong to either author; the offer to cease beating him in return for his consent to sodomy implies that the boy was sufficiently free of them to require persuasion. The following translation attempts to reflect the stilted nature of the communication. It comes with an illustration of the object of their desire, namely a crudely drawn anus (cf. **Illustration 11**).

> Says Apion
> and Epimas to Epaphroditus, (1)
> the Dearest, that
> if you were to grant us the opportunity
> to bugger you, (2)
> well will it go for you when no longer will we
> thrash you (3) if you grant
> us the opportunity to bugger you. Farewell.
> Farewell.

> *Back*: Deliver to Epaphroditus the Dearest.

Notes

1 The boy's name lit. means 'One Favoured by Aphrodite', with connotations of beauty and charm.
2 The verb *pugazein*: to bugger (repeated at *l.* 8); cf. Bain 67–70.
3 The offer to cease thrashing his buttocks in return for sodomy indicates that the acts usually performed on Epaphroditus were sadomasochistic in nature.

Pompeian graffiti: male prostitutes

82 Sexual Acts with Male Prostitutes

Pompeian graffiti provide a useful and informative source of information about the presence of male prostitutes and their sexual activities.

CIL IV 1825a
Narcissus, cock-sucker extraordinaire. (1)

CIL IV 1882
He who arse-fucks Accensus, burns his cock. (2)

CIL IV 2048
Secundus arse-fucks
sorrowing
boys. (3)

CIL IV 2319b
Vesbinus takes it up the arse, Vitalio fucks arse. (4)

CIL IV 5408
Felix sucks for one *as*. (5)

CIL IV 8940
Maritimus
licks cunt for four *asses*.
Virgins he ad-
mits (free). (6)

Notes

1 The inscription is vertical. The male prostitute's working name is Narcissus, after the beautiful youth of mythology who loved only his own reflection. A specialist *fellator*, his advertising declares him to be the very best (*maximus*) at the trade. His name, Narcissus Fellator Maximus, is presented in a form parodying that of a Roman aristocrat (*praenomen/nomen/cognomen* or *agnomen*).

2 *pedicare*; also at *CIL* IV 2048 (cf. n. 3). There is a pun on the name of the passive recipient, *Accensus* ('The Inflamed'), and the consequence of anal sex with him for the penis of the active customer.

3 Corte (108) suggests Secundus is Lucius Ceius Secundus, a prominent political figure at Pompeii. He likes to sodomise (*pedicare*) boys. That they are described as *lu{g}entis* (sorrowing) is a reflection of the size of his *mentula*, the pain it causes them, and possibly a preference for inexperienced boys. His name can mean 'Favourable' (in respect of his endowment?) or 'Following'/'Next' (he likes to be 'Behind'?). On the reading *lu{g}entis*, cf. Varone 122; Zangemeister 131. On Secundus with (Novellia) Primagenia (from Nuceria), cf. *CIL* IV 5358; Corte 101–20.

4 Vesbinus is the passive (*cinaedus*) while Vitalio is the active (*pedicare*).

5 Felix (Lucky) is a common Roman name. In view of the low price he charges for *fellatio*, it would seem to be something of a misnomer.

6 The name Maritimus lit. means 'Seaman' (perhaps 'The Fish-Pond' in view of his professional sexual proclivity). He licks cunt (*cunnus*) for a significant fee. Many graffiti attest two to three *asses* as a fairly standard price for fellatio; cunnilingus seems to command similar fees (Glyco for two *asses*, *CIL* IV 3999). But he readily licks virgins free of charge, an indication both that he enjoys the practice per se and has an eye for prospective clients of the future. The verb *ammittere* can mean either 'to admit' – as adopted above (free of charge) – or 'to send away'. Krenkel 1981 opines it could mean 'sends them away as virgins' (53), that is, he licks but does not have intercourse with them (thereby not impairing their marital prospects).

V

SAME-SEX RELATIONSHIPS

To love boys (*paidophilein*) is delightful ever since
  the son of Cronus, the king of immortals, loved (*eramai*)
  Ganymede
and captured him and led him to Olympus and gave
  divinity to him because he had the lovely blossom of boyhood.
So do not marvel, Simonides, when it is revealed
  that I am overpowered by love (*eros*) for a beautiful boy (*kalos pais*).
                                                                    Theognis 1345–1350

Reference to the story of Zeus and Ganymede occurs as early as the *Iliad* and *Homeric Hymn* 5, yet Theognis is the first extant writer to treat the abduction in sexual terms. The story provides a divinely sanctioned aetiology for boy-love in the historical Greek world. Subsequent writers from the Fifth Century onwards approach the origins of same-sex attraction from scientific (84) to mythical (83; 85) to quasi-historical perspectives (86).

Male same-sex relations occupied the minds of Greek writers working in a variety of genres. From Archaic times, writers extol the beauty of boys and detail the various criteria for young male desirability. It is not until the Sixth Century BC that male–male love, attraction and eroticism gained more widespread acceptance in the eyes of philosophers, playwrights and historians. Admittedly, not all sources (from any period) are positive in their attitudes, but usually criticism and censure were based on the transgression of specific ethical traditions for the *eromenos* and *erastes*. Censure of the older male in such a relationship was usually related to a reputation for passivity. The passive adult male (*kinaidos*) was regarded as one who had deviated from nature (84) and, as such, was associated with outrage or violence (*hubris*) and shame (*aischron*). Such moral attitudes extended to the *eromenos*, as the 'ideal' did not tolerate his participation in explicit sexual acts of any kind. Of course these views do not provide a complete or satisfying insight into the realities of individual relationships, for the endorsement of such ethical parameters in the public arenas of the stage, law court or published text cannot reflect what went on behind closed doors.

Same-sex attraction was extolled by Plato and revered in practice, as exemplified in the Sacred Band of Thebes (95). From Anacreon in the Sixth Century onwards, poets speak of their passion for boys and much subsequent lyric and epigram is devoted to the topos. In the Graeco-Roman era a convergence of the personal and the theoretic led to a seemingly ongoing 'debate' about the respective merits of boys and women as

110

objects of desire. Straton (89; 92) makes a stand on behalf of boys, Ovid (87) for women; and the proponents of the genre of dialogue, Pseudo Lucian (90) and Achilles Tatius (91), provide substantial debates on the subject.

Both the Greek and Roman cultures throughout the ages generally looked with distaste upon female–female relationships. Female poets, Sappho (96) and Erinna (97), reveal close female–female relationships with some sexual overtones and a positive intensity of feeling, while some male writers such as Anacreon (99), Asclepiades (100) and Martial (101) regard female–female relationships with a repugnance as distinct from the light-hearted voyeurism of Lucian (102).

The origins of same-sex relations

83 Plato *Symposium* 189d–192b: Plato's Myth About Same-Sex Attraction

Plato's *Symposium* (*c.* 384–79 BC) is an account of a conversation between a group of leading historical figures on the subject of *eros*. *Eros* between men is a focus of the speeches, reflecting the social environment of Classical Athens, in which intellectual, erotic and even romantic relationships – usually between an older man and a youth – were regarded as an important part of life among the upper class. In the speech delivered by the comic poet, Aristophanes, the reason behind an individual's sexual orientation is expounded in a fairytale that describes the beginnings of human-kind. (1)

"In the beginning there were three human genders, not two as now, male and female. [189e] There was also a third type that had a share in both genders, a type of which only the name now remains for the thing itself has vanished: this was the hermaphrodite, (2) one appearance, one name, having a share in both the male and female. Now it does not exist except as a word of insult. Secondly, each human's entire body was spherical, having back and sides in a circle, with four arms and legs and two faces on a cylindrical neck, faces similar in every way. [190a] There was one head for both faces, which were opposite, and four ears, two sets of genitals, and all the other parts as one would guess from this.

Aristophanes then describes how these creatures became arrogant and defiant. Zeus, in response, cuts them in two and orders Apollo to heal the wounds.

[191a] Since, therefore, their nature was cut in two, each half went about longing for its other half. Throwing their heads around and embracing each other, desiring to merge into one, they were dying of hunger [191b] and overall inertia because they did not wish to do anything without the other. And whenever one of the two halves died and the other was left, the remaining half sought and embraced another, whether it met a whole woman's half – what we now call a woman – or a man's half – and as a result they began to die. But Zeus, pitying them, adopted another strategy and moved their genitals to the

111

front, for they were previously on the outside, and they had begat [191c] and bore not in each other but in the earth as grasshoppers do. Through these changes he made it that their process of generation be in conjunction with each other, through the male in the female, for the following reason: firstly, in order that in the embrace, if a man met a woman, he might beget, and offspring might be born; secondly, if a man met a man, at least they might have their fill of each other, and they might rest and turn to work and care about the rest of life. (3) Ever since, therefore, [191d] erotic love of each other has been intimate in humans, a union of our old nature, an attempt to make one out of two and to heal human nature. Therefore, each of us is a half of a human being, having been cut in two like turbots, two out of one. Each man seeks his own other half. All men who are cuttings of the hermaphrodite, which was called man-woman, [191e] are lovers of women, and most of the adulterers come from this group. Women who are cuttings of women do not pay much attention to men but are more inclined towards women, and female lovers of women come from this group. (4) All who are cuttings of the male pursue male objects and while they are children, since they are cuttings of the male, they love men and enjoy lying with them and embracing men, [192a] and these are the best of boys and youths and are bravest in nature. Some people say they are shameless but they lie, for they do not do this from shamefulness but from boldness and courage and masculinity, welcoming what is similar to themselves. There is strong evidence: for when adult, only men such as these go into politics; when they become men [192b] they fall in love with boys (5) and do not by nature pay attention to marriage and begetting, but are compelled by the law to do so. (6) It is enough for them to live unmarried and with each other. (7) At any rate, this sort of male becomes a lover of boys and is fond of his own beloved, always welcoming what is similar. Therefore, whoever meets his other half, the lover-of-boys or the other kinds, they are wonderfully smitten with affection, kinship and erotic love."

Notes

1   Cf. Reckford; Penwill; Cohen 1991: 190–92; Carnes.
2   *androgunos*: a hermaphrodite; also used as an insult, i.e. a *kinaidos*.
3   The male is the begetter of life who plants his seed in the female; male union with male, while obviously infertile, is a source of pleasure recognised and ordained by Zeus.
4   *hetairistriai* (pl.): female lovers of women. Dover 1980 notes that this is 'the only surviving passage from classical Attic literature which acknowledges the existence of female homosexuality' (118). Cf. also Brooten 4–5, who points out that the term *tribas* is the more commonly used expression among later Greek (and Roman) writers.
5   *paiderastein*: to fall in love with boys, to be a *paiderastes* (lover of boys).
6   *physis* (nature) and *nomos* (law) are represented as areas that clash. The obligation of begetting children and the demands of society expressed in law as distinct from nature underpin these statements.
7   To Aristophanes the ideal companionship is male–male *eros*, between the *erastes* and *eromenos*. This ideal is that which conforms to nature.

84 Pseudo-Aristotle *Problems* 4.26: The Causes of Male Passivity

The author explores why some men enjoy being the passive partner, despite the possibility they may also enjoy being active, and provides the following answer. Winkler 1990a notes the importance of the text: '[it] contains the most complex and many-sided theory of "natural" sexual desire known . . . from ancient sources' (67). (1)

The men who are womanly by nature . . . have been constructed contrary to the natural order because though they are male they have been made in such a way that their rectum is essentially defective. When this defect is total it brings about destruction, but when partial, it causes perversion. (2) The first of these alternatives is not at issue, for such a man would then be female. It therefore follows that those under consideration are perverse and that the urge towards secretion of semen takes place elsewhere. (3) For this reason, just as in the case of women, they are sexually insatiable, for they produce very small quantities of liquid that does not force itself out of the body and rapidly loses its heat. This experience in some cases can be attributed to lifestyle and habit. (4) For this reason, whatever sexual activity they engage in, they derive pleasure and their semen is ejaculated as a result. Therefore they experience a desire to engage in sexual acts that generate this pleasure and through habituation these practices are very much like those generated by nature itself. Individuals, who have regularly been subjected to passive sexual intercourse, continue to want to undergo the experience. This occurs not prior to puberty but when they are undergoing puberty and comes about as a result of their recollections of having being treated this way, as well as recollections of the pleasure they experienced; lastly, their habituation to passive sex has become equated with nature. In most cases, however, the habit emerges in those who are naturally disposed towards it. If an individual combines both lustfulness and delicacy, such developments as these will become evident at a much faster rate.

Notes

1 On the passage and its importance, cf. Dover 1978 (169–70). The term most commonly applied to an individual being acted upon sexually is *aphrodisiazesthai*.
2 The rectum of the passive is defective in that it performs its normal function while also being the relocated focus of sexual pleasure.
3 Every secretion in the body has a natural location; in the case of the man who enjoys being passive, the seminal secretion does not necessarily form in the genitals but may be located in the rectum. This results in a sexual excitement in that area and with it the desire to be penetrated.
4 There is a keen interest in *physis* versus habituation (*ethos*). The author has briefly discussed the natural or physiological causes of passivity, and now considers the enjoyment of the activity through habit.

85 Phaedrus *Fables* 4.16: A Titanic Error

Phaedrus, translator of the *Fables* of Aesop in the Early Imperial era, provides an aetiological myth for the creation of individuals attracted to their own sex or, more specifically, masculine women and effeminate males. The narrator, an old (and therefore wise) man, explains that these two groups resulted from a mistake by the drunken Titan, Prometheus. (1)

Someone asked what were the circumstances that led to the
    emergence of
tribads and effeminate males. (2) The old man expounded:
"This same Prometheus, creator of common man made
    from clay,
as soon as he had offended against fortune was brought low:
one time, after he had been working for an entire day those parts
    of nature,   5
which a sense of shame (3) covers with clothing, doing them
    separately
so that he could soon adapt them to their appropriate bodies,
all of a sudden he was invited to a meal by Liber. (4)
After saturating his veins at dinner with a prodigious amount
    of nectar,
he returned home late with a rather unsteady step.   10
Then, being semiconscious, due to sozzled error
he welded maidenly genitalia onto the male species
and applied masculine members to the female.
As a result, nowadays their lust takes its enjoyment from depraved
    pleasure." (5)

Notes

1 Cf. Hallett 1989; Brooten 45–46.
2 Tribads are women who rub against each other; cf. 101; also 102. The term *molles* (soft, delicate; effeminate) is pejorative when applied to males.
3 *pudor*.
4 An indigenous Italian deity often called Bacchus and equated with the Greek god Dionysus.
5 The pleasure (*gaudium*) the masculine woman and the effeminate male receives is described as *pravum* (depraved), with connotations of something distorted, deformed, improper or bad.

86 Athenaeus 602f–603a: The Origins of Pederasty

The view that the Cretans invented pederasty was not uncommon in the ancient Greek world. It is implied, for example, in Plato's *Laws* 636a–b and several other authors note the Cretan predilection for the practice. (1)

Falling in love with boys (2) as a practice first came to the Greeks from Crete, as related by Timaeus. (3) Others say Laius initiated such erotic attachments

(4) when he was Pelops' guest and fell in love with his son Chrysippus; [603a] after seizing the boy and placing him in his chariot, he fled to Thebes. (5) But Praxilla of Sicyon (6) says Zeus snatched Chrysippus. Of the barbarians, the Celts, though they have very beautiful women, (7) enjoy boy-loves far more; so that often some of them sleep on animal skins with two beloveds at the same time. (8) In the case of the Persians, Herodotus asserts they learned to make use of boys as sexual partners from the Greeks. (9)

Notes

1 Cf. Dover 1978: 185–203; Bremmer; Sergent 197–213; Thornton 1997.
2 *paiderastein*: cf. 83 n. 5.
3 Timaeus of Sicily (*c.* 350–260 BC) was a historian.
4 *erotes*: the plural of *eros*, the term is used of love-affairs and erotic attachments.
5 The tale of Laius is the first one that details a mortal male's abduction of a young man for sexual purposes (cf. Sergent 67–73; Gantz 488–89). Hence, he was regarded as the inventor of male–male relations. On the significance of the story, cf. Thornton 1997 (102).
6 Female poet (fl. Fifth Century BC) who wrote drinking songs and hymns. Gulick (6: 250–51, n.b) alludes to the reading of Oedipus in lieu of Zeus.
7 *kallistai* (pl.): superl. of *kalos*.
8 Ath. uses *paidikai* (pl.) for 'boy-loves' and *eromenoi* (pl.) for 'beloved (boys)'.
9 Hdt. 1.135.

Males compared to females

87 Ovid *Ars Amatoria* 2.683–84: Sexual Pleasure with Boys is Unequal

The following passages (87–91) exemplify a fashionable literary topos from the Augustan age onwards, namely the comparison between boys and women as sexual partners. The debate commenced much earlier in the age of Plato, when philosophers began to examine male–male *eros* not only from a physical and spiritual viewpoint but also in terms of morality and social issues. Overall, such comparisons favour boys, but Ovid is definitely in favour of women when it comes to love and lovemaking. (1)

> I hate sex (2) that doesn't provide equal release for each partner.
> This is why I am touched less by the love of a boy. (3)

Notes

1 For Ov. the need for parity in the pleasure that sex provides is of utmost importance; cf. Verstraete.
2 In the *AA* Ov. has a preference for the term *concubitus* (lying together) when alluding to sexual intercourse; cf. Adams 1982 (177–78). His use of the strong verb 'to hate' is indicative of his convictions concerning unequal sexual pleasure.
3 *amor*. There is a clever pun on his use of *tangere*, to touch (here in the passive) with its secondary sense of having sex with someone.

88 Plutarch *Moralia* 751.4 [*Dialogue on Love*]: Love of Boys is Genuine

In the words of Protogenes, quoted by Plutarch's son Autobulus, women are inadequate sexual partners as are slaves when compared with the romantic pursuit of freeborn boys. This passage extols the love between a man and a boy as a heroic and virtuous relationship, one opposed to the effeminate and hedonistic love for a woman or a slave. (1)

". . . the love of boys is the one genuine Love, (2) not 'shining with longing' as Anacreon says the love of girls is, not 'full of myrrh, polished'. (3) But you will see it plain and unaffected in philosophical schools or I suppose in the gymnasium and wrestling-schools, in the hunt for boys, with a shrill and noble call, urging to virtue the boys worthy of its concern. But this soft love, staying at home, spending time in the bosoms of women and in women's beds, always pursuing soft things, unmanned by pleasures that are unmanly, and without friendship or passion – it is proper to reject this Love, as Solon also rejected it. (4) He forbade slaves to make love to boys and to rub themselves dry with oil, but he did not prevent slaves from having sex with women. (5) For friendship is a beautiful and refined thing, but pleasure is vulgar and unworthy of fine men. Therefore, it is not manly or refined to be in love with slave-boys, for this love is copulation, (6) as is the love of women."

Notes

1 One should keep in mind, however, that the words of Protogenes do not characterise the overall thesis of the text. Plut. explores *eros* in a unique and holistic way and presents a view that love for both boys and women each has its own merits; cf. Cantarella 1992 (70–73).
2 The ideal Love (Eros) is defined as by the adj. *paidikos* (lit. of a quality appropriate to a *pais*).
3 Anacr., *Fr.* 444 describes the emotion as *pothos*, a love that is *parthenios*. Protogenes, by introducing the words of the poet, attempts to establish that love for a woman is a base *pothos*. In contrast, love of boys is perfect, socially acceptable and characterised by virtue and excellence (*arete*) with its emphasis on athletic and philosophical activity.
4 The love of a woman is presented as the antithesis of manliness: it is *malthaka* (things soft to the touch, cowardly) and characterised by *hedone*. It is also wanting in manliness (*anandros*) and devoid of male friendship (*aphilos*). On Solon's attitude to same-sex love as a feature of men of higher quality and his ban on slaves having sex with boys, cf. Plut. *Sol.* 1; Sol. *Fr.* 25: 'until a man falls in love with a youth (*hebe*) in the full flower of boy-love (*paidophiles*) / possessed of desire-enhancing (*himeiroi*) thighs and a honey-sweet mouth.'
5 The equation of women with slaves in this context reduces sexual activity with them to simple carnal release.
6 *sunousia*: copulation; also social and intellectual union as well as sexual intercourse.

89 Straton *Greek Anthology* 12.7: The Differences Between Girls and Boys

As a poet commissioned to write erotic epigrams promoting pederasty (*AP* 12.258), Straton is a proponent of the joys of boys over women. His argument in favour of boys has a physiological as well as aesthetic basis.

In the case of a young girl there is no sphincter, (1) there is
    no simple kiss, no natural fragrance of the skin,
none of that lascivious chat so sweet to the taste, (2) no seductive
    glance, and even when she has been taught how, she is worse!
Finally, when being joined from behind, they are frigid. But, what is
    of greatest import, there is nowhere you can put your wandering
    hand. (3)

Notes

1 As females lack a prostate gland, he may be arguing that their enjoyment of anal intercourse (*l.* 5) is less than that of boys. In 11.43.11–12, Mart., despite his wife offering herself for sodomy, denies that women possess a *culus* (arsehole, i.e. sphincter): 'Cease, therefore, giving masculine names to your parts / and regard yourself wife, as possessing two cunts.'
2 Girls lack the capacity of boys for engaging in lascivious (*pornikos*) conversation (*logos*) during sex.
3 While acknowledging that girls can be sodomised, the argument is that they get no enjoyment from it, and furthermore lack what a man needs to gainfully employ his hands during the act, i.e. a penis.

90 Pseudo-Lucian *Amores* 25–28: Love of Women Versus Love of Boys

Lucian is regarded as the author of this work but it may have been written as late as the Fourth Century AD. It is in keeping with the author's satiric approach to subject matter and offers a modern reader further insight into the sexual mores of late antiquity. The protagonists are Lycinus and Theomnestus, the latter a young man who has enjoyed both males and females. When Lycinus asks his friend to speak of his lovers, Theomnestus poses a challenge instead. He asks Lycinus, as a more objective thinker in the matter, which gender is the better partner in sex. Lycinus then proceeds to tell the story of Charicles and Callicratidas – the former loved women and the latter loved boys. In this excerpt, the views of Charicles are reported with a view to assessing the pragmatic argument against same-sex preferences.

"Callicratidas, coming down somewhat from matters of excessive seriousness to your level of pleasure, (1) I will demonstrate that pleasure with women is much better than pleasure with boys. First of all, I think prolonged enjoyment is the more delightful. For pleasure taken swiftly escapes our notice, flying past, over before it is even recognised; delight is more intense in that which is prolonged. (2) If only this arbitrary Fate of ours had spun for us a long, fixed lifespan, and our health was entirely unbroken, with no grief feeding upon our mind! Then we would be holding feast and festival all the time! But since a malicious divine force has begrudged the greater good things to us, in the good things that are available to us the sweetest are the lasting ones. A woman, from virginity to middle age, before the last wrinkle of old age completely overruns her, is company pleasant to embrace, and even if the qualities of youth have passed away, experience, nevertheless, has something to say that is wiser than the young.

117

[26] But if a man were to make an attempt on a youth of twenty, in my eyes he is craving passive sex, (3) pursuing an Aphrodite that is unnatural. For, now that he has become a man, the build of his limbs is hard, and his chin, thickened with hairy growth, is rough, and his well-developed thighs are rendered grubby with hair. (4) The parts less visible than these I leave to your expert knowledge, since you have made a thorough examination of the subject. But the grace of a woman's skin glistens all over her, as do the many ringlets from her head, reddening like fair-flowing hyacinths, some pouring down her back as an ornament to her shoulders, others beside her ears and temples, much curlier than celery in the meadow. The rest of her body, with no hair growing on it, flashes, as they say, more transparently than amber or Sidonian glass. (5)

[27] Why is it not right to pursue pleasures that are reciprocal, where the passive partners experience pleasure equal to that of the active partners? For in general we do not, as the irrational animals do, gladly adopt solitary ways of life, but yoked in friendly and loving partnership, we consider good things sweeter and hardships lighter when shared with each other. . . .

Coming together with women has a similar reciprocity of enjoyment. For the man and the woman separate pleasurably after having an equal effect on each other, unless we ought to adopt the verdict of Tiresias that female sexual pleasure (6) exceeds that of the male by an entire portion. Although men are able to attain a 'good outcome' for themselves alone, namely, taking all the pleasure they want at the expense of another, I think it a far finer thing, not wanting to engage in purely selfish enjoyment, to render like for like, sharing what we encounter when we encounter it. (7) No one would say this is the case with boys, for he would not be quite so mad. The active party, if he were ever to consider this, after he has taken his exquisite pleasure, goes away. For the violated boy, however, there are pain and tears at the beginning, but, when the pain has eased a little under the influence of time, while you would not be causing him ongoing discomfort, as they say, there is still no real pleasure in it for him. (8) And, at the risk of saying something that may appear far-fetched – but I must, being in Aphrodite's precinct, Callicratidas – it is possible, using a woman in the fashion of a boy, to enjoy oneself, travelling along two roads to pleasure. But a male does not in any way provide the potential for enjoyment a woman gives a man. (9)

[28] Since, if she can give pleasure to men with your inclinations, then we men should wall ourselves off from each other; yet if for males associations with males are seemly, in future let women enjoy erotic love with each other. (10) Come now, New Age Lawmaker of Strange Pleasures, dreaming up new pathways of male luxuriousness, grant an equal right to women as well, let women associate with each other as men do. After they've yoked to themselves a contrivance made up of licentious implements, (11) a portentous riddle devoid of seed, let a woman lie with a woman as a man does. A name rarely coming

1. Cupid with bow. Roman copy of a Greek original by Lysippus. Capitoline Museum, Rome.

2. Wedding scene. Red Figure Loutrophoros. Athens *c*. 450–425 BC. Francis Bartlett Collection, 1903. Courtesy of the Museum of Fine Arts, Boston.

3. Wedding scene. Red Figure Loutrophoros. Athens *c*. 450–425 BC. Francis Bartlett Collection, 1903. Courtesy of the Museum of Fine Arts, Boston.

4. Married couple. Sarcophagus and Lid. Italy, Etruria c. 330–300 BC. Gift of Mrs Gardner Brewer, 1886. Courtesy of the Museum of Fine Arts, Boston.

5. Male with youth. The Warren Cup. 30 BC–AD 30. Courtesy of the British Museum. 1999.

6. Male with youth (and onlooker). The Warren Cup. 30 BC–AD 30. Courtesy of the British Museum. 1999.

7. Symposium scene. Pedieus Painter. *c.* 520–505 BC. Musée du Louvre. G13. Photographers: M. and P. Chuzeville.

8. Symposium scene. Pedieus Painter. *c.* 520–505 BC. Musée du Louvre. G13. Photographers: M. and P. Chuzeville.

9. Symposium scene. Euthymides. *c.* 515–500 BC. Musées Royaux Bárt et D'Histoire, Bruxelles.

10. Symposium scene. Athenian Red Figure Cup. Brygos Painter. *c.* 480 BC. Courtesy of the British Museum. E 68.

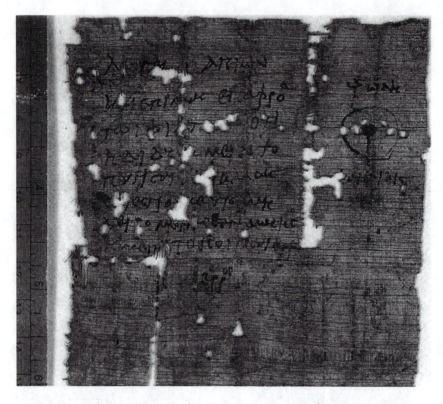

11. Provocative letter with crude sketch. P. Oxy. Courtesy of the Egypt Exploration Society.

within our earshot – I feel it disgraceful even to utter it – tribadic licentiousness. (12) Let it go on show in public procession without restraint. In all our women's quarters, let them be Philaenis, (13) behaving disgracefully in androgynous erotic encounters. How much better that a woman should force her way into the realm of male luxuriousness than that the noble quality of men should be turned effeminate like that of a woman."

Notes

1 *hedone* is translated as 'pleasure' throughout.

2 With women, the time for sexual relations extends throughout the whole of a man's life, unlike the brief and transitory period available to a boy-lover. Another consideration is that sex with a female can itself be prolonged and thereby a more enjoyable experience than sex with a boy or youth.

3 Chalicles deliberately chooses a youth of twenty rather than a prepubescent boy. The widespread antipathy towards sex with post-pubescent males renders the practitioner of passive sex (*paschetia*) subject to social condemnation.

4 In addition, by concentrating on a youth around the age of twenty, the author is able to present a visual image of the characteristically unattractive *eromenos*, a young man with hard limbs, a hairy chin and thick hairy thighs. Yet, the depictions on the Warren Cup, of a young man close to twenty (in the passive role, being penetrated) indicates the sexual appeal of post-pubescent youths in the Early Imperial age. Cf. **Illustrations 5–6**.

5 Sidon, on the coast of Phoenicia, was renowned for its production of purple dyed garments and glass blowing.

6 For Tiresias' experience of sexual pleasure (*terpsis*) in the shape of male and female, cf. Gantz 528–30. Cf. 102 n. 10.

7 Sexual activity with a woman, where each is attentive to the mutual pleasure of the partner, is regarded as a *kalon*.

8 The active party (*diatheis*) engaging in sex with a boy renders him a violated person (*hubrismenos*), who receives no *hedone* due to the painfulness of anal penetration.

9 As women enjoy penetration due to their nature, vaginal and anal intercourse are capable of providing them with equal pleasure and the active partner thus can achieve delight via both paths. In the case of a passive boy partner, his genitals play a limited part in the attainment of pleasure for the active male.

10 Chalicles proposes the radical view that women should also be able to enjoy same-sex relations. While his stated views on the abhorrence of tribadism are indicative of those of society as a whole, his main purpose is to expose the hypocrisy of Callicratidas' philosophical position. On male perceptions of what women actually 'do' together, cf. Brooten Ch. 2.

11 On the use of an *olisbos* (dildo) by women, cf. Kilmer 1993 (passim) with visual representations involving men and women; cf. 139–140.

12 On tribadism and the revulsion it arouses in men, cf. 85 n. 2; Brooten Ch. 2.

13 On the name Philaenis and her association with tribadic activities, cf. 101; for Philaenis as celebrated author of a *Handbook of Sexual Positions*, cf. 143 and H. N. Parker 1992.

91 Achilles Tatius *Leucippe and Clitophon* 2.35–38: The Merits of Boy-Love

The merits of women as well as boys are debated in this scene from Achilles Tatius' melodramatic novel. Clitophon and Clinias meet an Egyptian by the name of Menelaus, a lover of boys, who is returning to his homeland after three years in exile. Menelaus and Clinias share a common bond as both have experienced the death of their beloveds. This correlation of sexual preference sets the scene for the following debate: Clitophon, besotted by Leucippe, is an obvious supporter of love for women, while Menelaus puts forward a case for boy-love. (1)

Seeing Menelaus very dejected while remembering his own problems, and seeing Clinias weeping secretly from memory of Charicles, wishing to lead them away from their grief, I threw in a talk about erotic diversion. (2) Leucippe was not present, but was sleeping in an inner part of the ship. I said to them, smiling a little: "How far Clinias surpasses me! For he wanted to speak against women, as he is accustomed to do. He would now speak more easily, having found a sharer of his views on love. (3) For I don't know how nowadays love for males is fashionable." Menelaus said: "Isn't it much better than the alternative? For boys are simpler than women and their beauty is more piercing as a stimulus for pleasure." (4) "How more piercing," said I, "something that has hardly blinked when it has gone, and gives no time for the lover to really enjoy it, but instead is like the drink of Tantalus? (5) For often, while in the very act of drinking it, it has fled, and the lover (6) leaves, not having found anything to drink; what is still being drunk is snatched away before the drinker is sated. It is not possible for a lover to go away from a boy having pleasure without pain; for it leaves him still thirsting."

[36] Menelaus said: "Clitophon, you don't know the chief point about pleasure. The unsatisfied is always desirable. (7) The thing that is there longer for enjoyment, that thing of delight is withered by satiety. The thing that is snatched away is always fresh and more in bloom; for it possesses a pleasure not grown old, and the more it is shortened by opportunity, the more it is stretched out into enormity by longing. (8) The rose is shapelier than other plants for this reason, namely that its beauty flees. For I consider that two kinds of beauty wander among humans, one of them 'heavenly', the other 'common', like the two forms of the patron goddess of beauty. (9) The heavenly beauty is vexed, bound to its mortal tent, and seeks to flee quickly to heaven; the common beauty lies prostrate below on earth and spends its time on corporeal bodies. If one ought to take a poet as witness of the heavenly journey upwards of beauty, listen to Homer:

The gods snatched him up to pour wine for Zeus because of his
beauty, in order that he might be with the immortals. (10)

But no woman ever went up to heaven because of her beauty. Zeus associated with women too but grief and exile took Alcmene; a chest and the sea took Danae; Semele became food for fire. (11) But if Zeus falls in love with a Phrygian youth, Zeus gives him heaven, in order that he might live with the youth and have a pourer of nectar. (12) The previous female servant has been ejected from the honour; for she, I believe, was a woman."

[37] Taking up his words, I said: "The beauty of women seems more likely to be heavenly, since it does not perish quickly. For the imperishable is closer to the divine. What is roused in perishable corruption, imitating mortal nature, is not heavenly but common. Zeus fell in love with a Phrygian youth, and took the Phrygian to heaven; but the beauty of women took Zeus himself down from heaven. On account of a woman Zeus once mooed, on account of a woman he once danced the 'satyr', and he made himself into gold for another woman. (13) Let Ganymede pour the wine; but let Hera drink with the gods, in order that a woman may have a youth as a servant. I pity him and his seizure; a carnivorous bird went down to him, and seized, rendered humiliated, he looked like a man crucified. That is a most shameful sight, a youth hanging from talons. No savage bird but fire brought Semele up into heaven. Do not be amazed if someone ascends into heaven through fire; thus went Heracles. If you laugh at Danae's wooden crate, how are you silent about Perseus? This gift alone is sufficient for Alcmene that on her account Zeus stole three whole days. (14)

Leaving aside mythologies, I now must talk about the pleasure of the deeds themselves. . . . A woman's body is supple during the embracing process, and her lips are soft for kisses. For that reason she holds the man's body in her arms, and within her flesh she holds him completely fitted, and the man who is in her is engulfed with pleasure. She presses her kisses to his lips like seals, she kisses with skill, she contrives the kiss so that it is even sweeter. For she does not wish only to kiss with the lips, but meets the man with her teeth and grazes round the mouth of the kisser and her kisses bite. Her breast, too, when touched, has its own individual pleasure. In the grip of Aphrodite she is maddened by pleasure, gaping wide open while kissing, and is like a Maenad. During this time their tongues are in constant contact with each other, and employ force to kiss as much as they can. You make the pleasure greater, kissing with open mouth. Nearing the completion of Aphrodite, (15) the woman is naturally inclined to pant under the scorching pleasure. The gasp, rushing up with erotic spirit to the lips of the mouth, encounters the kiss that wanders and seeks to go down below. The kiss, turning back with the gasp and mingled with it, follows, and strikes the heart, which, being disturbed by the kiss, quivers. If it were not bound fast in the flesh, it would have followed and would have drawn itself up with the kisses. But boys' kisses are untrained, their embraces are unskilled, their capacity for Aphrodite is inactive, and in them there is nothing of pleasure."

[38] Menelaus said, "But you appear to me to be not a beginner but an old man with respect to Aphrodite. Such an amount of the superfluities of women you have poured all over us. Hear in turn the facts about boys. A woman's every word and every gesture is feigned. If she appears beautiful, (16) it is due to the fussy contrivance of unguents. Her beauty is of scented oil, or hair-dye, †or rouge†. (17) If you strip her of these many deceits, she is like the jackdaw

stripped of feathers in the fable. But the beauty of boys is not watered with scents of unguents or with deceitful and alien smells; the sweat of boys smells sweeter than all the scented unguents of women. You can meet him in the wrestling school, before engaging in the embraces of Aphrodite, and you can openly spread yourself round him, and the embraces have no shame. (18) He does not soften embraces in the midst of Aphrodite by suppleness of flesh; but bodies offer resistance to each other and they contend for pleasure. His kisses do not possess the wisdom of women, (19) and with his lips he does not artfully contrive a mischievous deceit, but he kisses as he knows how, and the kisses are not derived from skill but from nature. (20) This is the image of a boy's kiss: if nectar had solidified and become a lip, you would have had that sort of kisses. Kissing, you would not have satiety, for as much as you take your fill, you thirst still to kiss, and you would not draw your mouth away until, on account of pleasure, you fled from his kisses!"

Notes

1 On the passage cf. Cantarella 1992 (74); also, Reardon; Holzberg 1986 (87–93).

2 *erotike*: erotic material.

3 *eros*: love/sex at a broader level than usual, the subject matter of the dialogue. Unless otherwise noted, throughout *eros* is translated as 'love', while Aphrodite is used of the 'sexual act' (cf. n. 9 and 15).

4 Boys (*paides*) possess an uncomplicated nature and a *kallos* that inspires an undiluted form of *hedone*.

5 Tantalus was invited to dine with the gods, despite being a mortal: variant versions have him either revealing the secrets of the conversation that took place or giving to mankind the nectar and ambrosia he had savoured at the divine banquet table. He was punished in Hades; seeing food and drink that he was forever unable to reach. Sexual activity with a boy is too short-lived, as this comparison with Tantalus' experience of heavenly delight illustrates.

6 *erastes*: the lover, as distinct here from the *pais*.

7 *hedone* is linked with *terpsis*, which is associated with lack of fulfilment.

8 *pothos*.

9 Heavenly Aphrodite (born of the severed genitals of Uranus) was goddess of the higher forms of love (cf. 3), while Earthly Aphrodite (daughter of Zeus and Dione) was goddess of carnal love; cf. Pl. *Smp*. 180e–181c.

10 *Il*. 20.234–35.

11 For the stories of Zeus and Alcmene, Danae, and Semele, cf. 1; for detailed references cf. Gantz.

12 Aspects of the story of Zeus and Ganymede are treated at Theognis 1345–50 and (Anon.) *AP* 5.65. Ganymede replaced the previous, female wine-server, Hebe (*Il*.4.2); she was subsequently married to Heracles (Hes., *Th*. 950–55).

13 For Zeus and Europa cf. 1 n. 14; and Antiope 2 n. 5; for Danae, 2 n. 8.

14 On Semele, cf. n. 11. Heracles was transformed into a god after apotheosis by fire. Perseus was the son born of Danae and went on to become one of the greatest of heroes. Zeus enjoyed sex so much with Alcmene that he stopped the progress of time and extended the night. The point is that Zeus frequently sought delight with women rather than boys.

15 Aphrodite is the equivalent of intense sexual experience, culminating in orgasm.

16 A woman's appearance is illusory, based upon adornment and deception. The adj. *kale* and noun *kallos* are employed for beauty.

17 MSS corruption; the translation is based on the text of Gaselee (130–31).
18 The issue of shame (*aischune*) is designed to address the contrary argument that the passive partner is unmanned in male–male sex. By offering resistance in the sexual act, the recipient actually maintains and enhances his masculinity.
19 The *sophia gunaika* is not a compliment: a woman's wisdom comes from the knowledge of her power to draw and deceive males.
20 Boys lack the skill (*techne*) of women and respond to sex through innate *physis*.

Male beauty and eroticism

92 Straton *Greek Anthology* 12.4: The Ideal Ages for Boys

Straton is a prolific writer on the subject of pederastic love. There are over ninety of his poems in Book 12 of the *Greek Anthology* (known by the collective title *Musa Paidike / Puerilis*). This poem is essentially programmatic, outlining the various stages at which boys are at their most desirable. It is clear that late fourteen is the ideal age for boys in the case of mortal lovers. (1)

> In the prime of a twelve-year-old boy I take the utmost delight.
>> One of thirteen, however, is even more desirable. (2)
> He who is fourteen is an even sweeter bloom of the Loves. (3)
>> More delightful (4) is he not far from the beginning of his fifteenth.
> The sixteenth year is the property of the gods. The seventeenth
>> it is not for me to seek, but Zeus.
> But if anyone has a craving for one even older, he no longer sports, (5)
>> but is now in need, and 'answers him back'. (6)

Notes

1 On the works of Strat., cf. Maxwell-Stuart 1972, 1975; Cameron 1982.
2 The word for the longing, *pothos* (also at *l.* 7), is made even more emphatic here by the use of the adj. *potheinoteros* (even more desire-inducing).
3 Erotes: pl. of Eros, therefore 'the Loves'. Note the equation with the sweetness of a blooming flower.
4 The comp. adj. *terpnoteros* (even more inducing of sexual pleasure) represents the ultimate erotic impact a boy can generate.
5 *paizdein*: to sport or play with/as a boy. Note that mortals should not pursue boys after their fifteenth year; beyond the age of seventeen such a desire is seen as perverse obsession rather than delightful sport.
6 An ambiguous proverb, common in Homer (Paton 4: 285 n. 1).

93 Catullus 48: Kissing Juventius

The Juventius Cycle of Catullus contains up to eleven poems, although Juventius is named in only four – Poems 24, 48, 81 and 99. (1) The Cycle is not only the earliest but is also among the most sensitive and informative of extant Roman material on the eroticism of boy-love. Of the four cited poems, only this one can be regarded as essentially happy.

Your honey sweet eyes, Juventius, (2)
were anyone to allow me to kiss (3) them continuously,
continuously would I kiss them three hundred thousand times
and I would never consider myself going to be sated,
not even if the harvest of our osculation (4)
were to be denser than the dried ears of the corn-crop. (5)

Notes

1   Cf. Lilja (51–55); Quinn 1972 (242–55).
2   The Juventii were a distinguished noble family at Rome (cf. Neudling 94) and there are serious questions about Cat. having an active sexual relationship with a boy of such breeding. If he was the son of a freedman he could be considered an available sexual partner.
3   Cat. seems to have coined the term *basia* for passionate kisses (Cat. 5 and 7 to Lesbia) along with the verb *basiare*, also repeated in the following line.
4   *osculatio* means kissing or the process of kissing; a rare word in Classical Latin, it is found only here and in Cic., *Cael.* 20.49.
5   The reference is not just to the quantity of corn niblets but their sweet taste as well.

Same-sex love in militaristic societies

94   Aelian *Miscellany* Book 3: Pederasty at Sparta

Aelian (*c.* AD 170–235), relying on a wealth of source material, records the value the Spartans placed on the spiritual or moral aspect of love between the *erastes* and the *eromenos*. The Spartan ideal was for the *erastes* to demonstrate his virtue and temperance and thereby win the affection of the *eromenos*. Likewise, the *eromenos* was expected to look for a good man as a potential lover. This ideal, however, was just that, for we do not know to what extent the laws mentioned by Aelian were imposed. (1)

3.10

There are many other fine things I could say about the ephors in Lacedaemon, and now I will outline what I have selected. When one of the beautiful youths (2) among them chose a rich lover instead of a good man who was poor, the ephors imposed a fine on him, punishing him it seems for his love of money by fining him money. They also fined any man who was 'beautiful' (3) but was not in love with one of the beautiful youths. They fined him because, although a good man, he was not in love; for clearly the man would have moulded a youth like unto himself, and perhaps another youth as well. For the goodwill of lovers towards their boy-lovers is perfect for the creation of virtue, (4) when the lovers themselves are admirable. For this is also a Spartan custom, (5) that when a youth does wrong, they pardon the naivety of his character and the youthfulness of his age, and punish the lover instead, commanding them to be inspectors and examiners of the youth's activities. (6)

3.12:

Beautiful Lacedaemonian youths are not provocative or boastful towards their lovers, so one can learn from them the opposite of what one learns from other beautiful youths. The youths themselves ask their lovers to 'breathe into' (7) them; this is the Lacedaemonian word for love. Spartan love knows nothing base. For if a youth dared to submit to insolence (8) or a lover dared to be insolent, it would not profit either of them to pollute Sparta. They would rather forfeit their native land or their lives.

Notes

1 Cf. Dover 1978 (202); Cartledge 1981, who comments on the reference to legal punishment as deserving no 'special claim to our credence' (31 n. 19). On the importance of these relationships in the Spartan training (*agoge*), cf. Plut., *Lyc.* 17; X., *Lac.* 2; on punishment of boys for misdemeanours, cf. Plut., *Lyc.* 18.3.
2 *kaloi* (pl.): beautiful youths, used throughout. The age of the youth (boy) may have been approximately twelve years. The older *erastes* probably began the practice from the age of twenty onwards.
3 *kalos*: here as much respectable and eligible as physically beautiful.
4 *arete*.
5 The word *nomos* is used: at Sparta, as elsewhere, custom had the force of law.
6 On the responsibilities of the elder partner, cf. Plut., *Lyc.* 18.4.
7 I.e. to 'inspire them' or for the *erastes* to transfer his good qualities into the *eromenos*. For the suggestion that the concept could have involved the actual transfer of semen (an 'in-blower' of seed), which may have been regarded as a source of *arete* or some form of manly strength, cf. Devereux 1968 (80); Cartledge 1981 (23–24); Percy (88–89).
8 *hubris*. The context suggests submission to anal sex, which would bring opprobrium onto the participants.

95 Athenaeus 561e–f: Love Honoured in Military Societies

In this brief summation of the practice of sacrificing to Eros and the linkage with male–male relations within the military, Athenaeus provides three examples of communities where such unions were essentially institutionalised.

And in public libations, generally speaking, Love is honoured. Before the marshalling of troops, the Lacedaemonians sacrifice to Love, (1) thinking that safety and victory lie in the friendship of those men being drawn-up for battle. [f] The Cretans arrange the most handsome of their citizens in the front lines, then offer sacrifice to Love on their behalf, (2) as Sosicrates (3) relates. Among the Thebans the Sacred Band, as it is known, consists of lovers and beloveds. The Band reveals the worthiness of this god, since lover and beloved embrace glorious death rather than a shameful and blameworthy life. (4)

Notes

1 Eros binds the Lacedaemonians as it does the Cretans. Several sources allude to the practice of pederasty in both centres, for example, X., *S.* 8.35; *HG.* 4.8. For discussion on pederasty, cf. Cartledge 1981 (Sparta); Percy (Sparta and Crete).

2 Cf. Ogden 1996 (116–17).
3 Rhodian biographer of uncertain date.
4 The contrast is between a death that is *endoxos* (extremely glorious) and life that brings *aischron*. The Sacred Band of Thebes (formed in *c.* 378 BC) is the most renowned collective of soldiers bound by institutionalised same-sex unions. Plut. explains the rationale behind the organisation: 'For, in times of danger, tribesmen do not pay much attention to their fellow tribesmen nor phratrymen to fellow phratrymen, but a band that was unified by sexual love was enduring and unbreakable, since they stood firm when confronting danger because of each other, the *erastai* out of love for their *eromenoi* and the *eromenoi* out of shame in front of their *erastai*' (*Pel.* 18). Cf. Ogden 1996 (111–15); for a re-evaluation of the Sacred Band and its ideals, cf. Leitao.

Women in love

96 Sappho *Fragments*: Love and Friendship

Sappho not only explores the power of emotions between women but the pain of separation experienced by women. This is especially in evidence in *Fragment* 94, which also contains the nearest overt reference to sexual contact between Sappho and a woman in the surviving corpus. *Fragment* 49 draws attention to the beginning of her relationship with Atthis when she was an ungainly child, while *Fragment* 96 has Sappho reminisce about a relationship now gone, not between herself and Atthis, but that of an unnamed woman (now in Lydia) and Atthis.

Fragment 49
I loved (1) you a long time ago, Atthis, once. . . .
a small child, (2) lacking in grace, (3) to me you seemed to be.

Fragment 94.1–23
. . . "To be dead is what I honestly want." (4)
She, leaving me, was weeping   2

many tears, and said this to me:
"What a terrible thing we suffer
Sappho. Truly against my will do I leave you."   5

This is what I answered:
"Rejoice, go, and remember me,
for you know how much I cared for you.   8

But if not, I wish
to remind you
. . . and we experienced beautiful things: (5)   11

many wreaths of violets
and roses and . . . ,
you put on, alongside me,   14

126

and many garlands
woven out of flowers
you drew round your delicate neck,   17

and with much costly perfume,
appropriate for a queen,
you anointed yourself,   20

and on soothing (6) beds
tender . . .
you would satisfy your longing." (7)   23

Fragment 96.2–17
. . . often her thoughts turning this way   2

. . . (she honoured) you like
a goddess, conspicuous,
and she rejoiced in your song.   5

Now among Lydian women she stands out
as, the sun
having set, the rosy-fingered moon   8

surpasses all the stars; and her light spreads over
the salty sea
and flowery fields equally alike;   11

the dew is shed beautifully,
roses and delicate
chervil and flowery melilot bloom. (8)   14

Often going to and fro
remembering gentle Atthis with desire (9)
her tender heart is eaten by reason of your fate   17
. . .

Notes

1 *eran*: to be in love with, to have a desire for.
2 *smikra pais*: a tiny, small child.
3 *kacharis* (combining *kakos* and *charis*): lacking in grace.
4 The speaker of the opening line has been questioned by scholars: Burnett argues that it is
   the girl who delivers the line not Sapph.; contra Robbins 1990.
5 *kala* (pl.): 'beautiful, good things'. The images evoked of past times are romantic as well as
   erotic. Wilson observes: 'this song seems to be designed to give comfort in a way which
   would be almost maternal if it did not linger over erotic details' (127).

6 The adj. *malthakos* is frequently used pejoratively, esp. of men (= effeminate); here it evokes softness and comfort. It means much the same as the adj. employed in the next line, *apalos* (soft, tender).

7 The series of lines and images, culminating in the reference to the satisfaction in bed of their *pothos* (*l.* 23), is perhaps most informative for those who look for a definitive sign of the poet's sexuality.

8 On Sapph.'s use of natural imagery, cf. Winkler 1990a (180–87). Cf. also McEvilley 1973.

9 The intensity of the woman's love for Atthis is evoked in the depiction of her daydreams in Lydia; she remembers Atthis with heartache and *himeros*.

97 Erinna *Distaff* 13–55: Baucis

This fragmentary elegy illustrates the tenderness of friendship and the intensity of emotion over the loss of a friend, firstly through marriage and then death. The sentiments expressed by the poet reveal that same-sex love between young women is something that can and does transcend standard, stereotyped and narrow definitions. (1)

> You said you carded wool and yarn from Priene
> and I ran in a circle around you until into the waves you
> leapt from white mares with their madly running feet.   15
> "Alas for me," I shouted loudly; once again I became 'tortoise',
> and, leaping, I pursued <you> over the farmyard. (2)
> Baucis, unhappy and groaning deeply within, I grieve over these
>   things.
> These games of ours, so recent, lie stored in my heart,
> still warm. But these games we played before are now ashes: 20
> groups of dolls, in the inner rooms friendly
> nymphs, and at night carefree beds, and towards dawn
> my mother singing, when together with the gap-toothed wool
>   carders
> we came to our work. You were sitting beside cloth interwoven
>   with purple.
> The little girls arrived in a hurry: Mormo generated such great fear. 25
> There were big ears on Mormo's head, she moved on four feet,
> and kept changing from one shape to another. (3)
> But when you went into the bed of a man, then you forgot
>   everything
> you heard as a child, then, in my mother's house,
> dear Baucis. Aphrodite makes people forget many things. (4)   30
> Therefore, I weep for you, I groan, but I pass over other things.
> Right now, however, my feet are not permitted to leave the house
> and with my eyes I cannot look upon you dead, and I cannot lament
> with hair uncovered. (5) But crimson Shame (6)
> scratches my cheeks.   35
> Always standing before me, Shame, you address me:

"Your nineteenth year, standing beside you,
Erinna, sees you by the side of your dear mother, still a virgin,
watching the distaff.
Know that the revolving spindles of the Fates urge on threads   40
much more powerful than the hands of Gello." (7)
Shame always teaches me this beside my
virgin bed. With soft hands I raise my mirror
and as I gaze, I notice the fading of youth from my skin.
My beautiful hair worries me, and the approaching   45
grey hairs that gently warn me, the blooms of old age for mortal
    kind. (8)
Therefore, dear (9) Baucis, I have scratched both my cheeks raw,
weeping for you. My groans are twofold.
The entire household is at the funeral-pyre. But alone at home,
I listen to the lamentation that rends my inmost heart.   50
Ah, wedding day, that brings to girls much serenity
and enables them to experience many things
and gives to girls all delights in exchange
for one delight. Ah, wedding day.
Ah, poor (10) Baucis.   55

Notes

1 West 1977 is sceptical of authenticity. For further discussion, cf. Bowra; Barnard; Pomeroy 1978; Arthur 1980; Skinner 1982.
2 For details on the game, cf. Bowra 328; West 1977 (102).
3 The little girls had to help weave wool. A means of getting them downstairs to get on with their work was the fear that Mormo would catch them. Mormo was one of the archetypal child-snatching demons possibly used as an explanation for such incidents as cot-death; she is the ancient equivalent of the bogeyman.
4 The first separation occurred when Baucis married. Girlish pleasures are replaced by those that Aphrodite brought, along with the new husband.
5 The second separation is the death of Baucis. Erinna, as 'a young woman of childbearing age' (West 1977: 108), may not have been permitted to attend Baucis' funeral. It may also be a form of punishment, inflicted by her mother, or by herself.
6 Aidos: Shame personified.
7 Erinna has passed through the time when girls usually married, remaining at home engaged in the domestic tasks of a girl, as reflected in the rebuke of Aidos that she is still afraid of Gello, like Mormo, a female demon. The fate of an unmarried woman is of far greater weight.
8 At the age of nineteen it is likely that these thoughts are the anxieties of Erinna rather than the realities.
9 *phila*: dear, beloved.
10 The adj. *talain{a}* (fem.) evokes images of distress, much suffering and endurance.

98 *CIL* IV.5296: Entreaty to a Girl

The language employed may be that of a concerned older woman for a child of her own or for a close young female friend. The intensity and negativity of the feeling about desire for men and its consequences suggests that the girl is being pressed not so much by one expressing motherly considerations as one motivated by her own desire for the girl.

> Ah, would it were allowed to hold your precious little arms wrapped around
> (my) neck and to convey kisses to (your) tender little lips. (1)
> Go on, sweet girl, right this moment, entrust your joys to the winds,
> trust me: the intrinsic nature of men is capricious. (2)
> Often, in a state of despair, (3) have I maintained a vigil at midnight
> musing upon these things within myself: many are those chance (4) has hoisted high;
> she now bears down hard upon them, suddenly hurled headlong downwards.
> So, just as desire (5) suddenly joins together the bodies of lovers,
> the light of day separates them and †...........† (6)

Notes

1 The erotic vocabulary of the opening lines is conveyed via diminutives: *braciola* (precious little arms, *l.* 1), *labella* (liplets, *l.* 2), *pupula* (sweet girl-let, *l.* 3).
2 Reminiscent of Cat. 64.142; 70.4 (with gender reversal).
3 *perdita*: (fem.) 'ruined, destroyed' is a common image in amatory poetry, as is the idea of a distraught lover on vigil throughout the night. Usually it is a male who spends the night at the closed door of a beloved: here the vigil is indoors (as one would expect with a woman), dwelling upon her thoughts.
4 *fortuna*: could be the personified deity, Fortuna, which presides over the fate of humankind, or lower case 'chance' as adopted here.
5 *venus*: as with *fortuna*, it could be the deity, Venus, or desire, lust for sex.
6 The light of day separates lovers from their illicit pleasures. The remainder of the line is corrupt.

Representations

99 Anacreon *Fragment* 358: Girl Gazes on . . . Girl

The fragment has been the subject of much debate. Dover 1978 (183–84) sees the focus of the second stanza as the hair (silver/black, head/pubic) and conjectures that the conclusion alludes to the reputation women of Lesbos had for fellation. Cantarella 1992 (86–87) follows this line, citing others (especially Gentili), and places the action within the context of a banquet, where oral sex was more likely to be available from a professional in a quasi-public setting. The poem itself does not require such an artificially imposed context. The poet, clearly ageing, is smitten by Eros for a young, well-born girl, and the tone of the first stanza is decidedly erotic and play-ful, rather than overtly lustful. Her rejection of him on the basis of his silver hair is precocious and her gaze at 'another' does not, in itself, warrant any linkage with fellatory intent.

Once more with his rosy-hued ball
does Eros of the golden hair strike me (1)
and calls upon me to play a game with
    a delicately sandalled girl. (2)   4
She, however, for she comes from delightful
Lesbos, (3) criticises my hair in every way
because it is silver, and she
    stares open-mouthed at – another (girl). (4)   8

Notes

1 The playful tone undercuts the powerful impact of Eros conveyed in earlier lyric poets (cf. 11 ff.) and is a precursor of the lightness of touch found in the Augustans (16).
2 Her well wrought, fancy sandals indicate she is well-born (or a prostitute) and desirable.
3 Lesbos was famed for its beautiful women from the time of Homer (*Il.* 9.128–30). Here the island is described as *euktitos* (a derivative of *euktimenos*) 'good to live in, well endowed with resources'; cf. Campbell (2: 57) 'Lesbos with its fine cities'; West 1994 (104) 'noble island of Lesbos'; MacLachlan 1997 (202) 'well-founded with cities'. Anacr., however, is more likely thinking of Lesbos as a delightful and sophisticated place that produced a delightful girl.
4 The debate over the direction and focus of the girl's gaze hinges largely upon the reading of 'another' in the final line. Both Campbell and West 1994 (cf. n. 3) see the focus as another girl; contra, Dover 1978 and Cantarella 1992 (cf. the introductory above). A plausible reconciliation is offered by MacLachlan: '. . . Anacreon mocks not only the girl but himself; he doesn't have the credentials on two counts – he has white hair and the wrong physique' (1997: 208, also n. 35).

100 Asclepiades *Greek Anthology* 5.207: Two Women of Samos

In the following poem Asclepiades of Samos (born in the early Third Century BC) formally invokes Aphrodite to bring down punishment on two women, Bitto and Nannion, who engage in sexual practices contrary to the 'natural order' laid down by the goddess. (1)

The Samian women, Bitto and Nannion, are unwilling to follow
    the pathway set by the laws (2) of Aphrodite,
but desert to other courses, which are not beautiful. (3) Mistress
    Cypris, (4)
    look with hatred upon these fugitives from your bed. (5)

Notes

1 On the poem, their names, and the nature of their sexuality, cf. Dover 2002; also Brooten. According to Gow and Page 1965 (2: 122), these are names of *hetairai* found elsewhere. On Asclep. and women, cf. Cameron 1981a.
2 The poet assumes the part of a prosecuting lawyer, asserting their behaviour entails a reprehensible breach of the laws (*nomoi*) of Aphrodite (= nature).
3 *kala* (pl.): beautiful things.
4 He directly invokes the goddess, calling upon her to curse them. This is an indication of the

impotence felt by men in their dealings with women who seek sexual pleasure with their own sex: vituperation and an appeal to the gods are their only recourse.

5 The poet is evasive about the precise nature of the sexual 'offences'; cf. Dover 2002 (224–25).

101 Martial 7.67: Philaenis the Tribad

Martial ridicules Philaenis for being both active and passive in her sexual cravings. Philaenis is a bisexual freak of nature in the eyes of the poet in that she assumes a male role in her penetration of both boys and girls, while displaying a passive predilection for performing cunnilingus. (1)

Philaenis the tribad (2) buggers boys (3)
and with her 'erection', (4) more savagely than any husband,
she shafts eleven girls every day. (5)
Tucked-up from below, she also plays hand-ball (6)
and glows golden-hued from the sand; and, heavy as they are for
    bum-boys (7)   5
she swings the dumb-bells with a ready arm;
and, filthy from the putrid palaestra,
she gets flogged by the blows of the oiled-up instructor. (8)
She neither dines nor reclines prior to the time
when she has vomited seven measures of unmixed-wine; (9)   10
she thinks it proper for her then to go back for more,
when she has devoured sixteen servings of energy-food.
After that, when she is in the grip of lust,
she does not suck cock (10) – she thinks this to be insufficiently
    manly –
but solely guzzles on girls' groins. (11)   15
May the gods grant you your wits, Philaenis,
you who think it manly to lick a cunt. (12)

Notes

1 Cf. Howell 297–99; Hallett 1989; Brooten 47, 215–17. Cf. also Sullivan 1991 (186–88). On the paucity of references to female same-sex activities in Latin literature, cf. Howell 297. Note the equation of tribadism with the possession of a clitoris that acts effectively as a penis: Bassa is a *fututor* when she joins her cunt to another (Mart. 1.90.6–8).

2 On Philaenis, cf. 143 and H. N. Parker 1992; on *tribas*, cf. 83 n. 4.

3 *pedicare*: she anally penetrates young boys.

4 *tentigo*: lit. lust, overwhelming sexual desire; here used colloquially of an erection. Adams 1982 notes the term is a euphemism for the clitoris (104).

5 Her appetite for virgins is insatiable. The verb *dolare* conveys images of slicing or tearing open with force and bludgeoning (cf. *L&S* 607), a clear indication of her insensitive technique.

6 *ludere*: lit. she plays, sports, here with a hand-ball (medicine ball?). The emphasis is on the vigour with which she plays sport, corresponding to her penchant for rough sex.

7 *drauci* (pl.): usually sodomites, bum-boys (cf. *L&S* 612), not manly athletic types.

8 The post-exercise rubdown entails massage and a sound whipping to tone the muscles. This is the only intimate physical contact she has with an adult male.

9 Consumption of neat wine in large quantities to induce vomit is a means of cleansing the stomach. Her excesses of eating and drinking are justified as a training regimen.

10 *fellare*; cf. Adams 1982 (130–32). As a 'man' she would regard such an act as effeminate.

11 *media*: the middle places; between the girls' legs. The verb *vorare* (devour, gorge upon) is devoid of tenderness or eroticism: her oral sex is rough.

12 *cunnus*. The Greeks and Romans regarded cunnilingus as an unmanly as well as an unnatural activity and the practice was widely ridiculed (cf. 137 for an extreme example).

102 Lucian 5 [*Dialogues of the Courtesans*]: Clonarium and Leaena

While this late (Second Century AD) piece reflects long-standing male antipathy towards female same-sex relations, it does so with an overtly titillating tone. Here we are privy to the conversation of two *hetairai*, Clonarium and Leaena. The latter attended a party organised by two rich women living in a married relationship, Megilla and Demonassa. Clonarium seeks the details from Leaena, who, it transpires, was seduced by Megilla.

Clonarium

We've been hearing new reports about you, Leaena; that Megilla the rich woman from Lesbos (1) is in love with you like a man, and that you are living together doing 'I don't know what' with each other. What's this? Are you blushing? Tell me, is it true?

Leaena

It's true, Clonarium. But I'm ashamed because it's unusual.

Clonarium

For the sake of the Child-rearing-goddess, (2) what is it, and what does the woman want? What do you do when you're together? Do you understand? You don't love me, otherwise you wouldn't be hiding this from me.

Leaena

I love you, if I love any woman. But the woman is terribly butch. (3)

Clonarium

I don't understand what you're saying, unless she happens to be a practitioner of tribadism. (4) For they say there are such women in Lesbos, man-faced, not willing to have it done to them by men, but preferring to associate with women as men do.

Leaena

That sort of thing.

Clonarium
Well then, Leaena, tell me this, how did she make her intentions towards you known, how were you persuaded, and then what?

Leaena
She and Demonassa, the Corinthian woman who is also rich and practises the same art as Megilla, organised a drinking-party. (5) They took me along to play the cithara for them. After I had played it was late and time to sleep and they were both drunk. Then Megilla said, "Come, Leaena, it's time to go to bed. Sleep here in the middle between us two."

Clonarium
Did you sleep? What happened?

Leaena
At first they were kissing me just like men do, not only pressing their lips but opening their mouths a little, and they were embracing me and feeling my breasts. Demonassa was also biting me while she was kissing me. (6) I didn't know what to do with it all. Then, in time, Megilla, becoming rather heated, took off her wig, which is like real hair and fits very neatly, and I saw her shaved head, which is like the most masculine of athletes. I was thrown into confusion at the sight. (7) She said, "Leaena, have you ever seen such a fine young man?" "But I don't see a young man, Megilla," I said. "Don't make a woman of me," she said, "for I am called Megillus and long ago I married this woman, Demonassa, and she's my wife." I laughed at this, Clonarium, and said "Well, Megilla, you escaped our notice as a man, just like they say that Achilles, when hiding among the girls, escaped notice. (8) Do you have that male thing (9) and do you do to Demonassa what men do?" "I don't have 'that thing,' Leaena," she said. "I don't need it at all; you'll see me associating with a woman in a way of my own only much sweeter." "But," I said, "You surely aren't a hermaphrodite, as many people are said to be, the people having both things?" For I was still ignorant of such things, Clonarium. "No," she said, "I'm completely a man." I said "I heard the Boeotian flute-girl Ismenodora relating tales told around the hearth, how someone in Thebes became a man after being a woman, and this very man was also an excellent prophet. I think his name was Tiresias. (10) Surely you haven't suffered something like that?" She said "No, Leaena, I was born a woman just like you and other women, but I've the mind and desire and everything else like a man." I said, "Is desire enough for you?" She replied, "Come to me, Leaena, if you are disbelieving, and you will know that I don't fall short of a man in any way because I've got something instead of the male thing." (11) I did go to her, Clonarium, because she enticed me and gave me an expensive necklace and a dress of fine linen. Then I embraced her as if she were a man, and she began, and she kissed and panted and seemed to me to be enjoying herself incredibly."

134

Clonarium

What did she do, Leaena, and how did she do it? Tell me all.

Leaena

Don't interrogate me. Such things are shameful. By the heavenly goddess, I won't tell.

Notes

1 It is surely deliberate that Megilla and Demonassa are from Lesbos and Corinth, respectively, for the women from such places were renowned for their promiscuity and beauty.
2 Aphrodite; also referred to in the last line of the work.
3 *andrike*: man-like. It develops her earlier statement about the sex being unusual.
4 *hetairistria*. Cf. 83 n. 4 (for the pl.). The definition of tribadism by Clonarium focuses upon external appearance and aversion to men as much as the notion of 'rubbing'.
5 As a *hetaira*, Leaena was a symposiac entertainer. In addition to her musical contribution, she would be expected to provide sexual relief for male symposiasts (cf. **Illustration 10**), hence the overture from Megilla.
6 At the heart of Leaena's description of the women's activities is their active, dominant and sexually aggressive behaviour in their assumption of a male role.
7 The emphasis is on all that is artificial in the description of Megilla. The wig and Megilla's general appearance and behaviour reinforce the caricature, namely, she is *hosper andra* (like a man) and *deinos andrike* (terribly mannish) – but she is *not* a man. In this sense she represents transvestism as well as tribadism.
8 Achilles was hidden among the daughters of Lycomedes, king of Scyros, by his mother Thetis, in an attempt to prevent the youth from participating in the Trojan War. Cf. Gantz 580–81; Cyrino 1998.
9 Leaena is too polite and modest to use direct language for the penis, instead referring to *to andreion* (that male thing).
10 For the story of Tiresias, cf. 90 n. 6.
11 It is most likely that Megilla possessed an enlarged clitoris (a female abnormality); she may, however, have made use of an *olisbos* (cf. 139–140). Either would justify Leaena's sense of shame. Note that her consent to the sex came at the price of a necklace and dress as one would expect from a flute-girl.

VI

SEX AND VIOLENCE

The myths and legends of the Greeks and Romans are characterised by a recurring theme of violence, be it in terms of heroic quests, warfare or numerous stories of punishment and blood feud. Sex manifested through seduction, adultery and rape is often at the very heart of these tales; an overwhelming number of the heroic figures (as well as the gods themselves) are the product of such sexual unions (cf. 1–2). The behaviour of divine and heroic characters of both sexes is indicative of sexual mores in Dark Age and subsequent historical eras; Lefkowitz, however, notes 'that in the case of myths involving the unions of gods . . . with mortal . . . women, we should talk about abduction or seduction rather than rape, because the gods see to it that the experience, however transient, is pleasant for mortals' (1993: 17). A mortal male in the grip of *eros* faces the same alternatives as the gods of myth, but in the civilised world there are potentially dire consequences for the perpetrator as well as the object of desire.

Myths and legends expose fundamental attitudes – religious, social and moral – towards extra-marital sexual activity in antiquity. The story of Cassandra (103) entails multi-layered *hubris*. Locrian Ajax offers violence to the maiden, the code of suppliancy, the statue and precinct of Athena, thereby imperilling not only himself because of his frenzy but potentially all his allies in the Trojan expedition. The tale of Philomela (104) sheds further light on the consequences of extreme sexual violence. This story entails the violation of familial bonds and harmony by a man driven by lust who transgresses divine and natural order through barbaric psycho-sexual acts. At the heart of such stories, the genuine mortal fear of the powers of *eros* / *amor* in their most extreme and distorted forms are played out in dramatic renditions, which repeatedly acknow-ledge what volatile forces and reprisals are unleashed when a man is struck with an insane passion over which he has no control.

Sexual encounters in antiquity were to be carefully negotiated or else the perpetrator could pay dearly for his crime; he must tread cautiously in his dealings with freeborn males and females. Gratification of basic lust could be achieved through one's own slaves or prostitutes (66) and entailed, at worst, slight censure; but with the freeborn – unmarried or married – such gratification was unacceptable.

In Athenian and Roman law there were specific punishments for acts of adultery and rape predicated by the wrong done to the male responsible for the well-being of the victim (105–108). In the case of errant slaves and common thieves, sexual violation as punishment appears in literature to have been acceptable at both Athens and Rome (109–112).

136

The use of degrees of coercion in addition to persuasion in the seduction of a young girl sees the literary male tread a fine line. In the case of Archilochus' 'chance encounter' (113), the male has to demonstrate that he is not goaded by lust so much as a desire for the girl as a future partner: his desire and respect for her (as opposed to her 'fallen' sister) result in an unusual manner of gratification. Ovid (114) walks an even finer line between the erotic and the offensive in his argument that the male should start with persuasion and move on to less conventional means of overcoming resistance with 'rougher than usual handling', as the game of love is sport in his eyes, a match between equals, and forceful behaviour is an acceptable means of resolution in the eyes of both participants.

The sport motif is epitomised in the descriptive parody of contemporary combative athletic events by Aristophanes (115) and culminates in the ghastly re-enactment of a mythical tale of bestial lust as public spectacle on the occasion of the opening of the Colosseum (116).

Rape and violence in heroic legend

103 Alcaeus *Fragment* 298.4–24: Ajax and Cassandra

During the fall of Troy, Cassandra, a Trojan princess, daughter of Priam and Hecuba, sought refuge at the shrine of Athena and, as she clung to the image of the goddess, was dragged away by the Greek hero, Locrian Ajax. His crime is an example of *hubris*, a powerful concept in the Greek moral vocabulary, which entailed acts of violence so extreme as to offend freeborn men and women as well as, more importantly, the gods. The consequences for Ajax were dire. (1)

[Indeed] it would have been much better for the Achaeans	4
[if] they had killed the god-injurer;	
[in this way] sailing past Aegae (2)	
they would have met with a milder sea. (3)	
[But] in the temple, the daughter of Priam	8
was embracing the statue of Athena of	
Much Plunder, clinging to its chin,	
while the enemy attacked the city.	
[. . .] and Deiphobus too	12
[they kil]led, (4) and lamentation from the wall	
arose an]d the cries of children	
occupied the [Dardani]an plain;	
[and Ajax] with deadly madness entered	16
[the templ]e of holy Pallas, who,	
to sacrilegious [mortal]s,	
of all the blessed gods is most [awesome];	

and having taken the virgin (5) with both his hands,   20
(while she) was standing by the [solemn] statue,
the Locrian [violated] her, and did not fear
the daughter of Zeus, Giver of War,

Gorgon-eyed. (6)   24

Notes

1   Ajax committed *hubris* by doing violence to Cassandra (*l.* 8–11, 20–23) and to the image of
    the goddess; the other Greeks were enraged at the act and he barely escaped with his life,
    ironically as a suppliant at the same altar (cf. *Sack of Ilium* 1). On this fragment, cf. Campbell
    (1: 339–41); MacLachan 1997 (151); it appears to have been part of a polemic dealing with
    the tyrant, Pittacus, and contemporary issues at Mytilene.
2   In Southern Euboea opposite Locris, Ajax' homeland.
3   In her fury Athena generated a ferocious storm, which destroyed Ajax at the rocks known as
    the Capherides (cf. *The Returns* 1).
4   Deiphobus, brother of Cassandra and husband of Helen after the death of Paris, was brutally
    mangled (face, hands and ears torn off) and then slain by Menelaus and Odysseus (cf. Verg.,
    Aen. 6.494–534).
5   *parthenike.*
6   The epithets applied to Athena, *polylaidos* (Giver of Much Plunder, *l.* 10) and *gorgopis*
    (Gorgon-eyed, *l.* 24) highlight the fact that she generously confers riches on those who do
    not offend her and adopts a relentless attitude towards those who do.

104   Ovid *Metamorphoses* Book 6 Extracts: Tereus and Philomela

The story of the sisters Procne and Philomela and their treatment at the hands of
Tereus, Procne's husband, is arguably the most confronting of all the surviving
mythical stories of rape. Ovid's observations on violation, mutilation, sexual urges and
gratification create an unsettling yet insightful commentary on the unleashing of
primordial impulses once the veneer of civilisation is discarded. (1)

Tereus burst into flame at the sight of the maiden, (2) in a manner   455
not unlike someone applying fire to a dry field of corn
or setting ablaze foliage and hay stored in lofts.
Worthy indeed were her features, but in addition to them an innate
    lust
goaded him, as the race in those regions was prone
towards carnality: he flared up from his own vice and that of his
    race.   460
He had an urge to corrupt the dutifulness of her serving-maids
and the faithfulness of her nurse; or by very expensive gifts, to
    solicit
the girl herself, and to put on offer his entire kingdom;
or, lastly, to seize her and, once seized, keep her by means of cruel
    violence.

In the grip of unrestrained passion, there was nothing   465
he would not dare, nor could his emotions control the
    all-encompassing flames. (3)
And now he tolerates delays badly and with desire-filled mouth
    returns
to the instructions of Procne and, under guise of these, works to
    effect his own hopes.
Passion was making him eloquent, and as often as he pressed
more forcefully than was proper, he was saying Procne wished it
    such;   470
he also added tears, as though she had ordered these as well.

But the Odrysian king, (4) once he retired to bed, over that girl   490
writhes in heat, recalling her face, her movements, her hands,
whatever features he wants; parts which he has not yet seen, he
    imagines, and
his own fires he feeds, anxiety having removed sleep.

As soon as Philomela was placed aboard the painted keel,   511
once the channel was reached by the rowers and the land left behind,
He exclaimed: "We've won! I carry with me the fruits of my
    prayers!"
And he exults, and in his heart the barbarian can barely hold back
    from fulfilling
his joys and never does he turn his gaze from the girl,   515
in much the same way as when with hooked talons the predator
bird of Jupiter deposits a hare in its lofty nest:
the captive has no means of flight for, watching over its prey, is the
    captor. (5)

Now the journey was complete, now onto their shores from the
    weary
ships they disembark, then the king conveyed the daughter of
    Pandion   520
to a hut on high ground hidden by age-old forests
and there she, growing pale and trembling and fearing everything,
and now, with tears, asking where was her twin-sister,
he shut her inside – and having admitted his vile intent, the girl, a
    maiden and alone,
by force he overpowered; she, in vain, shouted often for her parent,   525
often her sister, and above all else, the great gods.
She trembled like a fearful lamb, which, torn, cast aside
from the mouth of the white wolf, does not as yet feel safe,
or, like a dove, feathers moistened by its own blood,

still shudders and fears the greedy claws, from which it had clung.   530
Soon, when her mind returned, having torn at her flowing locks,
like a mourner, having scratched her arms in lamentation,
holding out her palms, she cried: "What dreadful deeds, barbarous man,
cruel man! Neither the injunctions of my parent
issued with pious tears moved you, nor care for my sister,   535
nor my virginity, nor conjugal ties!
You have thrown everything into confusion: I am made the rival of my sister, (6)
you are spouse to two! I deserve the punishment due to an enemy!
Why, rather than allow any criminal act left undone by you, traitor, don't you
take my life? Would that you had done so before these abominable   540
sexual acts! (7) My shades would then have been devoid of recrimination. (8)
If, however, the gods above see these things, if the powers of the gods
are in fact of any substance, if everything has not perished with me,
at some point of time you will pay the penalties to me! With shame
cast aside I will speak of these deeds of yours: if opportunity is granted,   545
I will come before the people; if I am held imprisoned by forests,
I will fill the forests and I will move rocks to a sense of awareness.
The upper atmosphere will hear these things, if there is any god in it!" (9)

With words such as these, the anger of the fierce tyrant was roused
no less than his fear: goaded by each of these emotions,   550
from its sheath he freed his sword, by which he was girded,
and having seized the girl by the hair, with arms pinned behind her back,
he forced her to endure chains; Philomela was preparing her throat
and at sight of the sword had grasped at the hope of her own death:
with her tongue indignant and constantly calling out the name "Father,"   555
and striving to speak – he seized it with pincers,
he tore it away with the cruel sword: the last root of her tongue quivers,
it lies there and, trembling, murmurs to the dark earth,
and, like the tail of a mangled snake writhing about,
it twitches and, in the act of dying, seeks the feet of its mistress.   560
After this vile crime – I scarcely dare credit it – he is said to have
reached for her lacerated body again and again for the gratification of his lust.

Notes

1 Cf. Anderson; Stirrup; Curran 1978; Keuls 33–64; Richlin 1992c; Segal 1992; deLuce; Deacy.
2 Tereus' reaction (*l.* 455–85) to the sight of his sister-in-law is a masterpiece of psychological and physiological evocation. Ov. begins by utilising standard metaphors for lust, flame and fire (*l.* 455–57), and then partially explains the reaction in terms of the girl's beauty and the racial tendencies of the Thracians (*l.* 458–60). He describes Tereus' response by reference to his lust (*libido*, *l.* 458) and carnality (*venus*, *l.* 460).
3 Tereus' impulse is to corrupt the girl or her attendants, for he has been captured by uncontrollable passion (*effrenus amor*); *amor* here is passion or lust as opposed to love.
4 The Odrysae lived on the Hebrus, the main river of Thrace.
5 Philomela's fate is foreshadowed by the animal imagery of *l.* 516–18. Such imagery is a common feature of ancient tales of rape.
6 Her speech is filled with powerful value terms: she appeals to the *piae* (pl.) tears of her father, to the *cura* that Tereus should display for his wife, to her own *virginitas*, the conjugal bonds (*coniugialia iura*) that should transcend individual lust. Finally, she laments the fact that she has become her sister's *paelex* (concubine, rival to the legitimate wife), with a consequent sense of guilt. On the concubine as a member of the household for the generation of children, cf. 108.
7 *concubitus* (pl.): Ov. consistently uses this respectable term for the sexual acts in the *Met.* and the *AA*; here the adj. *nefandi* (pl., abominable) provides the judgemental component. Note that it is the word chosen by Philomela to describe her violation, highlighting her sense of responsibility for the betrayal of her sister.
8 Her acceptance of a share of the blame for the situation, implicit in her use of *paelex* (*l.* 537), is reinforced with this stated desire to be able to dwell in Hades without recrimination after her seemingly imminent death.
9 Philomela castigates Tereus for his unconscionable renunciation of the values that govern civilisation: he is the perfidious one (*perfide*, *l.* 539) and has committed a crime-stained sexual union (*l.* 540–41). He has violated every universal goodness but one: he has not taken her life (*anima*, *l.* 540; also rendered as 'soul'). This realisation empowers Philomela to tell her story.

Adultery, rape and the law

105 Plutarch *Solon* 23.1–2: Solon on Adultery and Rape

This passage and the following one from Lysias may be seen as supportive of the argument that the Athenians regarded rape as a lesser crime than seduction, although some have interpreted them as drawing the opposite conclusion. The first extant Athenian law on these matters is that of Solon (sole Archon in 594 BC). (1)

[Solon] made it lawful to kill an adulterer (2) caught in the act, (3) yet a fine punished the crime of rape (4) against a freeborn woman . . . [2] it is surely quite incongruous that the same crime is regarded in the one instance with the ultimate ruthlessness and in the other with a more understanding tolerance . . .

Notes

1 For treatment of the laws at Athens pertaining to sexual offences, cf. Dover 1973; Cohen 1984; Keuls; Just; Cohen 1991; Lefkowitz 1993; Stewart 1995.
2 *moichos*.
3 *echein*: lit. 'to be with', here in a sexual sense.
4 *biadzein*: to coerce, constrain; rape.

106 Lysias 1.32–33: Rape and Seduction in Athenian Law

In assessing the law as cited in Lysias' record, one must consider its context: Euphiletus is on trial for the slaying of his wife's lover, so it would be in his best interests to stress the law concerning the treatment of the adulterer, and this can be done in part by elaborating on the acceptable punishment of a rapist that can, as this law indicates, take the place of a fine. Lysias (in the mouth of Euphiletus) is possibly confused about the laws, consequently citing contradictory evidence. As above (105), Plutarch, writing centuries after Lysias, and perhaps having read the orator's record of the trial of Euphiletus, voices the same confusion confronting the modern scholar. (1)

You hear, members of the jury, that [the law] sets down that if someone rapes (2) a free adult or child, he shall be subject to damages twice over. If he rapes a woman in a case that carries the punishment of death, it is also permissible to kill him. Thereby, members of the jury, the lawgiver (3) deemed that rapists are deserving of a lesser punishment than those who seduce, (4) for he condemned the latter to death but doubled the damages for the former, [33] having considered that rapists are loathed by their victims while seducers so violate the souls (5) of their victims they make other men's wives more closely connected to them than they are to their husbands. [The former] make the entire household their own and it becomes confusing as to the identity of the children's father – the husband or the adulterer. (6) In view of this, the lawgiver assigned death to the adulterer.

Notes

1 Patterson offers a persuasive interpretation of such contradictions: 'An important feature of Athenian law of which Lysias has taken advantage here, and which puzzles Plutarch, is that it allowed several different kinds of legal action for what we might consider a legal offense. Thus for both rape and adultery there seem to have been several possible legal routes that an injured part or his/her advocates might take' (171). Cf. also Scafuro on the specific law of Solon: 'This law does not differentiate among rape, seduction of unmarried women, and adultery (i.e. the seduction of married women), nor does it mention the term *moikheia* or any of its cognates' (134).
2 Lit. to cause *aischron* to someone.
3 Solon.
4 The verbal form of *peitho*: persuasion, here seduction and *peisantai* (seducers) in the following line.
5 *psyche*.
6 *moichos*.

107 Demosthenes 23.53: Caught in the Act

Demosthenes is clearer in the information he provides about the issue concerning rape and seduction in Athens. Demosthenes simply refers to the law that stipulates the rightful punishment (in the form of death) of the man who comes across his wife or certain female kin 'with' a man. The vague terminology, which does not specify a vocabulary often associated either with rape or seduction, may lead one to reconsider the view that rape was (seemingly always) regarded as a lesser crime and thereby warranting lesser punishment than seduction.

If a man kills another accidentally in an athletic competition, or overwhelming him on the highway, or unintentionally in battle, or engaged in intercourse (1) with his wife or mother or sister or daughter or concubine kept for the procreation of legitimate offspring, he shall not be sent into exile as a murderer on such account.

Note

1 *echein*: cf. 106 n. 3.

108 Horace *Satires* 1.2.37–46: The Perils of Adultery

Adultery was regarded as a crime against the husband and at Rome the reprisals that could be taken, especially to an individual caught in the act, were extreme. Catullus threatens Aurelius with violation of his anus with radishes and mullets (Cat. 15.19) and oral rape (Cat. 21.13) if he were to molest a boy pet of his. While Horace does not condemn adultery on moral grounds (this Satire precedes the Augustan legislation against it), he argues that fear of apprehension diminishes the potential for pleasure. He cites the following six examples of painful outcomes to illustrate his argument. (1)

It is worth your while to make an effort to hear – you who have no
    desire for things
to go well for adulterers (2) – just how tough it is for them in
    every respect,
and how, for them, the pleasure, (3) tainted by a great deal of pain
(itself, in fact, a rarity), often occurs in the midst of grave perils.   40
This one hurled himself headlong from a roof; (4) that one was
    beaten
to the point of death with rods; (5) in the act of fleeing this one fell
    into the hands of
a fierce gang of thugs; (6) this one has paid money in exchange for
    his body; (7)
the stable-hands 'pissed all over' this one; (8) ah, in fact, it even
    happened
that one man sliced off the offending balls and randy prick (9)   45
with a sword! 'Justly so' says everyone: Galba lodged his dissenting
    vote.

143

Notes

1 'To be caught is wretchedness incarnate' (Hor. *Sat.*1.2.134); the best advice to those who must have sex outside marriage is to deal with professionals and women of the lowest classes above the rank of slave. Despite some lyric poems on the subject of sexual pleasure and a reputation for unusual sexual practices (142), Hor. does not return to the subject in his later works.

2 *moechi* (pl.).

3 *voluptas*.

4 The first example is of a suicide, presumably caught unexpectedly in the act and plunging to his death.

5 The second has received summary justice at the hands of the aggrieved husband's slaves; the term *ad mortem* could indicate that he was actually beaten to death.

6 Having escaped the irate husband, the third has been bashed by roving thugs; the event seems to be set at night.

7 The fourth has been forced to ransom his person by a cash payment.

8 *permingere*: to urinate over; to pollute. The pollution can also refer to sexual abomination and violation, including anal rape; cf. Adams 1982 (142). Cat. describes a man having sex with his daughter-in-law as 'pissing in the womb of his own son' (67.30). Note that this individual has been violated by stablehands, adding social humiliation to physical ordeal.

9 The sixth has endured the ultimate reprisal, full castration at the hands of the husband; the verb evokes agricultural imagery associated with reaping, cropping, and harvesting. The final observation reflects both Roman law and popular feeling in respect of adultery. Galba (an aristocratic family name in both Republican and Imperial times) is unknown and may simply be synonymous with the amoral behaviour of the great and powerful.

Rape as punishment

109 Aristophanes *Acharnians* 271–76: Punishment of a Slave-Girl

Acharnians, a comedy performed in 425 BC, deals with a private peace treaty arranged between an Athenian farmer, Dikaiopolis, and the Spartans during the Peloponnesian War. Here, pleased with his success, he sings a hymn to Phales the deified phallus. It is a source of pleasure for him to rape a slave-girl as a reprisal for her act of theft. Since the aggrieved party is owed compensation, the situation Dikaiopolis describes would have been regarded as justified punishment – not lust-inspired rape.

> For it is so much sweeter, O Phales, Phales, (1)
> upon finding a fair-breasted maiden stealing, carrying off wood, (2)
> Strymodorus' Thratta – (3) girl from the rocky uplands –
> to seize her around the middle, (4)
> then, lifting her up and throwing her down, to de-pit her grapes. (5)
> O Phales, Phales.

Notes

1 An alternative spelling for *phallus*, *phales* is not found elsewhere as a proper name (Sommerstein 169). The god is a fitting companion for the celebration of the Country Dionysia being undertaken by Dikaiopolis (Starkie 64). At *Ach.* 265, Dikaiopolis had

addressed the god as a *moichos* (adulterer) and *paiderastos* (lover of boys), which anticipates divine approval for the ensuing scenario with the slave-girl.

2 A serious offence in wartime.

3 Thratta (Thracian girl) is a common Greek name for a female slave. Her origin is also reflected in the name of her owner, the Strymon being a major river in Thrace. Since she is from the uplands, her violation will have few if any consequences for Dikaiopolis. Contra, Halliwell, 'a gross provocation against his neighbor' (121): he cites the sources for justifiable assault on slaves caught in the act of theft but argues rape is too extreme a reprisal (136 n. 6).

4 The 'middle' can refer both to the waist of the girl and to her genitals; cf. J. Henderson 1991 (156, and n. 25).

5 The expression 'removing the pips from her grapes' is a euphemism for taking the virginity of a young, inexperienced girl (cf. J. Henderson 1991: 166 n. 71; Halliwell 122); compare with the current expression, 'popping a girl's cherry'.

110 *Priapea* 13: Punitive Rape

As guardian of the garden Priapus issues a warning to those who might consider plundering its agricultural product. Essentially the sequence of punishment options is the 'back door' for boys, the 'front door' for girls, and the 'upstairs door' for bearded, adult males. Parker notes that 'this is the first of the poems to refer to *irrumatio*, oral rape. It is also the first of three . . . epigrams which succinctly state the "three-fold punishment" meted out to thieves by Priapus, according to their sex and maturity' (W. H. Parker 89). (1)

> I give fair warning: a boy – I'll bugger, (2) a girl – I'll fuck: (3)
> the third penalty remains for the bearded thief. (4)

Notes

1 The other two epigrams are *Priapea* 24 and 74.

2 *pedicare*.

3 *futuere*.

4 For an adult male *irrumatio* is implicit: 'for the bearded brigade, nothing except the highest hole will (my cock) seek' (*Priapea* 74.2). Note all three cases assume that such actions are justifiable and legal.

111 *Priapea* 28: Punitive Rape for Males

In the event that anal rape is insufficient deterrent, Priapus threatens oral rape as well for would-be thieves.

> You, who are not thinking straight and have evil
> thoughts about stealing from this garden,
> you'll be arse-fucked (1) by this arse-fucking prick. (2)
> But if so weighty and grievous a punishment
> has no effect, I will 'touch' (3) you in higher places. (4)

Notes

1 *pedicare*: here in the passive. At *Priapea* 31.3–4, the god warns a woman 'these weapons of mine will so loosen up your guts / that you will be able to make your way right out your own arsehole'.
2 *fascinum*: prick; lit. 'an amulet with the shape of a phallus worn around the neck for the purpose of warding off the evil eye', Adams 1982 (63). On occasion it is transferred to the penis, especially as in a case such as this where it is represented in statuary.
3 *tangere*: 'touch', euphemism for sexual penetration; cf. Adams 1982 (185–87).
4 The mouth.

112 Catullus *Poem* 56: Master Punishes a Slave-Boy

Catullus has apprehended a slave-boy involved in sex-play. Scholars debate whether the boy is engaging in solitary masturbation or in masturbatory, inexperienced 'rubbing' with a girl. There is further dispute about the identity of the girl, whether she is a slave of the poet or of his 'girl', Lesbia. That he is described as a *pupulus* (boy-pet) suggests that the boy is a *puer delicatus*, a sexual plaything. The subsequent act of anal rape is a ritual punishment, be it for an offending slave or an adulterer. (1)

> An incident oh so ridiculous, Cato, (2) and funny,
> and worthy of your ears and your laughter!
> Do laugh, Cato, if you love Catullus at all:
> the incident is ridiculous and very, very funny.
> Just now I caught in the act the girl's boy-pet
> rubbing (his prick); (3) the boy – if it pleases Dione – (4)
> in lieu of a weapon, (5) I 'slew' with my hard-on. (6)

Notes

1 On the poem, cf. Housman; Tanner; Rockwell; Bailey 1976; Adams 1982; Ferguson 1985. The possibilities are as follows: (i) Cat. has apprehended two of his slaves having sex and 'slays' the boy; (ii) he has apprehended Lesbia with her *delicatus* and plays the role of her 'outraged husband'; or (iii) Lesbia has used one of his slaves as a *delicatus* and Cat. exacts 'revenge' on the boy. In each scenario, the poet adopts a stance of mock indignation.
2 The reference may be to Cato Uticensis (95–46 BC), a staunch moralist. He is said to have walked out of a performance during the Festival of Flora because of its unseemliness (Val. Max. 2.10.8; Mart. Book 1, Praef. epigram, who declares it a publicity stunt); contra, Neudling (172–76), who suggests Publius Valerius Cato, a countryman of Catullus, grammarian and poet (especially in light of *l*. 3).
3 Understand *mentula* with the verb, rather than reading the girl as its direct object; cf. Adams 1982 (146 n. 1); Quinn 1973 (254). Some read *puellae* as dative (for, towards the girl) rather than genitive (possessive, of the girl).
4 As the mother of (Earthly) Aphrodite (*Il*. 5.370), Dione is a more authoritative source for an appeal for divine sanction and witness than her daughter; on Dione, cf. 91 n. 9.
5 *pro telo* 'instead of a weapon' (rather than *protelo*: 'straightway'; adopted by Housman; Rockwell; Bailey 1976; et al.). This reading draws attention to the master's right to kill a slave caught engaging in sexual activity with another; cf. Ferguson, 1985 (163–64).
6 Cat. exercised his right to compensation by sodomising the boy with his 'weapon' (*rigida* = *mentula*); cf. Adams 1982 (145–46). His decisive act of penetration may be in contrast to the

boy's clumsy efforts. Tanner (507) regards this as a *series triplex* with the boy in the middle; contra Housman (404) and others.

Turning 'no' into 'yes'

113 Archilochus *Fragment* 196a: An 'Erotic' Encounter

When viewed in conjunction with the works of near-contemporary poets, Hesiod and Semonides, the following piece reflects a growing ambivalence towards women during the Archaic period. A man lures a young woman with the prospect of sexual pleasure that will not necessarily involve her loss of virginity (*l.* 9–10). His clear preference, however, is to achieve the ultimate pleasure; note the ambiguity in 'I will come to a halt in the grassy/gardens' (*l.* 15–16). The young woman in question is possibly the sister of Neoboule, once engaged to the poet, but whose father, Lycambes, subsequently voided the agreement. This broken arrangement led to a series of tirades against the family, the context of the following piece. (1)

"Holding off entirely . . .
Endure it equally . . ."

"If you are in a hurry and your spirit is eager,
there is in our house a girl
who is possessed of intense desire,   5
a beautiful soft virgin. (2) In my view she has
a faultless appearance.
Make her your girlfriend." (3)

She said this much. I answered her:
"Daughter of Amphimedo,   10
an excellent and . . .
woman, whom now the
mouldy earth holds,
there are many sexual delights of
the goddess for young men
besides The Divine Thing. One of them will be enough. (4)   15
About these things, quietly,
when it becomes dark,
you and I, with the god's help, will take counsel. (5)
I will obey as you command me.
Much . . . me . . .   20
Under the coping-stone, under the gates . . .
Do not begrudge anything, dear girl, (6)
for I will come to a halt in the grassy gardens. (7)
Know this now. Neoboule (8)
another man may have.   25

147

Alas, she's ripe . . . Her
virginal flower has drooped
along with the grace that once surrounded her. (9)
For she has never had enough [sex].
Frenzied woman, she has displayed the full extent of [her need].   30
To the crows with her!
Keep her at bay. May this not . . .
Now, if I had a wife like that, I
would be a laughing-stock to the neighbours. (10)
I want you very much   35
for you are not faithless or duplicitous,
but she is too sharp.
She makes many men 'her beloveds'.
I fear that, pressing on in haste, I may beget offspring
that are blind and premature,   40
as a bitch bears blind puppies." (11)

I said this much. This girl, among the blooming
flowers, I took and
laid her down. With a soft
cloak as a covering for her, holding her neck   45
in the crook of my arm,
like a fawn . . .
Gently with my hands I touched her breasts
where her young skin
revealed the approach of youth,   50
touching all over her beautiful body.
I spurted forth my passion,
lightly grazing golden [hairs]. (12)

Notes

1 Cf. Gerber 1999b; also Rankin 1974; Van Sickle; J. Henderson 1976; Rankin 1977; Davenport. On Archaic Age views on the sexual urges of women, cf. C.G.Brown 67. On the family connections, cf. Fantham et al. 1994. C. G. Brown argues the poem represents an attack on both Neoboule and the girl, that any form of consensual sex on her part renders her disgraced and unmarriageable, and that the action of the man is designed as an attack upon the father, Lycambes (66–69). The speaking parts have been rendered thus: *l.* 1–2 (man); *l.* 3–8 (girl); *l.* 10–41 (man).

2 *thumos* (spirit, *l.* 3) is the conscious, driving force within an individual (equivalent of Latin *animus*); she has an intense *himeros* (*l.* 5) for sex; and she is a *kale parthenos* (*l.* 6).

3 The description of the girl who lives in the same house as the seducer's target sets the scene for the sexually charged narrative that follows. The fact that the object of desire describes the girl, whom she suggests as an alternative, establishes her own unreadiness for a sexual encounter (cf. Van Sickle).

4 He begins his seduction by praising the girl's mother and ends his attempt at enticement by claiming how he might have sex with her without taking her virginity (i.e. 'The Divine Thing').

5 He tries to persuade the girl by ideas of reciprocity (*l.* 16–19), which is hardly in keeping with what we know of the sexual power dynamics of the Archaic age.

6 *phile*: here 'dear girl', while at *l.* 8 read 'girlfriend'. Also *philoi* (pl.), male friends, lovers, at *l.* 38.

7 A series of euphemisms for the girl's pubic region: her pubic bone (*l.* 21), her openings (*l.* 21, vagina and anus), her pubic hair (*l.* 23); cf. Gerber 1999b (215 n. 6).

8 Neoboule appears to be the girl referred to at *l.* 4–8.

9 The two key advantages for a girl are her maidenly flower (*anthos partheneion, l.* 27) and her *charis* (*l.* 28). These have faded due to Neoboule's loss of virginity and craving for sex.

10 Cf. Hes., *WD* 701 (44); Sem., 7.73–74, 110–11 (45).

11 Because Neoboule is promiscuous, he believes there is a risk of begetting mis-shapen offspring if he allows his urgent need for mating (and marriage?) to be resolved with her.

12 *l.* 42–53 are erotic in tone and imagery. Scholars have debated the precise nature of the act described at *l.* 53: Van Sickle (10) argues that the male practises *coitus interruptus*; J. Henderson 1976 (174) believes full penetration is achieved prior to ejaculation. Alternatively, the reference could be to premature ejaculation. Cf. C. G. Brown 67 n. 94.

114 Ovid *Ars Amatoria* 1.663–80: Girls Like it Rough

In his handbook of advice on how to pick up women and what to do with them, the endorsement by Ovid of 'rougher than usual handling' has aroused much reaction in recent scholarship (cf. Curran 1978; Richlin 1992c). Here he begins by adopting the approach recommended by Theocritus in *Idyll* 27 (a seduction scenario in a pastoral setting): start gently, work up to more intimate caresses, then move on to apply mild forcefulness to achieve the ultimate goal. Ovid's attempt at interpreting female psychology – that 'no' means 'yes' and that women want to be taken roughly in spite of their objections – is provocative to Ovid's audience (as well as the modern one), a fact of which he was well aware.

> What wise man (1) would not mingle kisses with coaxing words of
> endearment?
> Should she not surrender willingly, then take what is not given.
> Perhaps at first she will struggle and will say "vile man"; (2)   665
>   still she will want, after a struggle, to be made to surrender. (3)
> Just be careful, lest, seizing her roughly, you damage her tender lips
>   and she is then able to complain about 'brutality'.
> He who seizes kisses, if he does not seize all the rest,
>   will deserve also to lose that which has already been yielded. (4)   670
> After kisses, how much remains before you get to fulfil all your
>   wishes?
> Ah me, rusticity, there is no need for a sense of shame! (5)

> You are allowed to apply force: that kind of force (6) has appeal (7)
>   for girls;
>   they often wish to give unwillingly what in fact is pleasing
>   (to them).

149

And whoever has been violated by a sudden forceful taking of
    sex, (8)   675
    rejoices, and considers the impropriety a kind of gift. (9)
But the one who withdraws untouched, when she might have been
    coerced,
    though she feigns joy on her face, will be miserable.
Phoebe endured force, force was employed against her sister; (10)
    and each rapist had appeal in the eyes of the one raped. (11)   680

Notes

1 The tone of serious philosophical discourse is set with reference to the sage (*sapiens*). The axiom is evident: kisses need to be mixed with blandishments.
2 To address a would-be ravisher with the equivalent of "you awful man!" (*improbus*) borders on the satirical.
3 Strong military imagery, in line with much Augustan amatory poetry. Love is a form of military campaign and the object of desire cannot be attained without much struggle and strategy.
4 If the ardent lover does not become forceful, after snatching kisses (with or without consent), he risks losing what he has already attained.
5 The moment Ov. doubts his own advice, he admonishes himself with the charge of *rusticitas*. There is no need for a sense of shame (*pudor*) or embarrassment here.
6 *vis*: a strong term for force and violence; also at *l.* 679.
7 Deep down girls find *vis* welcome (*grata*); also at *l.* 680.
8 A strong line, which matches the military imagery of *l.* 666. The sex (*venus*) has been sudden, violent and the result of an act of seizure (*rapina*).
9 This half of the couplet undercuts and softens the first half; 'impropriety' (*inprobitas*) is as ironic here as "you awful man!" (*improbus*) at *l.* 665.
10 Phoebe and her sister Hilaeira, daughters of Leucippus (or Apollo), were carried off by the Dioscouri; cf. Gantz 324–25.
11 Just as in the case of the girls seized by the Dioscouri, the victim will view her rapist not only with favour but as a semi-divine, 'real' man.

Sex as sport

115 Aristophanes *Peace* 894–904: Sporting Metaphors for Rough Sex

In this surrealist comedy of 421 BC, Trygaeus the hungry vine-grower plans to fly to Heaven on a giant dung beetle in search of food. At this point in the play he has met with Theoria, the personification of Lady Festival. He compares the vigorous sex he has in mind for her in terms evoking well-known sporting events. Wrestling, pancration and chariot racing were means by which athletic, dominant males could display their *arete*. (1)

Trygaeus
Now that you have her, you can straightway conduct a
very nice athletic competition tomorrow: 895
wrestle her to the ground, set her on all fours   896a

throw her on her side, bent forward, onto her knees; (2)   896b
then, well oiled up for the pancration, (3)
strike out with vigour, fist burrowing in with the cock. (4)
On the day after, you will hold a horserace,
and stallion will power alongside stallion, (5) and their   900
chariots, piled upside down on top of one another,
will be all entwined, with much gulping and gasping. (6)
Other charioteers shall lie prone with their foreskins
drawn back, having fallen at the turn into the straight. (7)

Notes

1   The technical terminology employed in these lines is taken from the three named sports
and applied to the forceful means by which coupling with the woman is to be achieved: cf.
J. Henderson 1991 (169–70 and n. 85); also Scanlon (269–70). On Theoria, cf. Scanlon
(269).
2   The imagery in *l.* 896a–b entails grasping her from behind, with rear entry intercourse
implicit. Note also the force with which the woman is moved into the four positions.
3   The pancration was regarded as the harshest and bloodiest of all athletic contests in Greece.
It combined wrestling and boxing in a 'no holds barred' contest of brute strength: the object
was to bludgeon an opponent into submission.
4   It could be that the woman is being struck (spanked?) while being taken from behind; in
light of the oiling up and burrowing imagery, it more likely indicates simultaneous fistic
penetration of her anus (or vagina) during intercourse. On 'burrowing' = 'buggery', cf. J.
Henderson 1991 (124).
5   The racing image implies either simultaneous penetration of the woman by multiple partners
or a contest involving several women with teams of riders.
6   The chariot race entails a neck and neck tussle to the turning post and a return dash to the
finish line. Often there are major pile-ups at the turn leaving some contenders crushed and
defeated in a mangled heap: they have been brushed aside by the stronger performers because
they have lacked the necessary stamina to go the distance and are now exhausted.
7   A 'race' involved rounding the turning post and heading in the opposite direction (of her
body). Some 'stallions' have come adrift at this critical moment in the manoeuvres, and,
although still in a condition to go on, are not in a position for intercourse.

116 Martial *On the Spectacles* 5: Pasiphae and the Bull

Roman spectacle advanced over time from religious expiation, gladiatorial combat,
public execution and displays of wild beasts to the exotic and elaborate shows of the
late Republic and Julio-Claudian eras – naval battles, beast hunts, and amazingly
innovative theatre – with much emphasis on bloodshed. Martial's *Book on the Spectacles*
was written on the occasion of the opening of the Colosseum by Titus in AD 80. Among
the many wondrous displays was an enactment of the Story of Pasiphae, wife of Minos
of Crete, who, enamoured of a beautiful bull, mated with it and gave birth to a hybrid
monster, half man, half bull, known as the Minotaur. A woman, presumably a slave
or a criminal, was joined to a real bull before the massive crowd in attendance. (1) That
sex was an essential by-product of Roman public entertainment is evident in the
salutary advice given by Ovid for finding potential long- or short-term sexual partners
at the theatres and the racecourse (153).

That Pasiphae was joined (2) to the Dictaean (3) bull, believe it:
  we have witnessed it, the ancient tale has acquired credit. (4)
Nor should age-old antiquity, Caesar, (5) marvel boastfully about itself:
  anything Story (6) sings about, the arena presents to you.

Notes

1 On the moral, social and cathartic aims behind enactments in the arena, cf. Coleman.
2 On sources for the story of Pasiphae, cf. Gantz 260–62. *iuncta*: lit. 'joined to, mated'.
3 Adj. derived from Mt. Dicte on Crete, hence synonymous with 'Cretan'.
4 *fides*.
5 Titus was Emperor between AD 79 and 81.
6 *fama*. Other mythic re-enactments on this occasion included versions of Prometheus, Daedalus, Mars and Venus, Diana and the hunt, Meleager and the boar, Jupiter carrying off Europa, Orpheus, Hero and Leander. On deviations from the myth in actual performance, cf. Coleman, 60ff.

VII

ANXIETY AND REPULSION

In sexual or gendered situations, when codes of correct behaviour were eroded, the surety of the adult male's self-image and sense of control became threatened. In these circumstances, real or imagined, the Greek and Roman male displayed a variety of behavioural attitudes, particularly aggression, as a response to anxiety and repulsion. The counterpoints to hyper-masculinity, namely lustful women (assuming masculine initiative and dominance) and passive men (despised by the active male), were consequently railed against as targets: such vituperation relieved sexual tension or inhibition and reinforced the male's sense of self (or ego). Philaenis (101) embodies the ultimate source of apprehension; described by Martial as both active (buggering boys and fucking girls) and passive (performing cunnilingus), she is a freak of nature and thus deserving of poetic (and therefore public) humiliation. The example of Philaenis is, in many ways, a thematic blueprint for the passages that follow: representative of the sexual deviant, the 'other', Martial's tribad performs acts that, to the Greek and Roman mind, contravene the natural order of things. In similar fashion, Horace's old whore, greedy for sex even though she is physically repellent (121), Aristophanes' Ariphrades, licking the vaginal secretions of prostitutes (129–130), Catullus' Gellius (136) and Nanneius (137), revelling in performing oral sex, are ridiculed because of their assumption of gender roles specifically forbidden them by societal mores. In such pieces, the poet embraces the role of public educator while perhaps simultaneously betraying not only his own ingrained and culturally-specific prejudices but his own unease and sense of sexual displacement. No doubt the targeted audiences of these poets found in such works the reinforcement of their own views.

The greatest single cause of anxiety was fear of impotence. To be impotent was to be unmanly and to be equated with passivity. Explanations for the condition range from the natural consequence of ageing (117), the intrusion of magical forces or bad luck (118), to blaming the bed-mate (121). The extreme to which a sufferer of the condition might go to achieve restoration of potency is amply illustrated by Petronius (119).

The aggressive female is a common topos in epigram, satire and comedy; indeed she appears as early as Semonides' *Poem* 7 (45) in which she assumes many guises, including the form of the weasel (the 'thrasher' in bed). Neoboule (113), avid for sex, is despised by Archilochus, not only in contrast with the desirable virgin sister, but also because of the potential for producing deformed offspring. Attacks on such women usually focus upon their abnormal sexual appetite, their ugliness, age and odour. Lack of desire for and inability to perform with such a woman is a frequent source of vituperation against her, often via reference to her voracious and defiled genitalia (epitomised by 124). The issue of filth and bodily orifices is inextricably linked with views of unnatural sexual practice: multiple partners in women (as seen in descriptions of prostitutes such as 131–132) and passive behaviour in men.

In the literature of both Greece and Rome, the passive adult male is among the most abhorred of figures. For centuries in the ancient world there were publicly sanctioned expectations and legislation that forbade passivity by adult male citizens; Aeschines, for example, writes of the sexually depraved Timarchus who lowered himself as a prostitute (77), while laws such as the *lex Scantinia* and the *lex Julia* reinforced the intense distaste for passivity (and effeminacy) held by the Romans. In satiric literature (137–138) and graffiti (82) in particular it is therefore not surprising that a frequent means of demeaning one's enemy (real or fictional) was to accuse them of occupying the role of the submissive partner. Such denouncements were also an effective public means of boasting of one's own virility.

The writers of antiquity also describe the physical effects of sexual deviancy, notably staining with faeces, urine, menstrual blood and other bodily fluids. Whether characters like Ariphrades, Nanneius and, perhaps the worst of them all, Hipponax' stinking, shit-splattered 'scapegoat' (134), who lends himself to a modern-day reading of sado-masochism (and whose poetic representation stands alone in this chapter by dent of its sheer perversity), actually existed or not is irrelevant. The fact they are described, parodied and dramatised points to the general disgust of such pastimes – a disgust that takes the poetic metaphor of the materialisation (in the form of staining) of depravity.

Impotence

117 Philodemus *Greek Anthology* 11.30: Partial Impotence

In the first couplet the poet addresses Aphrodite, as if in prayer, lamenting his loss of sexual potency. In the second couplet he spells out the extent of the problem, namely that while not completely impotent, he has reached a point of crisis; somehow he has offended the gods. In the last couplet his repeated address to old age is more a prayer of aversion, dreading that what a man could expect in old age has come upon him prematurely. (1)

> I, who in earlier times could manage between five and nine (2) in a
>   session, now, Aphrodite, can scarcely achieve one from dusk till dawn.
> And, unfortunately, the 'thing' itself (3) has, of late, been more often than
>   not semi-lifeless, and right now is on the verge of 'death'. (4) This is
>   the Termerion. (5)
> Old age, old age, (6) what do you have to offer later on, if you
>   do come, when even now I am wasted away?

Notes

1 Cf. Sider 1982; R. F. Thomas; Sider 1997.
2 Phld. engages in some macho bravado here, suppressing any need for a noun in *l.* 1 to go with 'five and nine'; understand 'performances'.

3 I.e. his penis; again there is no specific noun, just a pronoun ('this', translated as 'the thing').
4 From 'semi-lifeless' (sometimes hard, sometimes soft) in the course of the act, it is on the 'verge of death', that is, being permanently impotent.
5 The reference to Termerion is metaphorical: it conveys the notion of a punishment that befits a crime. Termerus, a highwayman, used to kill people by head-butting them; he met his match with Theseus, who caused Termerus to break his own head (cf. Plut., *Thes.* 11). The pun here is that the head of his 'thing' (the prepuce of his penis) has now been rendered permanently soft; cf. Sider 1997 (130–31). The question remains as to the nature of the 'crime' that has warranted this fate: is it pride or wanton behaviour?
6 *geras*: old age.

118 Ovid *Amores* 3.7: Equipment Failure

Ovid acknowledges the beauty, desirability and willingness of his partner and therefore laments his inability to perform. (1)

Ah, is she not beautiful, ah is the girl not truly refined? (2)
    Ah, is she not, I believe, the one I've often sought in my prayers?
But I embraced her to no advantage, being utterly limp-dicked;
    so I lay there, an indictment and a burden on the wretched bed,
wanting it, and, with the girl wanting it every bit as much, I could not even   5
    take pleasure in her rendering 'help' to that part of an effete groin. (3)
Indeed, she slipped beneath my neck her ivory
    arms, brighter than Sithonian (4) snow,
and with a yearning tongue she inserted writhing kisses
    and placed wanton thigh beneath thigh   10
and she spoke sweet enticements (5) to me and called me "master" (6)
    and, moreover, those vulgar (7) words that render pleasure.
Yet, as if touched by chilling hemlock, (8) my members,
    slow to action, put paid to my plan.
I lay there, an inert trunk, a mere semblance and useless weight,   15
    and it was not exactly clear whether I was corporeal or a shadow.
What kind of old age is coming my way, if indeed it is going to come at all,
    when youth itself is lacking its own 'components'? (9)
Ah, I am ashamed of my years. What remains for me, both as youth and man?
    My mistress had no experience of me either as youth or man.   20
Just like the eternal priestess off to tend the sacred flames
    she rose up like a sister worthy of respect from a beloved brother. (10)

Ah, just recently, I did my duty: twice with flaxen Chlide, thrice with

shining Pitho, and thrice with Libas, (11) all in unbroken
    succession,
and I recall, in one short night, Corinna extracted from me   25
    my keeping it up for nine courses.

Could it be my parts are sagging limply, cursed by a Thessalic poison?
    Could it be a spell and some herb are harming wretched me?
Has some witch affixed 'names' in red wax
    and driven a slender needle into the middle of my liver?   30
Once she's damaged by a spell Ceres withers into barren herbage,
    the waters of a fountain damaged by a spell dry up;
acorns fall from oaks; once 'sung', grapes fall from the vine and
    apples drop without anyone shaking the tree.
What is there to prevent male organs as well being torpid through
    magical arts?   35
    Perhaps it's for this reason my groin is not up to it. (12)

At this point shame (13) at the event set in: shame itself was
    causing harm;
    that was the second cause of my failure.
Ah, but what a girl I looked upon and how I touched her!
    In much the same way she was being touched by her own
    tunic.   40
At the touch of that girl the Pylian could act like a youth
    and Tithonus could be more vigorous despite his years. (14)
She was at hand for me, but a man was not at hand for her.

    What entreaties can I now conceive through fresh prayers?
I believe even the great gods have regretted the gift offered me,   45
    which I have employed so shamefully.
I certainly longed to be wanted, indeed I was wanted;
    to bring kisses, I brought kisses; to be alongside her, I was.
Where did so much good fortune take me? What are kingdoms
    without occupancy?
    Why, unless I'm a miser, have I held on to such rich resources?   50
It's much the same as the 'Divulger of a Secret' who thirsted while
immersed in
    water and possessed apples he could not touch. (15)
If someone were to rise up in this state in the morning from a
    tender girl,
    how could he directly approach the sacred gods? (16)

But in my opinion, did she not simply waste on me †coaxing†, (17)
    ultimate   55

kisses? Did she not strive to stimulate me by every means at her
    disposal?
That girl could rouse to action weighty oaks, hard adamant
    and deaf rocks by means of her coaxing techniques. (18)
Surely she was worthy of rousing to action those who are alive and
    who are men,
    but at that moment I was neither alive nor was I, as before, a man. 60

What pleasure would there be if Phemius were to sing to deaf ears?
    What pleasure does a painted board provide to wretched
    Thamyras? (19)
Ah, but what delights did I not fantasise about in my silent mind,
    what positions did I not frame and dispose!
Yet my members lay there as if prematurely dead   65
    shamefully more limp than yesterday's rose.

Ah, but right this moment they are vigorous and inopportunely
    potent!
    Right this moment they're demanding work and military service!
Would that you lie down now, you objects of shame, worst part of
    me!
    Just like before I have been taken in by your promises.   70
You have deceived your master: because of you, captured without
    a weapon,
    I have borne bitter losses with tremendous shame.
My girl did not even deem it unworthy to stimulate
    'the part' by a gentle motion of her hand;
but after she saw it was incapable of rising through any of her arts 75
    and continued to lie prone utterly oblivious to her,
she said: "Why are you making fun of me? Who ordered you, utter
    idiot,
    uninvited, to put your members in my bed?
Has either some Aeaean sorceress (20) hexed you by her drawn out
    wool-threads, or do you come weary with love for another?" 80

Without delay, she sprang down covered only by a loose tunic –
    and it was delightful to snatch a glimpse of naked feet.
So that her maids would not know she had been untouched,
    she concealed her embarrassment by splashing water over herself.

Notes

1 Cf. Sharrock.
2 To Ov., she is a *formosa* and *culta* (refined) *puella*. On *culta*, cf. Green 1979.
3 Ov. describes his impotence with a series of repetitive images: he is *languidus* (limp-dicked;

usually weak, languid); his penis droops (here the word is *iacere*: to lie drooping, to lie ill, to lie dead); and his groin is *effetus* (incapacitated; unmanly).

4 I.e. Thracian.

5 *blanditiae* (pl., also at *l*. 58) are sweet words exchanged between lovers; enticements; cf. also *l*. 55 (*blanda*, adj.: coaxing, enticing).

6 *dominus*: the term evokes master–slave bedroom games, where the girl will submit to anything asked.

7 *publica verba*: words in common use among the lower classes, rough language that stimulates in the bedroom.

8 This line sets the scene for the discourse on witchcraft at *l*. 27–35 (returned to again at *l*. 79–80).

9 For the literary debt to Phld., old age associated with impotence, cf. 117. The topos goes go back to Mimn. (35).

10 The girl may just as well have been a Vestal Virgin or his sister.

11 The names of the girls suggest they are professionals: *Chlide*, Delicacy or Luxury; *Pitho* (*Peitho*), Persuasion, also Obedience, a girl who will do whatever she is told; *Libas*, Fountain, a girl who 'trickles' for she is always ready for sex.

12 Ov. uses a series of technical terms to evoke the theme of witchcraft (*magicae artes*, *l*. 35) including *carmen* (spell, *l*. 28, 31–32) and *defigere* (to affix, i.e. to inscribe a name or names in wax in order to bind a person by means of magic). Cf. Ogden 2002.

13 *pudor* is used twice in this line to highlight his embarrassment and humiliation.

14 The Pylian (from Pylos in S-W Peloponnese) is Nestor and Tithonus is the mortal lover of Eos or Dawn. Both are archetypal figures of old age combined with youthful zest.

15 A reference to Tantalus whose crimes earned him a gruesome punishment in Hades: within reach of abundant food and water he can never get to either (*Od*. 11.582–92). The exact nature of his crimes is a matter of much debate: *taciti vulgator* (divulger of a secret) indicates he revealed something of import, and at *Am*. 2.2.44 Ov. says his fate was due to a *garrula lingua* (a tongue too talkative).

16 He was given good fortune by the gods (a *tenera puella*) but spurned their gift.

17 The text is corrupt.

18 Her words and actions have an effect upon inanimate objects similar to that of Orpheus' voice and lyre.

19 Phemius and Thamyras were minstrels: on Phemius, cf. *Od*. 1.153–55; 22.330–56; Thamyras engaged in a musical contest with the Muses and, defeated, was blinded, cf. Paus. 4.33.7; Apollod., *Lib*. 1.3.3.

20 *Aeaea*: of Colchis (Aea), an allusion to Medea.

119 Petronius *Satyricon* 138: Treatment for Impotence

In a parody of the wrath of Poseidon in the *Odyssey*, Encolpius, the hero of Petronius' epic, suffers from the anger of Priapus, which has predictable consequences. This explains his visit to the witch, Oenothea, who, in an attempt to remedy the malaise, practises a ritual both bizarre and painful. (1)

Oenothea produced a dildo (2) made of leather, (3) which she covered with oil and finely ground pepper and rubbed with nettle seed; little by little she began to insert it into my anus. . . . This cruellest of old women then sprinkled my thighs with this moisture. . . . Next she mixed the juice of nasturtiums with aromatic southern-wood and, having saturated my groin, took up a fresh nettle stalk and began to whip all the places beneath my navel with a rhythmic hand movement. . . .

Notes

1 On herbal remedies for impotence, where the offended deity is Venus, cf. also Mart. 3.75.3–4: 'Doses of rocket achieve nothing, nor lust-inducing bulbs, / nor does naughty savory any longer have an effect.' For the sadomasochistic elements, compare Hippon. (134).
2 The *fascinum* is usually an instrument used in witchcraft or a penis symbol hung round the necks of children for protection; here a dildo.
3 It is made of leather (*scorteum*), a clever pun on *scortum*, a term for a prostitute; for the association of prostitutes with sex-toys, cf. Kilmer 1993; 140.

The repellent woman

120 Lucilius *Fragment* 1182W: Menstrual Defilement

Hostile and at times obsessive verbal assaults on women are a persistent theme in Greek and Roman literature. From laments concerning marriage (43–45) to extolling virtues of boys over girls (89–91), male authors often depict women as the 'other' – the being who is misunderstood, disrespected and despised. The extreme revelation of such male anxieties is perhaps nowhere better encapsulated than in the writing dealing with female bodily functions and excreta. In this passage from Lucilius we witness the male's revulsion at menstrual blood – the epitome of a woman's bodily pollution – and possibly staining associated with anal penetration. (1)

Paulus, (2) citing Festus, 23: *Bubinare* is to defile with the menstrual blood of women.

Lucilius: 'She defiles (3) you with her blood, but on the other hand <he> (4) defiles you with <his> shit.'

Notes

1 On Lucil., cf. Richlin 1992a (169). On menstrual blood and sex, cf. Krenkel 1981 (47–48); cf. also 137.
2 Paulus Diaconus (Eighth Century AD) epitomised the etymological work of Festus (Second Century AD). The entry on *bubinare* is illustrated by this quotation from Lucil.
3 Lucil. uses the emphatic *inbubinare*, stressing just how messy the process can be.
4 Editorial conjecture (*ille*: 'he') is based on the grammarian's explication: '*inbulbitare* is to defile with a boy's shit'. It is possible that both acts are being performed with a woman and that, in either orifice, the client's *mentula* is going to be soiled. Cf. C. A. Williams 1999 for references to the potential dirtiness of the sexual act, both vaginal and anal. Williams quotes Marx' commentary on Lucil. (in Latin): '[Lucilius] says prostitutes are so greedy, that not even when they are befouled by their monthly outflow of blood do they spare either themselves or their lover(s), just the same as boys do not desist from sex (*venus*) when they are in the grip of sickness of the bowel' (271 n. 79).

121 Horace *Epode* 12.1–20: Old Whore

In *Epodes* 8 and 12 Horace discusses impotence. He is not ashamed of his condition; on the contrary, he uses it as an indictment of the hideousness of the woman (or women) he is addressing. The issue of age is an important factor in *Epode* 12 as Horace attacks the woman, a prostitute (*meretrix*), largely on this basis. Like many pieces from Greek and Roman poetry, it is debatable whether this reflects an actual situation and individual or whether it is an example of a fictitious scenario appropriate to the genre of iambics. (1)

> What are you after for yourself, woman most worthy of black
>   elephants? (2)
> Why do you send me gifts, why do you send me letters,
> as I'm neither a muscular youth nor possessed of a bloated nose? (3)
>   For I am unique in my sharp sense of smell –
> whether a polyp (4) or a heavy goat sleeps in your hairy armpits – (5)   5
>   sharper than a keen hound where the wild sow lies hidden.
> What a sweat! How vile a smell spreads all over her
>   shrivelled genitals, (6) while my penis has gone limp as
> she hastens to placate her uncontrollable frenzy. (7) Furthermore,
>   her moistening chalk does not sit in place, nor her 'face'   10
> painted with crocodile shit. (8) And now by her rutting (9)
>   she ruptures the stretched and canopied bed!
> In addition she disturbs my sense of delicacy with harsh words:
>   "You're nowhere near as slack with Inachia (10) as you are with
>   me;
> Inachia you can do three times a night; in my case, at a lone
>   performance,   15
>   it is always soft. (11) May Lesbia (12) perish a vile death!
> While I was looking for a bull, she pointed you out, limp-dick, (13)
>   at a time when Amyntas the Coan (14) was available to me,
> whose prick (15) in an indefatigable groin (16) stands more rigidly
>   than a vigorous young sapling gripping a hillside."   20

Notes

1 Cf. Carrubba; Clayman; Richlin 1984; Fitzgerald; Richlin 1992a (111–13); Mankin.

2 Hor. regards the woman as so repulsive that her most suitable partners would be black elephants; Mankin (206) offers several interpretative possibilities.

3 The adj. *firmus* implies power and potency (with the suggestion of a stiff penis), while *iuvenis* connotes a youth in his prime who can perform all night. The reference to the bloated nose indicates one who is unable to smell.

4 Sea creatures such as the polyp are known for their displeasing smell (Mankin 207).

5 In terms of physical aesthetics, women are expected to be smooth and have an appealing smell; on goat imagery, cf. Noonan; Nappa.

6 The word *membrum* (here, pl.) is, as Adams 1982 observes, 'largely restricted to the male organ' (46); hers are described as *vieta* (shrivelled).

7 Hor. conjures up the image of a woman out of control in terms of her sexual needs: *rabies* (uncontrollable frenzy) is used of humans and also dogs and other animals. Aged women are not expected to be active sexually, yet at the same time are a stereotype of insatiability.

8 Hor. is referring to the woman's makeup, which is made of chalk (*creta*) and crocodile dung; on cosmetics, cf. Leary; 151.

9 *subare*: to rut, to be on heat; used of sows, other animals and women.
10 Her name is an epithet of Io, daughter of Inachus, who is transformed into a cow by Zeus.
11 *mollis*, applied to his penis: limp, effeminate, unmanly.
12 Probably the name of another prostitute or madam (cf. Mankin 211). The name evokes the reputation of Lesbian women for unusual and insatiable sexual appetites (cf. 102 n. 1).
13 *iners* (adj.) can be something or someone sluggish or inactive.
14 Cf. Mankin 211.
15 *nervus*: lit. a tendon or nerve; also a bowstring; a metaphor for the state of erection.
16 *inguen*: the groin. The word was used euphemistically to denote the penis and the vagina; cf. Adams 1982 (47–48).

122 Martial 3.93: Vetustilla

Martial captures his sheer abhorrence at an ageing woman, Vetustilla (literally, 'That Old Woman'), by brutal vilification and the obsessive images of death associated with the idea of sex with her.

Vetustilla – although you have had three hundred Consuls, (1)
you still have three hairs and four teeth,
you have the breast of a cicada, the leg and the colouring of an ant;
although you bear a forehead more furrowed than a matron's robe (2)
and breasts equal to the sag of spider webs;   5
although compared to your gaping maw
the Nile crocodile has a narrow jaw,
and frogs from Ravenna (3) croak more musically
and the gnat from Atria (4) buzzes more sweetly,
and you can see as much as night owls see in the morning,   10
and you smell what the husbands (5) of she-goats smell like,
and you possess the tail of a scrawny duck,
and your bony cunt (6) would overwhelm an old man Cynic;
although the bathhouse keeper admits you, once the lamp has been
extinguished, amidst the graveyard whores; (7)   15
although winter in your case passes through the month of August (8)
and not even a raging fever can thaw you out –
you dare, despite two hundred dead husbands already, to desire to
    be married,
and go madly seeking yet another (9) to feel desire (10) for your
burnt out remains. What if he did want to hoe a rock?   20
Who will call you 'spouse', who will call you 'wife', (11)
you whom Philomelus had recently called 'grandmother'?
But if you have a need for your leathery carcass to be 'scratched', (12)
let a bed be laid out from the dining room of Orcus, (13)
which alone is appropriate for your wedding rite, (14)   25
and let the cremator of corpses carry the torches ahead of the new
    bride:
only a funeral torch could gain entry into that cunt.

Notes

1 During the Republic, the Romans dated their years by the names of the two Consuls. Although writing in the Imperial era (when more than two were appointed per annum), Mart. evokes the Republican tradition.
2 The *stola* was a long garment with pleats and folds (i.e. wrinkles) worn by married women.
3 A major centre built on marshy ground on the Adriatic shore in the territory of the Lingones.
4 A town among the Veneti not far north of Ravenna.
5 *viri* (pl.). On goat smell, cf. 121 n. 5.
6 *cunnus*: also at *l.* 27. It smells so badly that it would even overwhelm an aged Cynic, philosophers renowned for body odour due to their refusal to wash.
7 *moechae* (pl.): women who commit adultery, but the term can apply to those who give themselves for money. Poverty-stricken women who frequent graveyards, for food and prostitution, were known as *bustuariae*.
8 The height of summer in Italy.
9 *vir*.
10 *prurire*: to itch, to feel a craving for sex.
11 The terms employed are *coniunx* (spouse, partner of either sex) and *uxor* (wife).
12 Mart. plays on the range of meanings of *scalpere*: to carve and inscribe, to scrape and scratch, it can also mean to titillate or tickle. As a corpse is leathery and dry, the only impact on its skin will be scratch marks rather than caresses.
13 A god of the Underworld.
14 *thalassio* (or *talassio*) was the ritual cry that went up at the moment the bride (*nupta*) was brought to the bedchamber of her new husband.

123 Rufinus *Greek Anthology* 5.76: Ravages of Old Age

The theme of the ageing woman, the ageing *hetaira*, is a particularly satisfying one, psychologically speaking, for many of the male poets of the *Greek Anthology*. Once attractive, in demand and haughty, these fallen beauties provide a gratifying topic to the (possibly once thwarted) male. (1)

> Once upon a time her appearance aroused desire: breasts springing with
>   youth,
>   strong and healthy, tall, with fine eyebrows, hair like a goddess.
> The passage of time and old age (2) and grey hair have brought change,
>   and now she is not even a shadow of what she once was,
> but decks herself in wigs and her face is rutted with wrinkles,
>   and her features are like those of an aged ape. (3)

Notes

1 Compare the sentiments expressed by Mart. on Galla (70) and Athen. on Lais (71).
2 *geras*: also used adjectivally in *l.* 6.
3 On a comparison of a woman with an ape, cf. Semon. 7.71–82 (45).

124 *Priapea*: Vergilian Appendix 83.26–37: A Filthy Old Woman

Priapus threatens his inert penis: if it does not behave it will have to penetrate the vagina of a woman old enough to have remembered Romulus, instead of the orifices of girls and boys. (1)

> A mistress (2) endowed with two teeth, who remembers old man
>   Romulus,
> is ready and waiting, in the midst of whose gloomy groin (3)
> lies a cavern, hidden away by a loosely hanging paunch,
> and a roof covering, made of a pelt intertwined with year-round
>   ice, (4)
> filth (5) shrouded by cobwebs blocks up its entrance.   30
> She is ready and waiting for you, so that three or four times
> her bottomless pit (6) may swallow whole your slippery head. (7)
> Even if you lie there suffering, more sluggish than a serpent, (8)
> you will grind away (9) non-stop until – poor, poor wretch –
> you fill that cavern to the brim both three and four times.   35
> That vanity (10) of yours will have profited you nothing, the
>   moment you dip
> your meandering head deep in her slushy sloppy swamp. (11)

Notes

1 Cf. Richlin 1984 (72–74); Richlin 1992a (114–16).
2 *amica*: mistress; even prostitute, whore; here an enforced one.
3 *inguen*: lit. the groin, here synonymous with *cunnus*; cf. Adams 1982 (47–48).
4 Her belly hangs low enough to cover her loins, whose pubic area is matted with hair the colour and texture of ice.
5 *situs*: the location of something; but here, in its secondary meaning, bodily filthiness. The cobwebs are indicators of its lack of recent use.
6 *fossa*: pit; in an obscene sense, *cunnus* or *culus* (arsehole); cf. Adams 1982 (85–86).
7 *caput*: head (synonymous with one's life); used to personify the prepuce of his *mentula* (also at *l.* 37); cf. Adams 1982 (72).
8 The linkage of *mentula* and serpent is clever: in wintry conditions, the snake lies inert.
9 *terere*: an agricultural term, meaning to thresh or grind; often to rub in a sexual sense; compare with *permolere* (66 n. 4).
10 *superbia*: vanity, arrogance; male bravado.
11 *lutum*: mud, mire, or any kind of sloppy muck such as solid or liquid excrement; cf. Adams 1982 (237 n. 1).

Odours

125 Catullus 97: Aemilius Smells at Both Ends

Previous entries on disgusting body and genital odours serve to introduce one of the recurrent themes in epigram and satire, that of the *os impurum* (the impure mouth). Bad breath was regarded as an indicator of depraved oral sexual practice, including fellatio, analingus and cunnilingus. The name Aemilius belongs to a member of one of the most ancient and respected patrician families of Rome. (1) Beyond this, nothing more is available to assist in the identification of this particular object of Catullan vituperation. It may well be a case of Catullus using such a name to make a more general point at the expense of the Roman aristocracy, at whose hands he had experienced considerable personal humiliation: cf. poems about Lesbia (especially 79), Caesar (29, 57, 93) and Memmius (28).

> I did not – so may the gods go on loving me – consider it important
>   to inquire,
>   whether I ought rather to smell the mouth or arsehole
>   (2) in the case of Aemilius.
> His arsehole is in no way purer, and his mouth is no less pure,
>   but in the end, of the two, his arsehole is the purer – and
>   preferable:
> for it is without teeth. His mouth is possessed of a tooth half a
>   metre long, (3)   5
>   indeed it possesses gums like an old box-cart,
> moreover it splits open into a gape like that which the cunt (4)
>   of a donkey possesses when, on heat, (5) it is taking a piss.
> He fucks many girls and regards himself as one blessed by Venus,
>   (6) and yet
>   should he not have been handed over to the treadmill and the
>   ass? (7)   10
> If any girl were to 'touch' (8) him, should we not consider her
>   capable of
>   licking out (9) the arsehole of a diarrhoeic (10) hangman.

Notes

1 Cf. Neudling 1; Thomson 530 (the triumvir or the poet Aemilius Macer of Verona).
2 *os*: mouth rather than face (also *l.* 3, 5); *culus*, the orifice not the buttocks (also *l.* 3, 4, 12).
3 *sesquipedalis*: one and a half (Roman) feet, approximately half a metre.
4 *cunnus*.
5 *in aestu*: the Latin term *aestus* can refer (i) to the heat generated by the sun; (ii) heat generated by ovulation (as in being 'on heat'); (iii) swelling due to menstruation. Thomson (531) notes that (ii) is the appropriate image here: the animal's genitalia, swollen from being in season, gape even more while urinating at the same time.
6 *venustus*, an individual (male) who is endowed with the qualities of Venus (*venustas*); on the terminology, cf. Seager; Wiltshire.
7 He is the kind of person who should have been sentenced to the most servile form of labour in the grinding mill, either working with or instead of the wretched animal who drags the millstone in an endless circle.
8 *tangere*: in a sexual context means (i) to touch manually, orally, etc. or (ii) to fuck; cf. Adams 1982 (185–86).
9 *lingere*: to lick. Adams 1982 notes that it 'was not inherently obscene. It is common in the historical period in non-sexual applications. But it had a well-established use in reference

to oral stimulation of the sexual organs (*mentula*, *cunnus* and *culus* are all recorded as objects of the verb), and in this sense it no doubt acquired an offensive tone' (134).

10 *aeger*: sick, unwell; here a reference to weakness of the bowels or diarrhoea (as J. Lindsay observed in his translation). The *carnifex* (hangman, undertaker) was a social outcast who was not even permitted to live within the community.

126 Nicarchus *Greek Anthology* 11.241: Theodorus Stinks

Nicarchus takes up the theme of linking the respective odours of the mouth and the anus (*prōktos*) in the manner of Catullus in 125. The name of the victim of the attack means 'God-Given' and may well refer to the kind of arrogant aristocrat represented by Catullus' Aemilius.

> Your mouth and your arsehole, Theodorus, smell exactly the same:
>> it would be amazing even for specialists to differentiate them. (1)
> You should put up a sign – which one is your mouth, which your arsehole.
>> Right now when you are speaking <I believe you are farting>. (2)

Notes

1 Here *kalon* is not so much 'a beautiful thing' as something 'amazing'. The term *phusikoi* refers to scientists, natural philosophers, medical practitioners, today's scientific experts.
2 The text is uncertain: Paton's reconstruction (4: 184) has been adopted.

127 Lucillius *Greek Anthology* 11.239: Telesilla's Classically Foul Breath

The stench of Telesilla is so repugnant that Lucillius (First Century AD) must summon his extensive knowledge of mythology to describe the indescribable. The allusions to female monsters, defecation and putrefaction place Telesilla in a mythic category worthy of epic poets.

> Not even the Homeric Chimaera (1) exhaled such an evil (2) stink,
>> nor even, as the story goes, the fire-breathing herd of bulls, (3)
> nor the totality of Lemnos, (4) and the shit of the Harpies, (5)
>> not even the foot of Philoctetes as it putrefied. (6)
> In the eyes of all, Telesilla, you have prevailed over Chimaerae,
>> suppurating sores, bulls, birds, and the Lemnian women.

Notes

1 A monster in Lycia that breathed sulphurous fire (pl. at *l.* 5); cf. *Th.* 304–25.
2 *kakon.*
3 The fire-breathing bulls at Colchis, overcome by Jason; cf. A.R. 3.1246–1345.
4 Venus punished the women of Lemnos for the murder of their husbands in the form of a disgusting smell that emanated from their bodies; cf. A.R. 1.609–26.
5 The Harpies, half-women and half-birds, defecated on the food of their victims; cf. A.R. 2.178–93.

6 A hero, who on account of the stench from his wounded foot, was left by the Greeks on Lemnos (*Il.* 2.716–25).

128 Martial 6.93: Thais Stinks

The poet's adverse association of women's bodies with foul odours is well illustrated in this piece, which describes in graphic detail the stench of a prostitute called Thais. The irony in her name, evoking that of the famous courtesan of Athens, compounds this aggressive vituperation. Instead of being like the cultured Greek original, this Thais is as far removed from the civilised world as possible, having traits more in common with animals than humans.

> Thais gives off an odour, not only as bad as that which a miserly
>   fuller's old piss-jar
>   does, (1) but one just now smashed in the middle of the street;
> not even as bad as a he-goat fresh from rutting, (2) nor even the
>   mouth of a lion,
>   not even the pelt seized from a dog from across the Tiber,
> not even as bad as a chicken when it putrefies in an aborted egg,   5
>   nor even as an amphora befouled by rancid fish-sauce. (3)
> In order that this stench might seem to come from somewhere else,
>   she alters it:
>   whenever she makes for the baths, once her clothes are off,
> she is green with depilatory, or hides herself covered by a clay
>   steeped in vinegar,
>   or is concealed under three or four layers of greasy bean mix. (4)   10
> When she thinks she is made completely safe by these thousand or
>   so tricks,
>   having done everything possible, Thais gives off the smell –
> of Thais.

Notes

1 On fullers' use of urine, cf. 78 n. 4–5. The smell of an old jar would be bad enough, but one just smashed in the street, full of urine, is even more evocative; for a similar reaction (a donkey pissing in the street), cf. 125.
2 On the scent that goats make when rutting (here, ironically rendered *amor*), cf. 122.
3 *garum*: a sauce made from the intestines and offal of mackerels; cf. Bailey 1993 (1: 73 n.c).
4 On depilatories and other body treatments, cf. Ov., *Med. Fac.*

Contamination and staining

129 Aristophanes *Knights* 1284–87: Ariphrades' Tastes

References to deviant sexual practices and defilement had long been of special interest to comic and satiric writers. In keeping with the cathartic freedom of such genres, some authors discuss the taboos of sexuality, such as scatophagy (eating dung), and the resultant staining; cf. J. Henderson 1991 (192–94). The taint of cunnilingus, that most unmanly of sexual activities, is a particular favourite of Aristophanes and, in the *Knights* (424 BC) he mocks Ariphrades as a zealous practitioner.

> He defiles his own tongue in base pleasures
> in brothels licking up the disgusting dew, (1)
> dirtying his beard, (2) disturbing the hot coals, (3)
> and doing the deeds of Polymnestus, and associating with Oionichus. (4)

Notes

1 Ariphrades is cleaning the orifices of prostitutes by licking up their secretions. In itself, *drosos* is essentially a medical term for both vaginal and penile secretion; cf. J. Henderson 1991 (145 and n. 194). It is used of young boys at *Nu.* 978. On pathological practices such as those of Ariphrades, cf. Krenkel 1981.
2 In his enthusiasm he covers his beard with muck from her groin.
3 *eschara* (hot coals, the hearth) was also a common term for the labia; cf. J. Henderson 1991 (142); the metaphor suggests the movement of an implement (Ariphrades' tongue) in hot coals (their labia).
4 Polymnestus: Seventh Century musician; Oionichus: musician or poet. While little more than names, to the audience of Ar. they appear to have been representatives of gross sexual practices.

130 Aristophanes *Wasps* 1280–1283: Ariphrades' Talent

Ariphrades reappears in this comedy of 422 BC. Here the Chorus Leader cries out to the audience, asking if Automenes is present, for he has been made Father of the Year. Of his three sons named, the last is Ariphrades. The first three lines highlight the incredible natural wisdom developed by Ariphrades without the assistance of education or role models. The build-up is undercut by the ghastliness of the uses to which he puts this talent in the final line of the extract.

> Finally, there is Ariphrades, possessed of the most amazing wisdom
>   of spirit,
> whose father once said of him that he'd never had an instructor,
> but that being naturally clever on his own initiative had learned
> to ply his tongue in the brothel every time he paid a visit. (1)

Notes

1 *glottopoiein* means to ply or employ the tongue with gusto; Ariphrades has a taste for licking brothel workers after they have had sex with their customers.

131 *CIL* IV.1391: A Liquid Diet

Many inscriptions from Pompeii make reference to fellation, usually with an assessment of the quality and the price of the service being advertised. In this instance the notice takes the form of a judgemental epigram, carrying the theme of fellation into the realm of oral contamination.

> Veneria (1) drained all the muck (2)
> from his cock (3) for Maximus (4)
> to the extent of his entire vintage. (5)
> She left her stomach languishing (6)
> her mouth full of muck. (7)

Notes

1 Her name suggests one who devotes herself to the service of Venus.
2 *exmuccare* is a rare verb meaning 'to remove slime, to de-muck something'; the writer may be displaying a moralistic tone in equating semen with slimy filth, unless it is implicit that she also practises urolagnia.
3 *mentula*.
4 'The Greatest', a common Roman name from the Republic onwards; it is also indicative of his 'size'.
5 *vindemia*: lit. grape-gathering, vintage. Evidently Maximus' ejaculation was as substantial as his name.
6 The term *putris* has a range of meanings, including (i) stinking, rotten and (ii) languishing. The more likely of the two meanings is that her stomach is withering from lack of solid food.
7 *mucus* is any form of slime or muck. It is possible that Veneria does not swallow the ejaculate of her client.

132 *CIL* IV.1516: Female Muck

The Hesiodic view of a beautiful woman who conceals something terrible inside (17) is a standard theme in Greek and Roman literature. This inscription from Pompeii provides an extreme rendition of the concept of the 'beautiful evil' in which the visually appealing female body houses physical 'muck'. (1)

> Here just no[w I f]ucked a girl with a be[au]tiful body (2)
> praised by many, but slops (3) were inside.

Notes

1 On the inscription, cf. Richlin 1992a (82).
2 He has fucked (*futuere*) a girl (*puella*) possessed of a *formosa forma* (shapely shape).
3 *lutus* (usually *lutum*), lit. means 'mud'; cf. Adams 1982 (240). The writer has either encountered the remnants of a previous occupant (in which case the girl has not douched) or else she was carrying some kind of infection.

133 Martial 9.69: Unforeseen Consequences

Martial, within the context of 'home-grown humor', refers on numerous occasions to the 'physical realities of sexual practices' that are frequently graphic as well as explicit (C. A. Williams 1999: 29). The consequences of a loose sphincter are all too evident in the following epigram. (1)

When you fuck, (2) Polycharmus, you usually shit when you climax. (3)
When being buggered, (4) what, Polycharmus, do you do then?

Notes

1 On sexuality in Mart., especially same-sex between males, cf. Sullivan 1979, 1991; Pitcher; C. A. Williams 1999.
2 Polycharmus is initially portrayed as an active male through the verb *futuere*, to fuck (a woman).
3 The positive imagery is undercut by his expulsion of excrement at the moment of climax (*cacare*, to shit).
4 While the condition described in the first line might simply have been a joke at Polycharmus' expense, the physiological explanation for his habit is forthcoming in the second line. Polycharmus also enjoys the passive role (*pedicare*, to bugger). His sphincter is too loose to retain his waste at the moment of muscular release. Mart.'s sarcastic inquiry is purely rhetorical.

Sado-masochism

134 Hipponax *Fragment* 92: A Sound Thrashing

It may seem inappropriate to suggest that this fragment is masochistic or sado-masochistic considering, among other issues, its contextual hiatus. It may refer to a scapegoat ceremony or a ritual for the cure of impotence similar to the later description in Petronius' *Satyricon* 138 (cf. 119). Similar questions can be asked of Petronius in addition to a seemingly more appropriate one: was his intent to titillate some readers? On the similarity of the passages and their possible sexual intent, J. Henderson 1991 comments: '[Hippon. *Fr.* 92] shares with the Petronian account the same comic verve and delight in sexual sadism' (22–23). The piece stands out for its graphic and violent detail and while Hipponax does not indicate that either party receives sexual gratification from the exercise, it is worth considering why the poet chose to write such a confronting poem. Was it simply to shock? Was it to record an ancient ritual (inexplicable to modern readers)? Or, does it reflect a private fantasy of the author? (1)

> She spoke in Lydian: *Bask [. . .] krolea.* (2)
> In Arse-talk: 'Into the arse . . . ' (3)
> and [. . .] my balls [. . .]
> she flogged me with a branch of fig as if I were a sacrifice (4)
> fast[ened in] the stocks.   5
> And there [I was] between two torments:
> on one side the branch
> . . . coming from above,
> and [. . .] spattering shit.
> My arsehole reeked. Then dung beetles came buzzing   10
> at the stink, fifty or more of them:
> some of them attacked
> and others [. . .]

and others fell upon the 'gates'
of the 'Poo-gela' . . . (5)   15

Notes

1 Cf. Bremmer; Gerber 1999b (423 n. 1).
2 The transliteration of the Lydian phrase is based on the text of Gerber 1999b (423); cf. also West 1974 (144–45), 1994 (121). Its meaning is uncertain, beyond a connection with the anal imagery that follows.
3 The line introduces a series of variants on *puge* (arse).
4 *pharmakos*: translated here as 'sacrifice', but can be rendered 'sorcerer' or 'scapegoat'. Its verbal form can mean to require a remedy or to find a cure. It is clear from the context that a ritual of some sort is entailed.
5 The poet puns on the town of Pugela (=Pygela), near Ephesus. The metaphor of the door / gate (here pl.) for the anus is common; cf. J. Henderson 1991 (199); Gerber 1999b (423 n. 4).

Passivity and effeminacy

135 Anonymous *Greek Anthology* 11.272: The *Kinaidos*

The passive male, who receives a penis in his anus or in his mouth, is an object of ridicule in Greek and Roman literature. The male who practises cunnilingus is equally despised because this act is akin to debased sexual servitude. The following piece acts as a summary of the censure and belittlement levelled at those who, through such behaviour, are believed to have forfeited their manhood. (1)

> They denied they were men, and did not become women.
> They were not men when born, since they suffered the experiences (2)
>   of women.
> They are not women, since they obtained by lot the nature (3) of men.
> They are men to women, and to men they are women. (4)

Notes

1 On issues of male–male passivity in both cultures, cf. Dover 1978; Hoffman; Veyne; Halperin 1989, 1990; Fantham; Thorp; Richlin 1993a; C. A. Williams 1995, 1999.
2 *erga*: works; in this context, things that women do, that they endure.
3 *phusis*: the essential nature (and genitals) of a living being.
4 An echo of the remark made by Curio the Elder that Julius Caesar was 'the husband of every wife and the wife of every husband' (Suet., *Caes.* 52.3).

136 Catullus 80: Telltale Signs of Fellatio

Catullus' attacks on Gellius represent a high point of vituperative satiric epigram. Gellius, in the view of the poet, typifies the sexual deviant (elsewhere with much emphasis placed on his incestuous passion for female relatives) and here he is berated for assuming the passive role with a household slave. (1)

What can I say, Gellius, about how those rosy liplets (2)
    are rendered white more gleaming than winter snow,
when you rise in the morning at home and when the eighth hour
    rouses you from soft slumber during the long day? (3)
Something is up, I know not what: or does rumour (4) whisper truly
    that you are gobbling the stiffened enlargements of a male groin? (5)
Yes, that's what's up: the ruptured loins of poor unfortunate Victor (6)
    are shouting it, as well as lips marked with drained-out sperm. (7)

Notes

1 The group of poems labelled the Gellius Cycle include Poems 74, 80, 88–90, 91, 116; cf. Curran 1966; P. Y. Forsyth.
2 *rosea . . . labella*: 'rosy . . . liplets' is suggestive of both youth and femininity.
3 Gellius' life of slothful indolence is in stark contrast with the values of the upper classes, who rise before dawn to deal with their clients.
4 *fama*: a play on two meanings of the term, (i) reputation, what is said about one, and (ii) gossip.
5 Cat. avoids using any directly obscene terminology.
6 Victor is a slave in Gellius' household, if *misellus* (poor little wretched boy) indicates reluctance. To perform oral sex on a slave was seen as socially outrageous.
7 On the issue of pallor resulting from oral sex, combined with the fact that Gellius does not wipe away the traces of dried sperm from his lips, cf. Curran 1966.

137 Martial 11.61: Nanneius' Tongue

This poem is direct in its obscenity and is a clever and novel treatment of the theme of impotence. In most examples of impotence in satiric literature the victim is attacked as a practitioner of unmanly activity. In this unusual piece the effeminate target of Martial's abuse suffers from lingual rather than penile impotence. As a counterpoint to other passives, Nanneius ranks even lower on the scale of effeminacy due to his passion for cunnilingus.

With his tongue Nanneius is a married man, with his mouth an
    adulterer, (1)
filthier (2) than the faces of the Summemmian whores; (3)
when she saw him naked from her Suburan window (4)
wanton Leda closes the brothel
and prefers to kiss his middle-part rather than his upper-part. (5)   5
Up until recently he used to penetrate every passage in the belly (6)
and with a sure and knowing utterance used to declare
whether a boy or a girl was in the womb of the mother.
Rejoice cunts, for your work is done, (7)
now he is unable to get that 'fuckstress' (8) of a tongue to stand
    erect. (9)   10
For while stuck, fully embedded inside a swollen womb,
listening to the squalling infants inside,

a disgusting disease (10) paralysed his gobbling part.
Now he can neither be regarded as pure nor impure. (11)

Notes

1 When he is using his tongue, instead of his penis, he is acting the part of a *maritus*; with his mouth he is a *moechus* because he is performing cunnilingus, something a husband would never do.
2 *inquinatior*, a comparative of *inquinatus* 'defiled, impure, disgusting'. As the poem unfolds it becomes apparent that this is due to Nanneius' coprophagic tendencies.
3 A term derived from the brothel known as the Memmian Lupanaria (Juv. 3.66); cf. Kay 204.
4 The Subura lay in the valley between the Viminal and Esquiline Hills. As Rome grew it became crowded and dirty, and was often referred to as a brothel zone.
5 Leda is a common name for a prostitute. She closes the brothel out of embarrassment at having him as a client. She prefers to kiss (*basiare*) his cock rather than his mouth because it is clean, never having been put to use.
6 Lit. 'to make one's way along' all the passageways into her womb and belly.
7 The *cunni* (pl.) can rejoice because they will no longer be subjected to his attentions.
8 While *fututrix* is in the fem. form due to its linkage with *lingua* (tongue), it highlights the unmanliness of Nanneius using his tongue as a penis substitute.
9 *arrigere*: to stand upright, get an erection.
10 Cf. Kay (207) on the view that Nanneius has contracted a disease from contact with menstrual blood (and the arguments against this interpretation).
11 Now that he has a filthy disease he cannot be considered *purus* (pure). Because his impotent tongue no longer allows him to indulge his sexual proclivities, he can no longer be regarded as *impurus*.

138 Juvenal *Satire* 2.65–83: Haute Couture in the Courts

Part of the effectiveness of satire, in conveying its conservative messages concerning the need for social stability and adherence to traditions, is the presence of provocative and sometimes confronting visual depictions of deviants indulging in luxuriousness. In this instance, effeminate adornment of the male body within the top echelon of society is an indicator of abnormal behaviour and gender disorientation.

But what 65
will other men not attempt, when you yourself put on garments of
gauze, (1)
Creticus, (2) and with the populace at large expressing amazement
at this attire you
are declaiming against the Proculae and Pollittae? (3) Fabulla is an
adulteress,
let her be condemned; if you wish, Carfinia as well: such a garment
as your
toga, condemned though she be, she would not wear. (4) "But
'Julius' (5) burns, 70
I'm sweltering." You should perform in the nude, for insanity
is less disgusting.

What sort of raiment is that for you to be presenting laws and
    judgements in the
presence of a populace just now victorious in war with wounds still fresh,
    and that
a rustic mountain people with ploughs put aside should be hearing.
What would you not cry out aloud if you saw that sort of thing on
    the   75
person of a Judge? I ask whether garments of gauze would befit a
    witness. (6)
Vigorous and invincible and the master of freedom, (7)
Creticus, you are truly transparent. A contagion has bestowed this
    source of ruin
and will pass it on to many more, just as the entire flock in the
    fields
falls on account of the scabies of a single sheep and the mange of a
    single pig,   80
and as a grape takes on a mouldy hue from the mere proximity of
    its neighbour. (8)
Something more disgraceful than this attire you will dare some day;
no one achieves the ultimate in foulness (9) all at once.

Notes

1 *multicia* (pl.): material made of thin gauze; also at *l.* 76; cf. Walters.
2 Echo of an aristocratic honorific *agnomen* gained in Republican times by a major military victory over a people or region. This individual, Julius Creticus, was a well-known advocate.
3 The plurals suggest women such as Procula and Pollitta. The name Procula is ancient aristocratic; cf. Ferguson 1979 (130) and Johnson (50–51). Pollitta is either a dim. form of Polla or, as Ferguson 1979 (130) suggests, of Etruscan origin; the former would retain aristocratic connotations.
4 Fabulla, dim. of Fabia, is another famous family name from the Republican era. Carfinia is unknown, but the name is non-aristocratic. Having been condemned as a prostitute, she has to wear a toga in public, but even she would draw the line at wearing one like that of Creticus.
5 Julius is both the month named after Julius Caesar, the hottest part of the year in Rome, as well as the gentile name of the advocate himself.
6 A pun on the meanings of *testis* as both witness and testicle; male witnesses swore to tell the truth with their hands on their testicles.
7 The line contains strong value terms normally reserved for men of the highest calibre, including *acer* (keen, vigorous, sharp-minded), *indomitus* (incapable of being overcome) and *libertas* (freedom, the ultimate right possessed by a citizen of Rome, either in the Republic or the Empire).
8 Rome is prone to the adoption of fads and Juv. is fearful that Creticus' style will become popular, much to the detriment of public wellbeing; note the heavy emphasis on disease imagery.
9 *turpissimus* is the supl. adj.; *turpitudo*, the total absence of moral standards, is one of the strongest terms indicating disgrace or shameful behaviour.

VIII

AIDS AND HANDBOOKS

> Nature does not remain strong by being content with a single
> process, but delights in having varieties of change.
>
> Petronius, *Fr.* 17.9–10

All literature on sex and love is didactic, from the seeming misogyny of Hesiod (43) and Semonides (45) through to the scientific explanations in Lucretius and the lovers' guides of Ovid. Writers, regardless of era, context, mode of representation or even ideology were seeking explanations for the forces that lie behind the sex drive.

During the Hellenistic age there had been intense intellectual interest in the place of humankind within the natural workings of the cosmos, a curiosity reflected in works of history, geography and poetic experimentation in areas outside the traditional. Callimachus (fl. mid Third Century BC) wrote his *Aitia* (*Origins*) as a scientific inquiry via the medium of verse and had a profound influence on the amatory poets of the late Republican and Augustan ages.

A less intellectually didactic approach had previously been seen in the proliferation both of implements to enhance sexual pleasure (139–142) and illustrated handbooks designed for the benefit of newcomers and adepts alike. While none of the latter remain extant they were evidently valued by the more sexually adventurous in society (143–147).

The ancients saw Eros/Amor as a primal force over which mortals have little or no control. Humankind could fight it, surrender to it or find means to alleviate its impact. Explanation of Nature and the need to cope with the force of the sexual urge underpin the quite markedly distinctive approaches of Lucretius and Ovid. The Augustan era witnessed the greatest output by writers on matters pertaining to love and sex. Following the leads of Catullus and Lucretius, they provided their own answers by adapting the ethos of the contemporary world of military conquest to the competitive drive for success and survival in the sexual battleground of Nature.

The most overtly didactic works that emerged from this period are the *Ars Amatoria* of Ovid, three books of advice to the would-be lover, and his *Remedia Amoris*, effectively an adjunct for those who have tried, become infected, and now wish to withdraw from the competitive world of love. These works, however, are largely regarded as mock didactic.

Ovid acknowledges that desire and love are not the same. He stresses that there is more to love than beauty, that a tyro can acquire a love that lasts (152 n. 5), that plain

174

and awkward girls can be loved (157) and that moral fibre is a key ingredient for a prolonged love affair (151). All of this lies within the overarching context of the need for *cultus* (sophistication), in essence an attempt to enhance or circumvent whatever Nature has given.

In the final piece (160), Lucretius shows there is no meaningful role for the gods nor for mindless primal forces. There is no place for the deception of a Hera (1), driven neither by desire for sexual pleasure nor feelings of love, seeking to seduce Zeus solely as a means of securing her own agenda. In the end, the polemics of Hesiod and Semonides are silent and the cult of beauty is irrelevant. A long lasting, true love is built on companionship and mutual respect. Lucretius has elegantly and eloquently demonstrated that such a love is perfectly attuned to Nature.

Sex aids

139 Aristophanes *Lysistrata* 107–109: Dildos

There is ample evidence from pottery and literature of the use of dildos in the Greek world. Lysistrata speaks of women's sexual frustration during the Peloponnesian War due to the absence of their husbands (and boyfriends). At this point in the play, she discusses dildos, a not so uncommon joke in Old Comedy as Keuls writes: 'In comedy there are a number of jokes about the use, by women of a respectable class, of self-satisfiers, or dildos, made of leather. They were known as *olisboi*, a word derived from a verb meaning "to glide" or "to slip". Such objects must have been manufactured and marketed, but that they were put to the fantastic uses depicted by vase painters is less likely' (82). (1)

> Not even the spark of an adulterer has been left. (2)
> For since the Milesians betrayed us,
> I have not even seen a dildo eight fingers long. (3)

Notes

1 Keuls continues: 'Since the women using these instruments in vase paintings are usually naked, they may represent hetairai, or, possibly, they are not intended to belong to any special category but are imaginary figures' (82); for the visuals, cf. Kilmer 1993. On the issue of manufacture, cf. 140.

2 Comedy uses stereotypical sexual imagery in relation to the activities of wives. J. Henderson 1987 comments: 'How common adultery was in actual life cannot be determined, but its prominence as a theme is in large part attributable to male anxiety: a central concern of Attic family law was to ensure the unquestionable paternity of a man's offspring, and punishments for adultery were severe' (80). On adultery in Athens and the punishment of same, cf. 105–107.

3 Large scale naval operations against Miletus took place in 411 BC, the same year as the play was performed. Eight fingers equate to five or six inches (15 cm), small in comparison with the vase representations. The scarcity is so acute that she has not even seen a little one.

140 Herodas *Mime* 6.17–19, 58–79: Girl-Talk

Metro and Coritto conduct a confidential discussion about dildos for Coritto has recently purchased one and Metro, impressed, is eager to receive the name of the salesman. Comedy and satire often parody the sexual mores of the respectable woman in society, essentially the conservative and stereotypical mistress of the household. Prostitutes and sexually liberated women are regularly depicted in exaggerated sexual contexts, but here we gain further reinforcement of the male viewpoint, from the time of Hesiod onwards, that all women, especially together and in private, are potentially oversexed. (1)

Metro

I beg you, don't lie,   17
dear Coritto: who was the man who stitched for you
this bright red dildo? (2)

Coritto

I don't know if [Cerdon] is from Chios or Erythrae; (3)   58
bald, small – you'd call him a right 'Mr Tradesman'.

You'll think you're seeing the handiwork of Athena herself, not
    Cerdon's.   66
I – for he arrived bringing two, Metro –
at the sight of them, well, my eyes bulged;
men can't make their rods as rigid as this –
we are alone and can be frank – and not only that,   70
these are as soft as sleep; and the little leather straps
are as soft as wool, not like leather straps at all. (4) A kinder cobbler
to a woman you'll not find – even by putting-out.

Metro

Why then did you not take the other one as well?

Coritto

What didn't I do, Metro?
What sort of means of persuasion did I not apply   75
to him? Kissing him, stroking his bald head,
pouring out a sweet drink for him, calling him by a pet name,
giving him all but my body to enjoy. (5)

Metro

If he asked even that, you ought to have given it. (6)

1 On the proclivity of women to obsess about sex, cf. Semon. 7.90–91 (45). For additional comment on Herod., cf. Cunningham (160–74); on dildos, cf. Kilmer 1993 (98–102).
2 *baubon*: dildo. They were made of 'red leather like the phallus worn in comedy' (Cunningham 164).
3 She knows his name but is uncertain of his place of origin: Chios is a large island off the coast of Lydia, opposite the peninsula on which Erythrae is the major centre. Cerdon reappears in *Mime* 7 where his trade is confirmed as a shoemaker.
4 This dildo appears either to be a strap-on device for use in tribadic sex or to have straps designed to keep it in place within her body.
5 The reluctance to offer a sexual incentive is probably due to the class barriers; sexual preference may also be a factor.
6 While sharing her friend's preferences, Metro clearly believes the acquisition of the second one would have been worth the sacrifice.

141 Propertius *Elegies* 2.6.27–34: Visual Erotica

Propertius denounces the prevalence of erotic depictions within well-to-do households for the impact they have upon the innocent minds of the young, especially young girls. His objections are less to do with an anti-pornography stance per se as to the encouragement it gives them to practise infidelity in the pursuit of carnal pleasures. (1)

> The hand which first created painted panels depicting sexual acts (2)
>   and put up disgraceful sights (3) for display within a chaste household,
> that (hand) corrupted the tender (4) eyelets of girls (5) and thus refused
>   to allow them to remain inexperienced of his own wantonness. (6)
> Ah! Let him groan in painful sightlessness, (7) the one who revealed by
>   his art (8)
>   the secret rituals (9) that lie hidden beneath unspoken delight! (10)
> Once upon a time homes were not decorated with those sorts of
>   depictions:
>   at that time no wall was painted with any reproachable scene. (11)

1 On the issue of pornography in the classical world, cf. the essays in Richlin 1992b; on 'soft' and 'hard' core pornography in ancient art, cf. Kilmer 1993, Appendix II.
2 *obscaenae* (pl. fem.): 'depicting the sexual act or some of its preliminaries' (Camps 2: 95; also at 144 n. 2). Yet Goold 1990 (136–37 n. b) argues these are not the explicitly pornographic sex scenes on the walls at Pompeii, but 'the romantic depiction of adulteries such as *Mars and Venus*' (137). Ov., *Tr.* 2.521–28 mentions the practice of painting erotic scenes in respectable houses, citing an example of Venus barely concealing her nakedness in the waves: cf. the Venus from the Casa della Venere at Pompeii (Varone, Fig. 5).
3 *turpia* (pl.): things likely to cause shame or disgrace.
4 The eyelets are *ingenui* (pl.), freeborn, belonging to well brought up girls, hence tender or innocent.
5 *puellae* (pl.).
6 *nequitia*: here wantonness, rather than sense of worthlessness.

7 The text is corrupt. If *in tenebris* is adopted, it means the poet is wishing him to go blind as punishment for the corruption his pictures have engendered.

8 *ars*: here the skill of the artist, who is represented throughout by his hand.

9 *orgia* (pl.): while it can have the modern connotation, they were the cult objects employed by mystery religions.

10 *laetitia*: delight, pleasure. It was *tacita* because a sense of shame and modesty prevented discussion of sexual activity.

11 *crimen*: technically something for which an individual could be indicted or reproached.

142 Suetonius *Life of Horace*: Reflections

The *Life of Horace* is a brief survey of gossip about the great poet's life and relationship with Maecenas and Augustus. At one point the author describes his physical appearance (he was short and fat with a more than healthy appetite for food and wine) and makes a brief note on his sexual proclivities.

It is reported that he was very intemperate in respect of matters to do with sex. (1) It is said that he had prostitutes (2) in a mirrored bedchamber positioned in such a way that wherever he directed his gaze, there would be an image of sexual congress (3) being reflected for him from that location.

Notes

1 *res venereae*, lit. 'matters pertaining to Venus'.

2 The use of *scorta* (pl. prostitutes) is in keeping with his views on adultery in *Sat.*1.2 (cf. 66, 108) where he warns against sexual liaisons with women of the better classes; the issue is not so much a moral one as the risk of physical harm to the adulterer.

3 *coitus*: a polite term for sexual intercourse. The reflections were not just of women standing around in provocative poses, for *scorta* include males as well, a necessary adjunct for his viewing pleasure.

Sex manuals

143 Athenaeus 220e–f: Writers of Erotic Handbooks

Athenaeus attacks Socrates for consorting with flute-girls and the instruction on luring lovers that he provided for a *hetaira* called Theodote. In the process he lists some writers of sex manuals. According to Polybius (12.13.1), the historian Timaeus described such writers as *anaischuntographoi* (lit. 'those who write about matters that are a source of shame or disgust'). Such works are 'very strong stimulants towards matters of love (*erotica*) and sexual relations'. (1)

For he has [Socrates] recommending to Theodote a set of instructions [f] which Nico the Samian, Callistrate the Lesbian, Philaenis the Leucadian, and even the Athenian Pythonicus (2) had never dreamed up as enticements to passion, (3) for indeed all these writers were greatly occupied with such matters.

Notes

1 Attributed to Chrysippus at Athen. 335d, specifically with reference to the works of Philaenis and the *Gastronomia* of Archestratus.
2 Nico, Callistrate and Pythonicus 'are mere names', according to H. N. Parker 1992 (94). Philaenis of Leucadia is the most famous of the (mostly female) writers of erotic manuals. On the authorship of her 'unbridled written work on matters to do with sex' (Athen. 335b), cf. Tsantsanoglou (192), who argues that it was a 'pseudonymous' work. Athen. 335c cites an epigram (*AP* 7.345) attributed by some to Philaenis, which denies that she either wrote lewd books or consorted in a common or inappropriate way with men; he identifies the author as a Fourth Century BC iambic poet, Aeschrion of Samos; cf. Gow and Page 1965 (2: 3–4). For a tribad of that name, cf. 101.
3 *pothos.*

144 *Priapea* 4: Elephantis

Elephantis is either (i) a writer of this name (W. H. Parker 73), or (ii) materials from the city of the same name in Egypt (H. N. Parker 1992: 94).

> To the ever-stiff (1) god, obscene pictures (2)
> taken from the little books of Elephantis,
> Lalage offers as a gift and asks if he would test
> whether he could provide substance to the positions portrayed. (3)

Notes

1 *rigidus*: stiff, erect; for Priapus, a constant state.
2 *obscaenae . . . tabellae* were tablets on which words and/or pictures were presented to the viewer; here of a sexual nature; cf. 141 n. 2.
3 The most obvious means for the god to fulfil the request would be to perform them with Lalage. Scioppius (1606 AD) writes: 'The pictures taken from the books of (Elephantis), Lalage hangs from the little sac of Priapus' balls, asking him to be willing to sexually defile himself (*stuprare*) and put himself to the test, as to whether or not he could imitate faithfully all those depicted modes of sexual congress' (cited in Latin by W. H. Parker 72).

145 Martial 12.43: The Wanton Verses of Sabellus

Martial mentions a number of writers of erotic handbooks; cf. 146 and Sullivan 1991 (110); C. A. Williams 1999 (337 n. 102, 103). Sabellus, an otherwise unknown poet, apparently has succeeded in outdoing the established yardsticks of the genre, although Martial questions whether such clever erudition is worth the cost, for author or audience.

> Some exceedingly well crafted verses, Sabellus, on matters of a
> licentious nature (1) you have been reciting to me,
> such as neither the girls of Didyma (2) know
> nor the wanton (3) little books of Elephantis.
> There are in there radical positions for lovemaking, (4)   5
> such as a dissolute fucker (5) would dare,

what ageing male whores (6) both provide and keep quiet about,
in what configuration any five individuals may be joined up,
by what kind of daisy-chain (7) many more are held together,
what is possible once the lamp has been extinguished.   10
Your being so eloquent is not worth the cost.

Notes

1 *libidinosa*: emphatic adj., derived from *libido*.
2 Didyma, a city in Asia Minor near Miletus, had a temple to Apollo. If such *puellae* do not
   know the acts in question, endowed as they are with prophetic talent, then the *libidinosa* (*l.*
   2) are indeed unique.
3 *molles*: likely to encourage effeminate attitudes and practices. On Elephantis, cf. 144.
4 To the Roman mind, anything new was radical, dangerous, and likely to lead to a dramatic
   change in the status quo. These positions for sexual intercourse (*venus*) fit such a category.
5 *perditus fututor*: a sexual performer who is totally abandoned.
6 *exoleti* (pl.): lit. adult males; here passive adult whores. As they get older they are willing to
   perform the most debauched acts for a greatly reduced price (cf. 70 on the aged Galla and
   her services). Their silence is a valued commodity.
7 Lit. a chain of sexual linkages.

146 Martial 12.95: A Girl to Hand

The following is a rare acknowledgement of the practice of using erotic or pornographic
booklets for the purpose of masturbation. Martial urges Rufus to read the remarkable
works of Musaeus and Hemitheon, but to share the experience with a girl rather than
wasting his energy on his hand.

> The mega-raunchy (1) booklets (2) of Musaeus, (3)
> which rival the booklets of the *Sybaritica*, (4)
> and pages imbued with itch-generating (5) wit,
> you must read, Istantius Rufus: (6) but that girl (7)
> of yours should be with you, lest you proclaim with
> lusting hands your wedding exclamation (8)
> and you become a husband without a woman. (9)

Notes

1 *pathicissimi* (pl.): supl. adj. of *pathicus* (a male who takes another's penis in his mouth). The
   booklets need not have been exclusively devoted to male–male themes, *pace* Sullivan 1991
   (110).
2 *libelli* (pl.): lit. little books; slim volumes without much text but a lot of illustration.
3 Musaeus (variant Mussetius) is otherwise unknown.
4 Sybaris, a Greek city in southern Italy, was renowned for its luxurious standard of living.
   Ov. (*Tr.* 2.417) refers to a work called *Sybaritica* being a recent composition on salacious or
   shameful subject matter: its author was Hemitheon (a Greek), called a *kinaidos* by Lucian,
   cited Ker (2: 383 n. 4). Mart. refers to Sotades, a poet and a *cinaedus*, at 2.86.2; but it may
   be the man not the verse that is at issue; contra C. A. Williams 1999 (337 n. 103); cf. Ker
   (2: 156 n. 4).

5 The pages are saturated with *sal* (wit) that was *pruriens* (generating an itch), a common description for sexual arousal.

6 Istantius Rufus was Governor of Hispania Tarraconensis in the early Second Century AD. On the tone of Book 12 of the *Epigrams*, cf. Sullivan 1991 (52 ff.).

7 *puella*.

8 *thalassio*, a wedding salutation (often equated with an epithalamium), here addressed to his masturbating (*libidinosi*: lust-inducing) hands rather than a bride.

9 A *maritus* without a *femina* (woman), not the usual word for wife (*mulier, uxor*) let alone bride (*nupta*). Without the help of the girl, Rufus would be 'marrying' his hand. For Mart. on masturbation, cf. 2.43.13–14 (where it is inspired by some boys); 9.41 (critical of it in Ponticus' case).

147 Martial 10.35: Sulpicia – Erotica for the Respectable

Sulpicia and her husband Calenus were among the patrons of Martial (cf. 59). In addition to the theme of perfect marriage, which permeates this poem, Martial conveys a strong element of didacticism along with lofty praise for the erotic poetry of Sulpicia.

All girls (1) should read Sulpicia,
the ones who are desirous of pleasing one man;
all married men should read Sulpicia,
the ones who are desirous of pleasing one bride. (2)
She does not take as her theme the frenzy of the Colchian, (3)   5
nor does she retell the feastings of dreadful Thyestes; (4)
Scylla, (5) Byblis (6) she does not believe existed:
but she propagates chaste and honourable love,
sportings, delights, and clever pleasantries. (7)
He who properly understands her songs,   10
will have asserted no girl was more wanton,
will have asserted no girl was more morally upright. (8)
Such were the pastimes of Egeria –
I believe – under the dripping cave of Numa. (9)
With her as fellow-student or with her as teacher   15
you would have been more learned, Sappho, as well as chaste:
but had she been seen alongside you at that time,
emotionless Phaon (10) would have been in love with Sulpicia.
To no avail: for this girl, not as the wife of the Thunderer,
nor that of Bacchus, nor as the girl of Apollo,   20
would she go on living, once Calenus was taken from her.

Notes

1 *puellae*: most likely young wives or possibly girls who wish to be pleasing to their man (*vir*, *l*. 2). The Roman ideal woman was the *univira*, one who 'knew' only one man throughout her life (cf. Prop. 4.11, Funeral Elegy for Cornelia).

2 Mart. advises couples to read her works for an insight into a happy, harmonious and sexually satisfying marriage.

3 The intensity and honesty of her poetry are attested by the absence of mythical allusion. There is no Medea, the anti-heroine, epitome of the uncontrollable passion (*furor*) of a woman scorned.

4 Thyestes paid dearly for the seduction of his sister-in-law (Aerope, wife of Atreus) by unknowingly eating the flesh of his children.

5 Scylla betrayed her father Nisus, King of Megara, being obsessed with desire for his enemy Minos, King of Crete.

6 Byblis, daughter of Miletus, fell in love with her brother Caunus, with tragic consequences.

7 The mythological allusions centre upon disastrous sexual relationships: the love promoted in the poetry of Sulpicia is both chaste (*castus*) and respectably proper (*probus*), but still has erotic content, characterised by sporting (*lusus*), delights (*deliciae*) and pleasantries (*facetiae*).

8 *l.* 10–12 capture the spirit and essence of the perfect wife as revealed in her verse: she is both more wanton (*nequior*) and morally upright (*sanctior*) than others, but within the confines of marriage.

9 Egeria was a goddess of fountains and childbirth. Legend has it that Numa, the second King of Rome, met Egeria at her sacred spring. Livy (1.21.3) records that she was the king's lover and mentor.

10 A mythical ferryman made young and beautiful by Aphrodite. Sapph. is said to have fallen in love with him (cf. Str. 10.2.9; Ov., *Her.* 15).

Sex and science

148 Lucretius *On the Nature of Things* 4.1101–20: Lust – Never Enough

On the Nature of Things expounds the scientific theories of Epicurus. An important element in the creation and ongoing maintenance of the cosmos is the powerful force of the sex drive, a subject that dominates the concluding section of Book 4. In the following extract, Lucretius describes the frenzied futility of the lovers' attempts to fuse with the body of the beloved. (1)

Venus sports with lovers in the grip of love (2) through images:
they cannot gain satiety by gazing upon the bodies before their eyes,
nor with their hands can they rub off anything from tender limbs,
as they hesitantly rove in all directions over the entire body. (3)
Finally, with limbs intertwined, they revel in the delightful flower   1105
of youth, when, now that the body has had a foretaste of sexual
    delights (4)
and Venus is at the point where she will sow the furrows of
    women, (5)
avidly they press their bodies as if glued and mingle each other's
    saliva
in their mouths and gasp for breath, pressing mouths with their
    teeth –
to no effect, since they can rub off nothing away from there   1110
nor can they penetrate and pass into another body with their entire
  body;

for at times they appear to be wanting and striving to achieve this:
so completely in the grip of lust (6) do they cling in the shackles of
    Venus,
while their limbs melt, shaken by the impact of the sexual pleasure.
    (7)
At length, when the compacted lust has escaped from the 'sinews',
    (8)   1115
there might be a small respite from the violent passion – for a
    little while.
Soon the same frenzy returns and that madness comes back, (9)
when they seek to comprehend just what it is they crave to obtain
    for themselves
and are unable to discover a device which might overcome that
    'evil'; (10)
so, completely bewildered, they waste away from an invisible
    wound.   1120

Notes

 1 On the violent impact of *eros/amor* cf. 10–15; on the futile search for fusion, cf. 83; for a
   detailed analysis and commentary on the views of Lucr., cf. R. D. Brown.
 2 *amantes* (pl.): those in or making love (*amor*). Throughout the passage, Lucr. uses 'Venus'
   for the sexual urge (*l.* 1101, 1107, 1113).
 3 The rubbing, here and *l.* 1110, is a desperate attempt to link with the body of the beloved.
 4 *gaudia* (pl.).
 5 Reference to a woman being at her fertile period; note the agricultural imagery of furrowing
   and ploughing.
 6 *cupide* (lit. lustfully); also *cupido* (lust) at *l.* 1115.
 7 *voluptas*.
 8 *nervi* (pl.): sinews, flexible muscles; used here for the penis and its associated linkages.
 9 Lucr. employs three powerful terms to describe the forces at work here: *ardor* (passion), *rabies*
   (frenzy) and *furor* (madness).
10 *malum*, equivalent of the Greek *kakon*.

149 Lucretius *On the Nature of Things* 4.1153–76: Lust is Blind

Lucretius posits that in the grip of lust a lover is rendered blind to the physical realities
of the object of desire, a source of derision in the eyes of others. He notes that in reality,
all women have foibles, a fact well known to other women (cf. also 156).

For, in the main, mortal men do this blinded by lust (1)
and they manufacture positive attributes that do not truly belong
    to them.
As a result we see women, bent and disgusting in many ways,
    being   1155
held as 'darlings' (2) and thriving in the highest regard.
And some men ridicule other men and egg them on so that they render

sacrifice to Venus, since they are afflicted by a disgusting form
  of 'love'; (3)
and often these wretches do not see their own massive misfortunes.
  (4)

The dark complexioned is 'honey-skinned'; the shit-stained and
  fetid is 'natural',   1160
the odd-eyed a 'little Pallas', (5) the sinewy and wooden 'an
  antelope',
the tiny little one is 'elfin', 'a veritable Grace', (6) 'undiluted wit
  throughout',
the bulky and ungainly is 'a wonder' and 'filled with esteem'.
A tongue-tied one unable to speak is 'a lisper', a mute is 'bashful';
but the hot-headed, odious chatterer becomes a 'bright spark'.   1165
A slight one becomes 'a little sexpot', when she can barely any
  longer go on
living due to emaciation; 'slender' is one all but dead from a
  hacking cough.
But the bloated and huge breasted is 'Ceres herself as a result of
  Iacchus'; (7)
the pug-nosed is 'a Silena' and 'a Satyress', (8) the puffy-mouthed is
  'kissable'.
It would be tedious were I to attempt to list the remainder of this
  kind of thing.   1170
But just let her be whatever you want by way of distinction for
  facial features,
let the pull (9) of Venus rise up from each and every one of her
  limbs:
even so there are other women as well; without her we lived
  beforehand;
she does all the same things, and we know she does them, and
  foully at that,
and she drenches her wretched self with disgusting odours: 1175
her maids avoid her from a distance and they laugh at her in secret.

Notes

1 *cupido*: lust.
2 *deliciae*.
3 *amor*. The mockery of a friend who has an unfortunate lover is the issue here. The implication
   is that it is malicious (cf. R. D. Brown 279–80). Here read Venus as the deity.
4 *mala* (pl.), the equivalent of *kaka*.
5 The reference is to unusual eye-colouring, which might otherwise be seen as a defect. Pallas
   Athena was said to be grey-eyed; cf. R. D. Brown (285).
6 She is one of the Charites.
7 Ceres was the mother of Iacchus and synonymous with the figure of an earth mother. On the

variant versions of the parentage of Iacchus, who is associated with the Eleusinian Mysteries, cf. R. D. Brown (292).

8 The god Silenus was a regular member of the entourage of Dionysus, renowned for his drinking and dissolute lusts. Satyrs likewise were perpetually lustful.

9 The term *vis* conjures up images of force, power and irresistible strength. Here read Venus as the sexual drive.

Grooming and the natural look

150 Propertius *Elegies* 1.2.1–8: Talent Needs No Adornment

The question of the need for additional adornment of natural beauty goes back to the earliest erotic literature. Homer has Hera go to great lengths to enhance her divine beauty as a prelude to the seduction of Zeus (1). While Ovid wants a girl naked and natural when making love (20), he regards presentation and sophistication (*cultus*) as essential elements in the process of allurement (151). Propertius argues that in nature there is no need for this, nor is there in the stories from mythology that witness beautiful, unadorned girls being the object of desire for gods. Note, however, here it is a question of the girl stepping out in her finery – but not for his benefit.

> What use is it, [my] Life, (1) to go out with an ornate hairstyle
> and to set to movement [your] smooth curves (2) in a Coan
> creation? (3)
> What use is it to drown your ringlets with myrrh from the Orontes, (4)
> and to sell yourself with fineries foreign to you? (5)
> What use is it to ruin the glorious charm of Nature by purchased
> refinement, (6)
> and not allow your limbs to shine with their own innate merits?
> Trust me, your figure is in no need of treatment: (7)
> naked Love does not love beauty augmented by artifice. (8)

Notes

1 *Vita*, a term employed frequently of the beloved in Roman amatory poetry.

2 *sinus*: technically the folds of a (woman's) garment, synonymous with the breast and the lap; here, more likely the curve and sway of her hips and body as she walks (compare the effect of Anactoria's walk on Sapph. at 18).

3 Sheer fabrics from Cos were highly prized, and expensive. A garment made of this would be the equivalent of a Parisian creation today.

4 Myrrh was a particularly fine perfume; the Orontes was the major river of Syria. The emphasis is on it being expensive, exotic and imported.

5 The line could read 'to put yourself up for sale for the gifts of foreigners', but in this context it is unlikely that Prop. is saying she is playing the whore; cf. Camps 1961 (1: 46).

6 *cultus*, as opposed to the merits (*bona*) that natural beauty has provided.

7 *figura* in the modern sense. She needs no adjustment, improvement or treatment (*medicina*) to what she already possesses.

8 *Amor* is described as naked and unadorned in his simplicity, a theme visited frequently by Prop.; cf. Goold 1990 (47 n.a). Beauty (*forma*) here is external; *artifex* (adj.) evokes ingenuity and cleverness, something manufactured.

151 Ovid *Treatments for the Female Face* 1–7, 11–29, 31–50: Importance of *Cultus*

Published before 1 BC, this work of indeterminate length (we have but a hundred lines) is a learned treatise on a vital aspect of the game of love in a sophisticated society, namely feminine grooming (*cultus*) with a special focus upon the face. (1)

You must learn what application (2) will set off the face to
  advantage, girls, (3)
    and by what means your beauty (4) must be protected.
Cultivation (5) commanded the barren earth to produce the gifts
    of Ceres, (6) the stinging bramble-bushes to perish.
Cultivation alters the bitter juices of fruit,   5
    and the grafted tree receives 'adopted' wealth. (7)
Cultivated things are providers of pleasure . . .

Perhaps the Sabine women of long ago under king Tatius (8)   11
    would have preferred to cultivate their father's fields rather
    than themselves:
when the matron, ruddy-complexioned, sat on her high chair,
    with her hardened thumb spinning the constant work,
and the lambs, which her daughter had pastured, she used to shut
    in their pens,   15
    and she put twigs and chopped wood on the hearth. (9)

But your mothers have given birth to tender girls. (10)
    You want your bodies covered with garments inlaid with gold,
you want to vary the styling of your scented locks,
    you want to have hands admired for their gemstones: 20
you adorn your neck with precious stones sought from the East,
    and of such a size that it is a burden for the ear to bear two of
    them.
Still, it is not an unbecoming thing if your concern is to give
    pleasure,
    since our generation possesses men of elegance. (11)
Your husbands are embellished in accordance with feminine style   25
    and the bride scarcely possesses more in respect of cultivation.
    (12)
The person for whom each girl beautifies herself and what love
    affairs (13)
    are being pursued, is of significance; elegance (14) warrants no
    reproaches.
Even those hiding in the countryside shape their tresses. . . .

There is also pleasure (15) in pleasing oneself, whoever it might be;   31
    in the case of maidens (16) their own beauty is very dear to their
    heart.
The bird of Juno (17) fans feathers that are praised
    by mankind, and many a bird exults in its own beauty.
Thus it is more likely that love (18) will set us afire than powerful
    herbs,   35
    which the witch (19) plucks by way of the frightful art of her hand.
Don't place any trust in grasses nor a cocktail of juice,
    don't put to the test the deadly venom of a mare on heat; (20)
snakes are not split down the middle by Marsian incantations, (21)
    nor does the wave flow backwards to its own fountainhead; 40
and even if someone has made a clatter with Temeseian cymbals,
    (22)
    the Moon will never be shaken loose from her own chariot.

The first priority for you, girls, should be safeguarding your moral
    fibre. (23)
    The face is pleasing when it is in accord with character.
Love of moral fibre is assured: age will ravage beauty, (24)   45
    and a once pleasing facial appearance will be ploughed by
    wrinkles.
There will be a time, in which it will grieve you to look at a mirror,
    and that grief will become yet a further cause for wrinkles.
Probity (25) suffices and it endures for a very long period of time,
    and it is here, throughout the duration of its years, that love sits
    well.   50

Notes

1 On the importance of *cultus* in Ov., cf. Green 1979; Myerowitz, Ch. 2. On the dating of the
    poem, cf. Holzberg 2002 (39). On the treatments suggested in the second half of the poem,
    cf. Green 1979. 'The poet chose . . . ingredients for his cosmetic recipes which are effective
    and in some cases still in use' (Dalzell 134). Ov. revisits this material at *AA* 3.200–30, and
    refers to this poem at *AA* 3.205–08.
2 *cura*: taking good care; application; also anxiety, concern (*l.* 23).
3 *puellae.* Ov. addresses his audience as girls, here and at *l.* 43
4 *forma*: also at *l.* 32, 34, 45.
5 *cultus*, a term borrowed from agriculture, connotes careful attention paid to every respect
    of appearance, both in private and in public. It, and its derivatives, have been rendered as
    'cultivation'; cf. *l.* 5, 7, 12, 26. Its opposite is *rusticitas*. Ov. has more to say on the subject
    of the need for *cura* and *cultus* in his advice to girls in *AA* 3.
6 Ceres was an Italic goddess of the harvest, identified with the Greek Demeter.
7 Adopted because they are products of the grafting process and not the product of nature.
8 Titus Tatius, King of the Sabines, was a contemporary of Romulus.
9 Sabine women, here both mothers and daughters, are treated as the epitome of old fashioned,
    upright behaviour, hard working in the household and rendering much assistance around

the farm. They thus represent a combination of all the womanly (and wifely) virtues, especially dutifulness and chastity, but pay little or no attention to their appearance.

10 *tenerae puellae*: these girls are a much gentler lot, incapable of the hard working lifestyle of their forebears; that work ethic is nowadays applied to beautification. They do appeal to Ov. (rather than the old fashioned Sabines, the epitome of *rusticitas*) on account of their love of cultivated refinement.

11 Strictly speaking 'men (*viri*) paying attention to the hair'.

12 Ov. is addressing married, respectable girls, indicating that refinement is as much a part of a married woman's world as that of the unmarried; female practice, in this context, has the force of law (*lex*). The *nupta* and her *vir* are equal in both their appearance and their love of *cultus*. Note the echoes of Sapph. (47) and Cat. (49 *l*. 189–92).

13 *amores* (pl.); Ov. moves to the world of the unmarried.

14 *munditia*: elegance.

15 *voluptas*. Ov. advocates dressing to please oneself, as distinct from doing so to gain approval in the eyes of others.

16 *virgines* (pl.).

17 The peacock (cf. Ov., *Met*.15.385).

18 *amor*; also at *l*. 45, 50.

19 *maga*: female practitioner of magic, a witch. Ov. has little time for magic, spells and incantations as *l*. 35–42 indicate. The power of Amor / Eros is as old as the universe and mere magical processes have no real influence over it.

20 *amans*: in the mood for love, often used as a substantive for lover. The substance is called *hippomanes* (cf. Ver., *Geor*. 3.280–83; yet note Theoc., *Id*. 2.48–49 'Hippomanes is an Arcadian herb, and, on account of it, all / the foals and all the swift-footed mares run maddened around the hills').

21 The Marsi, a formidable tribe from central Italy, S-E of Rome, were renowned for incantations and magic.

22 Temese in S Italy had copper mines, from which cymbals were manufactured.

23 *mores* (pl.); also at *l*. 45. These go to make up one's character (*ingenium*, *l*. 44).

24 Here *amor* is used in the broader sense of love for good *mores*. The enemy of *forma* is the ageing process.

25 *probitas*: moral uprightness, rectitude.

The art of love

The *Ars Amatoria* was written some time 'between 1 B.C. and 4 A.D.' (Holzberg 2002: 39) and is arguably the most famous treatise on the game of love to emerge from antiquity. Written in three books, it outlines the processes whereby young men can find and attract girls (Book 1), how to keep them once they have found them (Book 2) and how young women can attract and keep young men (Book 3). Many regard it as the *carmen* to which Ovid (*Tr*. 2.207–11) refers as a major factor, the other being an *error*, in his *relegatio* to Tomis where he spent his final years in wretched exile.

152 Ovid *Ars Amatoria* 1.35–38: The Task

Ovid establishes both his audience and his purpose in writing. This is not a work for the eyes of a bride or a respectable matron. The love affairs are, however, licit and not aimed at the corruption of the innocent. The motifs of military campaigning and hunting are established from the outset. The first step is the commencement of the search. (1)

To begin with, strive to find what you wish to love, (2)
    you who come as a soldier bearing new weapons for the first time; (3)
the next task after this is to win over a pleasing girl; (4)
    the third, that love (5) might last a long time.

Notes

1 On military imagery in Ov., cf. E. Thomas; Cahoon.
2 *amare*. Compare with Sapph. Fr.16.4 (18).
3 Young men entering into amatory campaigning for the first time, not experienced veterans, are his target audience.
4 The *puella* being sought must be agreeable and appropriate; at this point beauty is not being stressed.
5 Ov. aims at finding *amor* that is durable and not transient. In this he is in line with Lucr. (cf. 160).

153 Ovid *Ars Amatoria* 1.45–50, 89–100, 135–70: Where to Find a Girl

The would-be lover has much to learn from the world of the hunter, one in which skill and knowledge, as well as patience, are of crucial importance. As the first place to look, Ovid cites the theatre, followed by the Circus and gladiatorial shows where girls are wont to throng.

The hunter knows well, where to spread his nets for stags;   45
    he knows well, in what gully the gnashing wild-boar lurks;
to bird-catchers the shrubs are known; the man who holds the hook,
    knows what waters are swum by swarms of fish:
you too, you who seek the material for a long love affair, (1)
    learn in advance in what place a girl (2) frequents.   50

In particular you should go hunting in the curved theatres;
    these places are very bountiful as regards your hopes.   90
There you will find what you can love, what you can sport with,
    and what you can touch only once, and what you can wish to
    keep. (3)
Just as a bustling ant returns and passes through a long column,
    carrying its customary food with grain-bearing mouth,
or as bees, having gained their own thickets and sweet-smelling   95
    pastures, fly around through the flowers and the tops of the
    thyme-plants,
thus the best dressed woman (4) rushes to the crowded games;
    quite often their numbers have clouded my judgement.
They come to see, they come that they themselves might be seen;
    that place contains the seeds of destruction for chaste Modesty.
    (5)   100

And do not allow the contest of noble horses to escape your
    attention: 135
  the Circus, filled with people, holds many opportunities.

Take a seat nearest to your mistress with no one offering opposition;
    join your side to hers as much as you can.   140
And this is good since, if you are hesitant, touching sides is
  necessary,
    for by the law of that place the girl has to be touched by you.

Little things captivate light-hearted minds: it has been a useful
  device for many
    to have arranged a cushion with an easy hand;   160
it has also proven helpful to stir the breezes with a slender fan
    and to have provided a stool beneath a slender foot.

And so the Circus will offer these avenues for a new love affair (6)
    as well as the sorrowful sand sprinkled over the busy Forum. (7)
Often has the boy of Venus fought on that sand (8)   165
    and a youth who watched the wounding has received a wound:
while he chats and touches her hand and asks for a programme
    and enquires, while laying a bet, which one is winning,
he groans in pain and feels the winged weapon
    and he himself is part of the display on display.   170

Notes

1 Upon setting out, the aim is to achieve an *amor* that is durable.
2 *puella*.
3 The ideas are complementary: (i) *amare* and (ii) *ludere* in *l.* 91, and (iii) *tangere*, touch (or fuck?) and (iv) *tenere*, hold on to in *l.* 92. Ov. claims the theatre caters for both kinds of relationship, the long-term and the short-term.
4 *cultissima*: superl. adj. of *culta*. She is the epitome of refinement in both looks and deportment.
5 *Pudor*. The Romans had a propensity for deification of concepts.
6 *amor*.
7 Gladiatorial displays were conducted in the Forum prior to the construction of the first stone amphitheatre in 29 BC (Hollis 62).
8 There are artistic representations of Cupid fighting as a gladiator (Hollis 62).

154 Ovid *Ars Amatoria* 1.611–14, 621–26: Sing Her Praises

All girls, even chaste, modest ones, enjoy being praised, hence Ovid's emphasis on persuasive speech (*blanditiae*) as an integral weapon in the pursuit of the object of desire.

> You must act the part of a lover (1) and feign wounds with your
>   words;   611
> by every kind of artifice (2) her trust (3) must be sought by you.
> It is no great effort being credible: each of them feels she must be
>   loved; (4)
> be she the ugliest, there is none to whom her own shape (5) is
>   not pleasing.

> Nor should you tire of praising her face, her hair,   621
>   and her graceful fingers and delicate foot: (6)
> pronouncements about beauty please even chaste girls; (7)
>   for virgin girls their beauty is a source of worry and yet
>   pleasure. (8)
> For why does it even now embarrass Juno and Pallas   625
>   that they did not win the judgement in the Phrygian forests? (9)

Notes

1 *amans*: one who is in love.
2 *ars*.
3 *fides*: here trust, confidence, rather than loyalty.
4 *amanda*: the verbal adj. 'she who must be loved'.
5 *forma*, in contrast with a girl who is *pessima* (the worst, ugliest).
6 The four areas nominated for attention are the face, hair, fingers (hands) and feet, those that are always visible to the eye of the would-be suitor.
7 Not only available girls enjoy being praised. Ov. notes that chaste girls (*castae*, pl.) enjoy pronunciations about their *forma* and draws on mythical precedent by way of illustration.
8 *forma*. For virgins it is both a *cura* and a source of pleasure (*grata*).
9 The goddesses defeated in the Judgement of Paris were both renowned for their chastity, Juno as the model *matrona* and Pallas Athena as the patron of womanly arts, yet both were prepared to display themselves naked in the hope that their *forma* would result in approval and praise. The Phrygian forests, synonymous with Mt. Ida.

155 Ovid *Ars Amatoria* 1.753–54: Trust No One

Love is no different to any other aspect of life. Competition is about victory and every available means is employed to ensure success. Rivals are everywhere when beautiful girls are the prize.

> Beware kinsman and brother and dear friend; (1)
>   this crowd will provide you with real grounds for fear.

Note

1 In the field of love every male is a potential enemy or rival, be he a close relative (*cognatus*, sharer of one's bloodline), a brother (echo of the destructive rivalry between Romulus and Remus) or closest friend (*sodalis*).

156 Ovid *Ars Amatoria* 2.657–66: Avoid Talk of Her Flaws

Lucretius (149) had already addressed the susceptibility of the love-struck admirer for putting the best possible construction on the physical or personal flaws of the object of desire. Ovid takes up the issue, with a slant essentially his own, since he regards this as a tactic rather than a conviction on the part of some lovers.

> It is possible to soften the bad (1) by names: let her be called 'swarthy',
>   she whose blood is blacker than Illyrian pitch; (2)
> if she has a cast in her eyes, 'just like Venus'; (3) if flaxen haired,
>   'just like Minerva';
>   let her be 'slender', whose very life is endangered by emaciation;
>   (4)   660
> say she is 'trim', whoever is short; she who is bloated, call her
>   'plump';
>   and let a flaw (5) be hidden by its proximity to something good.
> And do not ask how many years she has nor under what Consul
>   she was born, these are the duties the stern Censor has, (6)
> especially if her flower has wilted, and the better part of her life   665
>   has passed and already she is plucking out greying hairs.

Notes

1 *mala* (pl.). If there are shortcomings, change their names to positives.
2 *sanguis*: lit. blood; its hue has seeped through the surface and given colour to the skin.
3 Lucr. uses the same image (cf. 149 n. 5).
4 Also at Lucr. (149, *l*. 1166–67).
5 *vitium*: a vice; flaw of character as well as appearance; it can be screened by placing it next to one of her assets (*bonum*).
6 Cf. 122 n. 1.

157 Ovid *Ars Amatoria* 3.255–86: Tips for the Plain or Awkward

The truth is that there are more plain girls than beautiful ones, but even the really beautiful are rarely without some flaw. Although they may have no urgent need for his advice, Ovid argues that all girls can benefit from close attention to *cultus*.

> A crowd comes to learn, attractive and plain girls, (1)   255
>   and the plainer ones are always more numerous than the fair.
> Beautiful girls (2) do not seek the assistance of art and precepts; (3)

their own dowry is there for them, a beauty (4) without art that
is powerful.

Yet rare is the face (5) lacking a blemish: hide the blemishes and,   261
as much as you are able, conceal any defect (6) your body might
have.
If you are short, sit down, lest while standing you appear to be sitting,
and however small you are, make sure you recline on your couch.

Let a girl who is excessively slender choose garments with full   267
compactness, and let her robe go loose from the shoulders.
Let a pale girl 'colour' her body with purple stripes, (7)
and you, darker girl, resort to the assistance of the Pharian fish.
(8)   270
A misshapen foot should always be hidden in a snow white leather
shoe,
and do not release withered ankles from their bonds.
Slender suspensory padding is suited to high shoulder blades,
around a narrow chest there should be a broad band. (9)
Let her signal with slight gestures, whatever she happens to be
saying,   275
if she has fingers that are fat and a nail that is rough.
She, who suffers from halitosis, should never speak without having
eaten
and should always stand back from the mouth of her man.
If you possess a black or excessively large tooth, one that will not
grow in its
proper place, you will suffer the greatest losses by laughing.   280
Who would credit it? Now girls are even learning to laugh,
here seemliness (10) is sought by them in this area: their mouths
should be slightly open and the dimples on either side should be
small,
and let the bottom part of the lip cover the top part of the teeth.
And they should not overstrain their flanks (11) with continuous
laughter,   285
but only a light and oh so feminine (sound) should be heard.

Notes

1 *puella* (pl.): also at l. 281. The attractive girl is *pulchra*, the plain one *turpis*, a somewhat
blunt expression in view of its connotations of ugliness and foulness, even disgrace.
2 *formosa*: here pl.
3 Ov. refers to his *ars* and his *praecepta* (teachings); neither is really needed by the truly
beautiful girl.
4 *forma*.

5 *facies*: the face is the most important ingredient in beauty and is subject to more scrutiny than any other feature.

6 *vitium*: fault, defect; vice. It is something that usually needs to be extracted (as with a plant, its original context), but here to be concealed.

7 Variegated coloured clothing to offset her complexion.

8 The reading *piscis* (fish) is awkward but adopted by most edd. Possibly the 'fish of Pharos (Alexandria)' is the crocodile; either its skin, worn as an accessory, or some by-product used as a skin toner or lightener is at issue. If *vestis* (garment, cloth) is read it would entail light clothing offsetting the dark skin of the girl.

9 Cf. Athen. (68) on the art of concealment of flaws in the case of prostitutes.

10 *decor*: adornment that is appropriate.

11 *ilia*: technically the loins, groin area; here rendered flanks. Uproarious guffawing makes for a 'bad look' in a girl.

158 Ovid *Ars Amatoria* 3.769–808: Best Positions for Sex

These lines constitute a literary version of the materials found in the illustrated handbooks of the type attributed to Philaenis and Elephantis (143–144). To Ovid the positions are not simply designed for sexual variation and pleasure but are recommended within the spirit of Book Three. The practice of *cultus* and his earlier advice on how to minimise a woman's visible bodily flaws, which might lead to the diminution of pleasure, are at the core of the segment. As Dalzell claims, if '[t]he object of an elegiac affair is to get the woman into bed' (162) and the woman herself is agreeable to that, here is Ovid's advice, ostensibly given to her but intended for the man as well, on what to do now that the aim of the exercise has been attained. (1)

> The things remaining it embarrasses me to teach, but bountiful
>   Dione (2)
>   says, "That which embarrasses is especially my concern!"   770
> Let each girl be known to herself; (3) take up sure methods from
>   your body:
>   the one style does not suit everyone.
> She who is striking in her face, lie on her back;
>   for those whose back is attractive, let them be watched from
>   behind.
> Milanion up on his shoulders bore the legs of Atalanta: (4)   775
>   if they are good, let them be looked upon that way.
> A small girl should be carried on horseback: because she was very
>   tall, never
>   did his Theban bride sit astride Hector as her horse. (5)
> A woman needing to be looked at for a long flank should press the
>   bedspread
>   on her knees, with her neck bent back a little: 780
> she whose thigh is youthful, and whose breasts as well lack
>   blemishes,
>   let her man stand, while she is spread-eagled on the couch at an
>   angle.

194

And do not think it shameful to loosen your hair, as did the
     Phylleian mother, (6)
     and bend your neck in the midst of flowing locks.
You as well, for whom Lucina (7) has marked your belly with
     wrinkles,   785
     just like the swift Parthian make use of stallions from the back.
     (8)
There are a thousand fun-filled ways for sex; (9) a simple one, of no
     great effort,
     is when she lies semi-reclined on her right flank.
But neither Phoebus' tripods nor horned Ammon (10)
     will sing more truths to you than my Muse;   790
if there is any trust, then put it in my art, which I have
     accomplished
     from long usage: my songs will exceed trust. (11)
Let the woman feel the sexual urge, released from the very depths
     of
     her marrow, and let that act be equally pleasing to both.
And do not let sweet words and charming murmurs cease   795
     and do not let risqué words be silent in the midst of the
     fun-making. (12)
You too, for whom nature has denied the sensation of sex,
     feign the sweet joys with counterfeit sound –
unhappy the girl, (13) for whom that place dozes devoid of feeling,
     in which a woman and a man (14) deserve to be delighted.   800
Only, when you are pretending, beware lest you be exposed:
     effect credibility through your movements and your eyes.
What does help is both to gasp words and breath from your mouth;
     Ah, what an embarrassment! That part has its own secret signs.
She who asks a gift of a lover after the joys of sex,   805
     does not wish her prayers to have any weight.
And do not let light enter your bedroom by each and every window: (15)
     it is preferable that most parts of your body remain hidden.

Notes

1 On the significance of the passage for the view that Book Three is a 'circular route' that
  'begins and ends in [the woman's] bedroom', cf. Myerowitz (97).
2 On Dione as mother of Earthly Aphrodite, cf. 112 n. 4.
3 The Delphic Imperative.
4 Atalanta outran (and killed) her would-be suitors, until defeated by Milanion. She is
  described as *pernix* (leggy) at Cat. 2b.1.
5 Hector's Theban bride was Andromache (cf. 58 n. 6).
6 Phyllus was located in Thessaly. The woman (*mater*, mother) is unknown; *L&S* suggest,
  unconvincingly, that it may be Laodomia (1373).
7 Juno as Lucina presided over childbirth.

8 The Parthians, when retreating on horseback, turned backwards to fire arrows at their pursuing enemies.

9 *venus*: also at *l*. 793, 797, 805.

10 Reference to oracles of Apollo (at Delphi, Delos) and Zeus at Ammon in the Libyan desert.

11 *fides*: also at *l*. 802.

12 *ioca*: fun times.

13 The *puella* is ill-starred, unlucky (*infelix*) if she is incapable of pleasurable sensations in her genital area.

14 *femina* and *vir*.

15 Compare with the prepared setting for his afternoon with Corinna (20).

Cures for love

159 Ovid *Remedia Amoris* 135–54, 161–70, 197–98: Healing the Disease

This work was written after the *Ars Amatoria* and some time prior to his *relegatio* to Tomis. It opens with a plea to Cupid not to regard the poet as a deserter from his military standards. He wishes the successful lover happiness (*l*. 13–14) and justifies the penning of this poem as bringing aid to the wretched, lest he utterly perish from the tyranny of an unworthy beloved (*l*. 15ff.). Love is a sickness and finding a means of healing is essential. (1)

Therefore, whenever you feel ready to be healed by this skill (2) of
    mine,   135
    see to it that, on my advice, first and foremost you avoid times
    of leisure. (3)
These lead you to fall in love, (4) these [then] guard over what they
    have done;
    these are the origin and the nourishment for the pleasurable evil.
    (5)

If you remove leisure times, the bow-wounds of Cupid come to
    nothing,
    and his firebrands lie spurned and devoid of light.   140
Just as the plane tree takes delight in wine, or the poplar does in
    water,
    or the swamp reed in the sodden earth (of the marsh), (6)
so does Venus love leisure times; you who seek a termination of
    love – (7)
    Love yields to activity – engage in activity (8) and you will be
    safe.
Languor and excessive sleep-ins without interruption,   145
    and dice games, and brows befuddled with a lot of wine
snatch away all sensations from the spirit (9) without inflicting a
    wound;

Love the ambusher flows with ease into those devoid of caution.
That boy (10) is habituated to chasing after sloth, (11) he hates
those who are busy:
give to an empty mind some task, to which it can cling.   150

There are the activities of the Forum, there are the Laws, and
Friends to protect: (12)
make your way through the rewarding campaigns of the City
toga; (13)
or take up the youthful 'gifts' of bloody Mars: (14)
soon pleasurable sources of delight will offer their backs to you.
(15)

Is there any question as to why Aegisthus was turned into an
adulterer? (16)   161
The reason is ready at hand: he was slothful.
Others were fighting in the drawn out clash of weaponry at Ilion;
(17)
the whole of Greece had transferred her resources of manpower.
If he had wanted to give attention to warfare, none was being
waged;   165
if to the Forum, Argos was devoid of litigious activities.
What he could do, lest he be doing nothing there, was make love.
This is the way that boy comes along, this the way that boy
hangs around.
The countryside and the pursuit of cultivation also delight the
spirit; (18)
whatever care there is yields to this care. (19)   170

There follows a series of pastoral images, echoes of the Georgics

When this particular pleasure (20) starts to soften up the spirit,   197
upon crippled wings does Love, frustrated, make an exit!

Notes

1 'Its inspiration came from the same sources as [the *AA*] had, the native elegiac and the
Hellenistic didactic traditions' (A. A. R. Henderson xiii); '. . . the *Remedia*, teaching how
to heal oneself of love, represents the extreme development of elegiac poetry and brings to
a symbolic close the brief period of its intense existence' (Conte 346).

2 *ars*. It is what Ov. claims he possesses in respect of love: the skill to impart lessons and to
compose great poetry.

3 *otia* (pl.): leisure time. It can be rendered 'idleness', depending on how an individual spends
periods of relaxation: Cic. wrote, Cat. lounged around the Forum with friends (Cat. 10.1–2)
or fantasised about Lesbia (30). Also at *l.* 139, 143.

4 *amare*: also at *l.* 167.

5 Being in love is seen as an evil (*malum*), albeit a pleasurable (*iucundum*) one.

6 On the imagery, cf. A. A. R. Henderson (59–60).

7 *amare* (also at *l*. 167) and *amor*.

8 *res*: an all-purpose word; here important business or activity.

9 *nervi* (pl.): nerve-endings, areas where we experience sensation; in the sing. it is used of the penis (cf. **148** n. 8); *animus*, here the mind.

10 Throughout Cupid (*l*. 139) or Love (Amor, *l*. 144, 148, 198) is described as a boy (*puer, l.* 168); cf. **Illustration 1**.

11 *desidia*: sloth, laziness; cowardice. It is a negative value as it represents the antithesis of *virtus*. Used as an adj. (*desiodiosus*) at *l*. 162.

12 The key areas of involvement in public life within Rome were the world of the Forum, the Law Courts, and the need to protect and look after one's friends and clients.

13 Ov. equates the activities of a participant in public life at Rome as military campaigning in a toga.

14 The other major area of serving Rome is on campaign, waging war (Mars) on behalf of the state; it is a career to be embarked upon in youth.

15 *deliciae*. The act of turning one's back is to flee from the battlefield.

16 The story of the adultery between Aegisthus and Clytemnestra was a popular one in Greek tragedy. Although he had a motive, gaining revenge for the wrong done to his father and siblings by Atreus, father of Agamemnon, Ov. attributes this adultery to having too much time on his hands.

17 Troy.

18 The final area of activity for men of substance was to occupy their *animi* in farming.

19 *cura* is used twice in this line, for 'concern, anxiety' and 'area of concern'.

20 *voluptas*. Pleasure of this kind softens the manly *animus*.

A last word

160 Lucretius *On the Nature of Things* 4.1278–87: Long Lasting Love

Throughout his treatment of the sex drive in Book 4, Lucretius sees it as a force over which humankind has little or no control, but makes a clear distinction between an urge for sex and love. Lust is blind (149) and sex is urgent, even brutish (148), but love between two people is a matter of habituation and affection.

Sometimes – and not due to divine intervention and the arrows of
  Venus –
it happens that a little woman (1) of inferior shape (2) is loved. (3)
For sometimes a woman herself achieves it by her own actions   1280
and by her agreeable ways and cleanly groomed (4) body,
so that quite easily she gets <you> accustomed to spending your
  life with her.
As for what is left, habit generates love; (5)
for that which is beaten, however lightly, by a repeated blow,
still, in the long term, is overcome and succumbs.   1285
Can you not see, too, that the drops of moisture falling upon
rocks in the long term beat their way right through those rocks?

Notes

1 The dim. *muliercula* indicates she is of adult age but on the small side. At *l.* 1280 he uses *femina* (any woman).
2 A *forma* of an inferior (*deterior*) kind suggests she does not meet widely held standards of beauty, such as those outlined by Cat. (27); her body may even be misshapen.
3 *amare*: here in the passive.
4 The key factors are her regular ways of doing things and her bodily deportment (*cultus*, used adj. with her body).
5 *consuetudo* means habit, practice, getting used to someone, which in time can lead to *amor*.

GLOSSARY OF AUTHORS

Achilles Tatius, Greek novelist from Alexandria. Second Century AD. *The Story of Leucippe and Cleitophon*, his only extant work, tells the story of two young lovers who elope, experience numerous adventures (common in the genre of novel), become separated and are finally reunited.

Aelian, Claudius, Born in Praeneste. AD 165/70–230/5. A Greek writer whose extant works are *On the Nature of Animals, Miscellany* and *Rustic Letters.* The *Miscellany* is largely comprised of historical and human interest stories designed for the moral enlightenment of the reader.

Aeschines, Athenian orator and statesman. *c.* 397–*c.* 322 BC. He was a rival and political enemy of Demosthenes. His speech *Against Timarchus* (345 BC) is one of three extant orations delivered in response to Demosthenes and Timarchus' attempt to prosecute him.

Alcaeus, Born in Mytilene on Lesbos in *c.* 625 BC, contemporary of Sappho. A lyric poet, his work incorporated a variety of themes including love, politics, hymnal pieces, as well as myths and legends.

Alcman, Of disputed birthplace: Laconia (or Lydia). *c.* Seventh Century BC. Lyric poet. He composed *partheneia* (maiden songs) for Spartan girls to perform at festivals as well as *epithalamia* (marriage hymns), and amatory and erotic verse. Fragments survive.

Anacreon, Born in Teos in Ionia. Sixth Century BC. Lyric poet. The extant work reveals the primary themes of love and eroticism (with both male and female objects of desire), as well as poetry extolling wine.

Apollodorus, Born in Athens. Second Century BC. The *Epitome* is a historical, philosophical and biographical work written in metre, which covered the period following the fall of Troy down to the author's own time. The *Library*, a compendium of Greek mythology, is also attributed to him.

Apuleius, Born at Madaurus in Africa in *c.* AD 125. A writer and orator, his major work is the Latin novel, the *Metamorphoses* or *Golden Ass*, a tale of magic, sensuality and comedy.

Archilochus, From Paros in the Cyclades. Seventh Century BC. A famed iambic poet whose work contains explicit sexual and erotic material as well as treatment of themes of a political and military nature.

Aristophanes, Athenian comic playwright. *c.* 448–*c.* 380 BC. Alone of the writers of Old Comedy, eleven of his plays have survived intact. His work was extremely popular in his own time and is characterised by its explicitness, obscene humour and brilliant social and political insights.

Aristotle, Born at Stagirus in Chalcidice. 384–322 BC. He moved to Athens in 367 BC and studied at Plato's school. In 335 BC he established the Lyceum. Many of his works of a philosophical, political, literary and scientific nature are extant, including material by his students attributed to his corpus.

Asclepiades, Born at Samos in *c.* 290 BC. Writer of epigrams, mainly on love, and the originator of the genre of erotic epigram.

Athenaeus, From Naucratis in Egypt. fl. *c.* AD 200. Collected anecdotes, quotations and stories and reproduced them in the form of conversations in *Deipnosophistae* (*Connoisseurs in Dining*), a work extant in fifteen books. His collection is invaluable for its preservation of many authors who would otherwise be lost and in its representation of Greek manners.

Callimachus, Born at Cyrene, later moved to Alexandria. *c.* 310/305–240 BC. Arguably the most influential of the great Hellenistic poets, fragments of his *Aitia* (*Origins*) have survived, his *Iambi* on contemporary morals and some 60 epigrams.

Cato, Marcus Porcius (The Censor), From Tusculum. 234–149 BC. Statesman and author of works on history (*Origines*), agriculture (*De Agricultura*) and fragments of published speeches.

Catullus, Gaius Valerius, From Verona. *c.* 84–*c.* 54 BC. Came to Rome *c.* 62 BC. A member of the *neoteric* circle, he provides the earliest extant corpus of romantic and erotic lyric poetry at Rome. His influence upon the Augustans and the Imperial epigrammatist Martial was profound.

Cicero, Marcus Tullius, From Arpinum. 106–43 BC. Consul in 63 BC. Roman politician, lawyer and statesman. Prolific author of texts including speeches, rhetoric, philosophy and epistles.

Demosthenes, Athenian statesman and orator. 383–322 BC. Many of his works are extant. The *Erotic Essay* and *Against Neaera* are of doubtful authenticity.

Erinna, Greek poet. Fourth Century BC. Her most famous work is entitled *The Distaff*.

Euripides, Athenian tragic playwright. *c.* 485/480–406 BC. Nineteen plays survive. Euripides challenged his audience in confronting ways and questioned traditional mores. Many of his plays are characterised by powerful women and strong emphases on the consequences of love, lust and betrayal.

Festus, Rufus, From Tridentum. Fourth Century AD. Historian and senator. Author of a work on the significance and meaning of words.

Gallus, Epigrammatist, possibly of the First Century BC.

Greek Anthology (Palatine Anthology), Collection of poems by various authors dating from Seventh Century BC–Tenth Century AD. Arranged in fifteen books, two comprise collections of verse on erotica (Book 5) and boy-love (Book 12). The poets included in this sourcebook are: Anonymous, Asclepiades, Gallus, Honestus, Lucillius, Nicarchus, Nossis, Philodemus, Rufinus and Straton.

Herodas, Probably *c.* Third Century BC. His extant work, the *Mimiambi*, consists of some eight pieces designed for performance, some of which have erotic and romantic motifs.

Hesiod, From Cyme in Aeolis, migrated to Ascra in Greece. Eighth Century BC (possibly later than Homer). Two major works, *Works and Days* and *Theogony*, are extant. His treatment of the myth of the creation of woman-kind (Pandora) and his views on marriage have given him an enduring reputation for misogyny.

Hipponax, Poet of Ephesus and Clazomenae in Ionia. *c.* late Sixth Century BC. Much of his work deals with sexual and farcical topics in vivid, vulgar language.

Homer, Born traditionally somewhere in Maeonia in Asia Minor. *c.* Eighth Century BC. Author of the *Iliad* and *Odyssey*, he is regarded as the greatest and most influential Greek poet.

Honestus, Greek poet, possibly born in Corinth. fl. during the reign of Tiberius. Author of ten epigrams in the *AP*.

Horace, Quintus Horatius Flaccus, From Venusia in Southern Italy and educated in Rome. 65–8 BC. Augustan age poet whose work demonstrates great versatility ranging from epodes, satires, odes to epistles on literary criticism.

Hyginus, *c.* Second Century AD. Two Latin texts are attributed to him: the *Fables* and an astronomical work.

Ibycus, From Rhegium. Sixth Century BC. Fragments of his erotic lyric poetry, especially on the love of boys, survive.

Juvenal, Decimus Junius, Possibly born in Aquinum. *c.* AD 60–70. Author of sixteen satires that provide valuable insights into the Roman lifestyle during the reigns of Trajan and Hadrian.

Livy, Titus Livius, Born at Padua. 59 BC–AD 17. Author of a monumental history of Rome, *Ab Urbe Condita*, from its foundations to the reign of Augustus. Thirty-five of the 142 Books are extant.

Lucian, From Samosata on the Euphrates. *c.* AD 115/120–*c.* 200. Settled at Athens. Author of quasi-philosophical works, satirical dialogues and eccentric, fantastic tales. A number of works of dubious authenticity are attributed to him.

Lucilius, Gaius, From northern Campania. *c.* 180–102/1 BC. Writer of vigorous satires in Latin in the iambic tradition of Archilochus.

Lucillius, Greek epigrammatist of the Neronian age whose essentially satirical pieces on people and events are well represented in the *AP*. His work strongly influenced Martial.

Lucretius, Titus Lucretius Carus, Likely from Rome. *c.* 94–55 BC. Poet and philosopher. Author of a didactic epic, *On the Nature of Things*, which expounds the theories of Epicurus with a focus on the laws of nature.

Lysias, Born at Athens. 458–378 BC. In the aftermath of the fall of the thirty tyrants in Athens, he gained renown for the elegant speeches that he composed for others.

Martial, Marcus Valerius, Born in Bilbilis in Spain. *c.* AD 40–*c.* 104. Came to Rome in AD 64. Famed writer of epigrams that reflect a keen interest in the social and private habits and foibles of humankind.

Mimnermus, From Smyrna in Asia Minor. *c.* Seventh Century BC. Writer of love poetry on the pleasures of boys, girls and beauty; preoccupied with the theme of old age.

Nicarchus, From the First Century AD. Writer of satiric epigrams, of which forty are represented in the *AP*.

Nossis, From Locri in Southern Italy. *c.* Third Century BC. Female epigrammatist who wrote dedicatory poems about the gifts offered by women to goddesses.

Ovid, Publius Ovidius Naso, From Sulmo, educated at Rome. 43 BC–*c.* AD 17. The last and greatest of the Augustan amatory poets. Banished to Tomis by Augustus in AD 8.

Oxyrhynchus Papyri, From Egypt. Fourth Century BC to Late Antiquity. The papyri include fragments of Homer, Sappho, Bacchylides and Aristotle. Many pieces provide insights into aspects of life, including marriage, divorce and related family matters.

Petronius, Arbiter, d. AD 65. Author of a fragmentary novel, the *Satyricon*. It deals with the adventures of the lovers Encolpius and Giton, providing an offbeat and at times informative insight into the sexual practices of the age. In addition, some thirty extant poems are attributed to his authorship.

Phaedrus, Gaius Julius, Greek slave from Thrace who became a freedman in the household of Augustus. Latin author of the *Fables*, five books in the style of Aesop.

Philodemus, From Gadara in Syria. *c.* 110 BC–*c.* 40/35 BC. He moved in the circles of Piso Caesoninus (Consul 58 BC) and Cicero as a devotee of Epicureanism. He is the author of thirty-eight extant epigrams, mostly on erotic themes.

Plato, Athenian philosopher. *c.* 429–347 BC. Twenty-five dialogues are preserved, including his insightful treatises of the nature of love and desire, the *Phaedrus* and the *Symposium*.

Plautus, Titus Maccius, From Sarsina in Umbria. *c.* 251 BC–184 BC. Roman comic playwright. Twenty-one plays are extant and deal with the themes and characters of New Comedy: love interests, reunions, mistaken identity and deception.

Pliny the Younger, Gaius Plinius Caecilius Secundus, Born at Comum.

AD 61/62–*c*. 113. The nephew of Pliny the Elder. A distinguished orator and Govenor of Pontica. His extant works included the *Panegyric* of Trajan and ten books of *Letters*.

Plutarch, From Chaeronea. *c*. AD 46–*c*. 120. Greek, best known as an author of (i) biographies of famous Greek and Roman statesmen and (ii) philosophical treatises known as the *Moralia*.

Priapea, A collection of poems focused on the phallic god Priapus. Scholars suggest dates ranging from the beginning of the Hellenistic age to the Fourth Century AD.

Propertius, Sextus Aurelius, Born probably at Assisi. *c*. 54/48 BC–*c*. 16 BC/AD 2. Augustan age erotic poet. Author of four books of *Elegies*.

Quintilian, Marcus Fabius, Roman rhetorician. *c*. AD 35–*c*. AD 90s. Major extant work is entitled *Institutiones Oratoriae* (*Training in Oratory*).

Rufinus, Greek epigrammatist of uncertain date. There are thirty-seven of his erotic poems in the *AP*.

Sallust, Gaius Sallustius Crispus, From Amiternum. 86–*c*. 34 BC. Author of the *Bellum Catilinae* (43 BC) and *Bellum Jugurthinum* (*c*. 41 BC). His *History*, written in five books, survives in fragments.

Sappho, From Mytilene in Lesbos. Born *c*. 612 BC. Author of nine books of lyric of which one complete poem remains extant in addition to many fragments. Her work deals with a feminine world of friends and perhaps lovers in addition to *epithalamia*. Known in antiquity as 'The Tenth Muse'.

Semonides, From Amorgos. Seventh Century BC. Greek iambic poet, author of a controversial and provocative satire on women.

Seneca, Lucius Annaeus (The Younger), Born at Corduba in Spain. *c*. 4 BC–AD 65. Author of philosophical tracts showing the strong influence of Stoicism as well as prose epistles, satire and tragedies.

Solon, Born at Athens. Sixth Century BC. Statesman, lawgiver and poet.

Strabo, A Greek from Amaseia in the Pontus. 64/63 BC–AD 21. Historian and geographer. His major work the *Geography* is extant.

Straton, From Sardis. *c*. Second Century AD. Writer of erotic epigrams mostly on pederastic themes, he is well represented in Book 12 of the *AP*.

Suetonius, Gaius Tranquillus, Born probably in Rome. *c*. AD 69–*c*. 140. Historian, biographer and author of other scholarly works. In addition to his famous *Lives of the Caesars* from Julius Caesar to Domitian, a collection of *Lives of Poets* is attributed him.

Theocritus, From Syracuse, spent time in Cos and Alexandria. *c*. 310–250 BC. The founder of the pastoral genre, his most famous work is called the *Idylls*.

Theognis/*Theognidea*, From Megara. fl. 544–541 BC. Greek poet, with subjects ranging from politics to erotica. The extant text contains many disputed pieces that are collectively called *Theognidea*.

Tibullus, Albius, Born in Rome. *c*. 48–19 BC. Augustan age elegiac poet whose work focuses on love and pain.

Tyrtaeus, Greek elegiac poet, most likely from Sparta. Mid-Seventh Century BC. Surviving fragments of his *Eunomia* deal with exhortations to the young to fight and die bravely on behalf of the community.

Vergil, Publius Vergilius Maro, From Andes (in Mantua). 70–19 BC. Roman poet and author of the *Eclogues*, the *Georgics* and the *Aeneid*.

Xenophon, Born at Athens. *c.* 444–mid-Fourth Century BC. Famous general and philosopher, contemporary of Plato. His extant works range from history to biography and hunting, as well as a *Symposium*.

GLOSSARY OF TERMS

Greek terms

agapesis higher form of affection and love.

agathon (neut.) a good thing.

agathos noun and adj: a noble; well-bred, excellent; *agathe*: a well-bred woman.

aidoios modest.

aidos a sense of shame, modesty; *Aidos*: personified Shame.

aischron shame, disgrace.

aischune shame; the shame done to a person.

anandros quality of being a man.

andrike mannish.

androgunos hermaphrodite.

arete excellence; character of the highest order.

baubon dildo.

biazdein to constrain, apply force; to rape.

binein to fuck.

charieis (masc.)/*chariessa* (fem.) gracious, graceful, beautiful; it can also denote one who is accomplished and elegant.

charis (sing.) beauty, physical grace, charm; *charites* (pl.) all of the graces, charms, qualities that attract. *Charites*, personified Graces (occasionally used in the sing., *Charis*).

dia bright; also heavenly.

dike the strongest Greek value term for justice.

doron (sing.)/*dora* (pl.) gifts, love-gifts, bribes.

drosos vaginal secretion.

echein to be with; to have sexual intercourse with.

eleuthera (sing.)/*eleutherae* (pl.) free-born women (of the lower classes); among the most sought-after class for (illicit) sexual encounters outside marriage.

epithalamium (sing.)/*epithalamia* (pl.) wedding song.

eran to be in love with, to have an erotic desire for; *eramai* to love, to be passionately in love, to lust after.

erastes (sing.)/*erastai* (pl.)   the older male partner who occupies the active role in a same-sex relationship; the lover.

erga   works.

ergasterion   lit. a workshop; brothel.

eromenos (sing.)/*eromenoi* (pl.)   the younger male who occupies the passive role in a same-sex relationship; the beloved.

eros   a powerful, mindless, sexual desire; *erotai*   sexual encounters.

Eros   personified *eros* (the god of sexual desire). *Erotes*   the Loves.

erotike   erotic material.

erotikos   amatory. *ta erotika*   what concerns *eros*; erotic matters.

esthles   excellent; also *esthlos*; *esthlon* (adj.)   good, noble; often equated with *agathos*.

euandria   a supply of good men; manliness; display of manliness and courage.

euexia   bodily fitness; good health.

gambros   bridegroom.

gamos   wedding; the state of wedlock; *gamein*   to marry.

geras   old age.

gunaikomanes   mad for women; preference for vaginal sex.

gune (sing.)/*gunaikai* (pl.)   usually woman, but also wife.

hebe   the prime of youthful beauty. *Hebe*, personified Youthful Beauty.

hedone (pl.)   pleasure.

hetaira (sing.)/*hetairai* (pl.)   a female companion (prostitute of the highest quality).

hetairein   to prostitute oneself.

hetairike (adj.)   that which befits a companion or prostitute.

hetairesis   prostitution.

hetairistria   a female lover of women; tribadism.

hetairos   male companion.

himeros (sing.)/*himeroi* (pl.)   desire for sex. *Himeros*, personified Desire.

hora   beauty; a period fixed by natural laws (year, month, day); the season or, more commonly in the pl., the seasons; *horia*   in season, the appropriate time.

hubris   violence that is offensive in the eyes of gods and men; *philubristes* passion for violence.

hubrizein   to cause outrage; to inflict shame or humiliation on another; *hubrismenos*   one who is violated.

hymenaios   wedding or bridal song; also, the wedding itself. *Hymenaios*, personified Bridal Song (the god of marriage).

kakon (sing.)/*kaka* (pl.)   evil, misfortune, disgrace.

kakos (masc.)/*kake* (fem.)   evil, bad, disgusting, ugly.

kallisteia (pl.)   beauty competitions.

kallistos (masc.)/*kalliste* (fem.)/*kalliston* (neut.)   fairest, most beautiful (from *kalos*); adj. and noun.

kallos   beauty.

kalos (masc.)/*kale* (fem.)/*kalon* (neut.) beautiful, lovely especially in relation to the body; it also carries connotations of goodness. In the neut., 'a beautiful thing'.

kestos something stitched or embroidered; Aphrodite's girdle.

kinaidos (sing.)/*kinaidoi* (pl.) a submissive male; one who submits to anal penetration; generic term for effeminate male.

kore (sing.)/*korai* (pl.) virgin; it can also mean daughter and can be used of a bride and young wife.

kyrios guardian.

lusimeles limb-relaxing; a frequent epithet of Eros.

malthakos soft; also faint-hearted or cowardly; also associated in a negative sense with *kinaidos*.

mela (pl.) limbs.

meriones (pl.) thighs; the area between the legs.

moicheia adultery.

moichos lover, adulterer.

moira destiny; fate; one's lot in life.

morphe shape; face; equivalent of *forma*.

neanis girl, maiden.

neos young man.

neoteroi (pl.) young men; collectively, the avante garde.

nomos (sing.)/*nomoi* (pl.) traditional sanctioned behaviour; an ordinance, a law, a custom, something assigned.

nothos (sing.)/*nothoi* (pl.) illegitimate or low born (from a slave or concubine).

nymphe bride; clitoris.

oiketis housewife.

oikos (sing.)/*oikoi* (pl.) the essential family unit and its possessions in the Greek world from Homer onwards; *oiketis* a housewife.

olisbos (sing.)/*olisboi* (pl.) a dildo.

paiderastein to love a boy; to make love to a boy.

paiderastes (sing.)/*paiderastoi* (pl.) boy-lover.

paiderastia love of boys.

paidika (sing.)/*paidikai* (pl.) boy-love, darling; *paidikos* (adj.) love of boys.

paidophilein to love boys.

paidophiles (adj.) the quality of a boy's capacity to induce love; a boy in full flower.

pais (sing.)/*paides* (pl.) a child of either age, more frequently a boy; occasionally a young male; a slave; *paidiska* (sing.)/*paidiskai* (pl.) young girl, maidens or young female slaves.

pallake whore or concubine.

partheneiosa (adj.) maidenly.

parthenia virginity.

parthenios (adj.) lit. of a girl or maiden; virginal; unsullied.

parthenos girl or virgin; unmarried female.

208

parthenike girl or virgin; unmarried female.

peitho persuasion. *Peitho*, personification of Persuasion.

philein to love, to be in love with, to care deeply for; to kiss.

philerastos amorous; also dear to lovers.

philia friendship, friendly affection.

philommeides laughter-loving; a common epithet for Aphrodite.

philopais loving boys; preference for anal sex.

philos (masc.)/*phila* (fem.) dear one, beloved; the word suggests tenderness and love as well as meaning friend or kin; *philoi* (pl.).

philotes (pl.) shared love, affection, friendship.

physis essential nature; soul.

polis (sing.)/*poleis* (pl.) the community and territorial entity under its control in the historical Greek world; often but not accurately translated as 'city state'.

porne female prostitute; harlot; *pornos* male prostitute; *porneion* a low class brothel.

porneia prostitution.

pornikos sexually arousing, lascivious.

pothos (sing.)/*pothoi* (pl.) desire, longing, yearning.

proskinein to thrust or screw.

psyche the soul.

puge (sing.)/*pugae* (pl.) rump, buttock; arse.

pugizdein to bugger.

pupulus (masc.)/*pupula* (fem.) 'boy-pet', 'girl-pet'.

sophos wisdom.

sophrosyne self-control; good conduct.

symposium (sing.)/*symposia* (pl.) male drinking party.

techne art, skill; a trade, sometimes prostitution.

terpsis pleasure, mostly sexual; *terpnon* the object of pleasure; *terpein* to take delight in.

thalamos marriage-bed, bedchamber.

thiasos a female group, often social, sometimes religious.

time possessions, status, and the right to compensation of a Greek aristocrat. *atimos* devoid of *time*, without honour, worthless.

thumos the heart as the seat of emotions, thoughts, passions; also soul or spirit.

tribas tribad; tribadism involved women rubbing their genitals together in a parody of conventional sexual intercourse; female lover of women; a term of contempt used by male writers. Term also used in Latin.

xenos (sing.)/*xenoi* (pl.) stranger; guest; host; *xeneia* guest-friendship.

zona cf. Roman terms.

Roman terms

adulterium adultery; a punishable crime at Rome.

amans (sing.)/*amantes* (pl.) loving; lover.

amare to love.

amator (sing.)/*amatores* (pl.) lover; in the pl. it denotes lovers and regular clients of a prostitute.

amicus (masc.)/*amica* (fem.) male friend; female friend; girlfriend; concubine, mistress or courtesan; *amici* (pl.)/*amicae* (sing.).

amor love: for one's parents, friends, and also in an amatory sense. Also an intense and passionate desire or lust. In the pl. (*amores*) it can depict the object of desire itself. *Amor*, personified amor (Roman god of love; also *Cupido*); equivalent to the Greek *Eros*.

amores pl. of *amor*, translated in the sing. as beloved; (pl.) love-affairs.

anima the soul, the life-force.

animus spirit, the heart, conscious self-drive.

ardor flame, fire, impatience, desire; *ardens* burning.

ars (sing.)/*artes* (pl.) skill, talent.

as (sing.)/*asses* (pl.) the lowest unit of Roman currency; *denarius* (ten *asses*); *sestertius*/*sesterces* (pl.) between 2.5–4 *asses*.

basia (pl.) kisses.

basiare to kiss.

bellus (masc.)/*bella* (fem.)/*bellum* (neut.) beautiful; *bellus homo* (sing.)/*belli homines* (pl.) one of the beautiful people, endowed with good luck, looks.

blanditia (sing.)/*blanditiae* (pl.) word(s) of love, flattery, allurement, seduction.

blandus (masc.)/*blanda* (fem.) coaxing, endearing.

bonus (masc.)/*bona* (fem.)/*bonum* (neut.) good; *bona* (neut. pl.) good things (in contrast to *mala*).

bubinare to defile with menstral blood.

candidus (masc.)/*candida* (fem.) shining; fair; the overall glow of beauty; similar to the Greek *dia*.

carmen (sing.)/*carmina* (pl.) poem; song; chant, spell.

carus (masc.)/*cara* (fem.) dear, precious, esteemed.

castus (masc.)/*casta* (fem.) chaste, morally pure, unpolluted.

cinaedus (sing.)/*cinaedi* (pl.) a submissive male; one who submits to anal penetration; generic term for effeminate male.

coitus polite term for sexual intercourse.

concubinus bed-boy.

concubitus lit. 'lying together', or 'sharing a bed'; the act of sexual intercourse.

coniunx spouse; applies to both husband and wife (lit. 'conjoined').

cultus (masc.)/*culta* (fem.) (1) adj.: refined; one who is cultivated and generally well educated. The word also indicates one who dresses well, one who is glamorous; (2) noun: refinement; sophistication; grooming.

culus (sing.)/*culi* (pl.) anus, arsehole.

cunnus (sing.)/*cunni* (pl.) cunt.

cupido lust, desire. *Cupido*, personified Cupid, equivalent of *Amor*.

cupidus (masc.)/*cupida* (fem.) yearning, longing, desiring, loving; also passionate and lustful.

cura burden; also care, trouble, concern; love.

decus honour.

dedecus disgrace, dishonour, shame, infamy; that which causes shame, a shameful deed; moral dishonour.

delicatus (*delicati*, pl. masc.)/*delicata* (fem.) one who is a giver of pleasure, a charmer; also voluptuous and wanton; soft and delicate.

deliciae (pl.) darling, sweetheart, beloved; delights; life of indulgence and luxury.

desiderium a longing, an intense desire.

diligere to cherish, to esteem highly, to love.

dolor grief, angst.

domina mistress of slaves; mistress of the house. In Latin love elegy the term came to denote one's mistress.

dominus master, lord, especially master of the house and slaves.

domus the house and all household members.

drauci (pl.) bum-boys.

exoletus (sing.)/*exoleti* (pl.) lit. adult males; used for passive whores.

fama reputation; fame and related concepts; also gossip, rumour, report, what people say about you.

familia family; household; household slaves.

fascinum (sing.)/*fascina* (pl.) penis symbol hung round the necks of children for protection; instrument used in witchcraft; the evil eye; dildo.

fellare to suck; to suck cock.

fellatio Act of taking a penis in the mouth; oral intercourse.

fellator (masc.)/*fellatrix* (fem.) cock-sucker.

femina generic term for woman.

fides faithfulness, trust, good faith. *fidelis* (masc./fem.) faithful. *fidus* (masc.)/*fida* (fem.) true, loyal, dependable.

flagitium outrageous activity; a shameful action done in passion.

forma physical appearance, shape; beauty.

formosus (masc.)/*formosa* (fem.) beautiful; denoting form, shape and sexuality.

fossa pit; vagina or anus.

furor a madness, fury or raging desire.

futuere to fuck.

fututor male fucker; *fututrix* female fucker.

gaudium (sing.)/*gaudia* (pl.) joy, delight.

gens (sing.)/*gentes* (pl.) a family line.

glaber (sing.)/*glabri* (pl.) a male smooth, devoid of hair.

hymenaeus wedding-song. *Hymenaeus*, god of marriage.

ilia (pl.) the loins; flanks.

improbus (masc.)/*improba* (fem.)/*improbum* (neut.)   antonym of *probus*; *improbitas* antonym of *probitas*.

impurus (masc.)/*impure* (fem.)   impure; defiled.

incensus (masc.)/*incensa* (fem.)   set on fire, inflamed, burning (with passion).

infamia   infamy; ill-repute, bad reputation.

inguen (sing.)/*inguina* (pl.)   the groin; used euphemistically to denote the penis and the vagina.

irrumare   to orally penetrate in a forceful manner.

irrumatio   oral rape.

iucundus (masc.)/*iucunda* (fem.)   delightful, pleasant.

iungere   to join in marriage; intercourse.

ius (sing.)/*iura* (pl.)   law; bond.

iuvenis   a young man in his prime.

labella (neut, pl., dim. of *labia* [lips])   little lips.

latus (sing.)/*latera* (pl.)   flank; loins (pl.).

leno (masc.)/*lena* (fem.)   pimp.

lex (sing.)/*leges* (pl.)   laws; equivalent of the Greek, *nomos*.

libido (sing.)/*libidines* (pl.)/*libidinosus* (masc. adj.)/*libidinosa* (fem. adj.)   lust or lustfulness; also inordinate or unlawful desire or wantonness; desires.

lingere   to lick.

ludere   to play, to have fun, to frolic; also to sport in a sensual or sexual sense.

ludus (sing.)/*ludi* (pl.)   game, diversion, pastime; delight of a sexual nature; alternative form *lusus*.

lupanar (sing.)/*lupanaria* (pl.)   brothel.

luxuria   indulgence in excess; luxury.

maiestas   treason.

malum (sing.)/*mala* (pl.)   evil, misfortune; equivalent of the Greek, *kakon*.

marita   married woman, wife.

maritus (sing.)/*mariti* (pl.)   husband.

mater   mother.

matrona (sing.)/*matronae* (pl.)   a respectable married woman, frequently denoting those with children.

media (neut. pl.)   the groin.

membrum (sing.)/*membra* (pl.)   a limb, a part of the body; the penis.

mentula   the usual obscene term for the male organ.

meretrix (sing.)/*meretrices* (pl.)   female prostitute.

moechus (masc.)/*moecha* (fem.)   lover; also a fornicator or adulterer.

mollis (sing.)/*molles* (pl.)   soft; delicate and gentle but also effeminate and unmanly; *mollitia* (noun) softness; effeminacy.

mores   moral standards, established customs and precedent.

mulier (sing.)/*mulieres* (pl.)   woman (sometimes used of a wife); *muliebris* womanly, the quality one expects in a woman.

munditia   elegance.

nequitia   wantonness; moral worthlessness.

nervus tendon, sinew; penis.

nupta bride.

osculatio (sing.)/*osculationes* (pl.) a kissing/kissings.

paelex a mistress who replaces a wife; rival.

pater familias the male head of a Roman household.

pathicus a male who takes a penis in his mouth; a submissive male.

patria potestas the power of the *pater familias* over all members, free and slave, within the family unit.

pedicare to penetrate anally; to bugger.

penis the penis, a milder term than *mentula*.

permingere to urinate over; to pollute; to sexually violate (especially via ejaculation into the body).

pius (masc.)/*pia* (fem.) godly; loyal; having respect for the gods, one's parents and country.

pravus (masc.)/*prava* (fem.)/*pravum* (neut.) depraved; deformed.

probus (masc.)/*proba* (fem.) respectable, upright; *probitas* upright character.

prostituere to put on display; to prostitute oneself.

prurire to itch; to long for; to display wantonly; *pruriens* (adj.) generating an itch.

pudicitia a sense of shame; modesty; chastity. *pudicus* (masc.)/*pudica* (fem.) modest.

pudor a sense of shame. *Pudor*, personified Sense of Shame.

puella (sing.)/*puellae* (pl.) girl; standard word in the repertoire of the elegiac poet.

puer (sing.)/*pueri* (pl.) child, most often a boy; *puerilis* (adj.) boyish, childish.

pulc(h)er (masc.)/*pulc(h)ra* (fem.) handsome, beautiful. *pulcerrima* utterly irresistible.

pulc(h)ritudo physical beauty.

purus pure, chaste, undefiled.

rabies frenzy.

rapere to carry off, to carry off by force; to rape.

rusticitas country ways; lack of sophistication (as opposed to *urbanitas*).

scortum (sing.)/*scorta* (pl.) leather; tart, slut, whore, prostitute; *scorteum* made of leather; a sex toy or dildo.

sedere lit. to sit; often in regard to prostitution.

sponsa a betrothed girl.

stola a long garment worn by married women.

stuprum (sing.)/*stupra* (pl.) sexual depravity. A powerful word in the Roman sexual vocabulary, it originally meant disgrace in a general sense but came to mean abominable sexual disgrace.

superbia arrogance; male bravado.

taberna (sing.)/*tabernae* (pl.) tavern, a place of low repute.

t(h)alassio nuptial cry.

tangere to touch; to touch in a sexual sense.

tener (masc.)/*tenera* (fem.)/*tenerum* (neut.)   tender, delicate, gentle.

thalamus   bridal-chamber, marriage-bed.

toga   garment worn by Roman males upon reaching manhood; it was also required to be worn by female prostitutes when appearing in public.

tribas   cf. Greek terms.

turpis (sing.)/*turpia* (pl.)   shameful, disgraceful.

turpitudo   shamefulness; ugliness, baseness.

univira   a woman who has had only one husband; who has known only one man.

urbanitas   ways of the city (i.e. Rome); sophistication.

uxor   wife.

veneres   the gifts of Venus; sexual allure.

venus   the desire for sex; the sex drive. *Venus*, the goddess of desire.

venustas   sensuality; the qualities of Venus; inner charm and grace; *venustus* a male endowed with such qualities; *venusta* (fem.).

verecunda (sing.)/*verecundae* (pl.)   shy (girl or woman), one who possesses a sense of shame, modest, bashful.

vir (sing.)/*viri* (pl.)   man. (i) an adult man; (ii) a true man (one possessed of *virtus*); (iii) a husband.

virginitas   virginity, maidenhood.

virgo (sing.)/*virgines* (pl.)   virgin, maiden.

virtus (sing.)/*virtutes* (pl.)   manliness. The concept embodies all aspects of manliness, courage, excellence, as well as the ability to be and act like a man.

vis   violence; rape.

vitium   vice; something needing to be pruned.

voluptas (sing.)/*voluptates* (pl.)   sensual encounter; pleasure.

zona   belt worn by a girl, symbolising her virginity.

ALPHABETICAL AUTHOR
INDEX OF PASSAGES

Author	Reference	Chapter	Passage/Number
Achilles Tatius	*Leuk-Kleit* 2.35–38	5	91
Aelian	Misc 3.10	5	94
	Misc 3.12	5	94
Aeschines	*Tim* 1.21	4	77
Alcaeus	*Fr.* 298.4–24	6	103
Alcman	*Fr.* 59a	1	11
Anacreon	*Fr.* 358	5	99
	Fr. 413	1	14
	Fr. 444	5	88
Anonymous	*AP* 11.272	7	135
	AP 12.96	2	26
Apuleius	*Met* 4.28	2	23
Archilochus	*Fr.* 196a	6	113
Aristophanes	*Acharnians* 271–76	6	109
	Clouds 1010–1019	2	32
	Knights 1284–87	7	129
	Lysistrata 107–09	8	139
	Peace 894–904	6	115
	Wasps 1280–83	7	130
	Fr. 141	4	61 n. 2
Ps-Aristotle	*Prob* 4.26	5	84

Inscriptions and Papyri

BIBLIOGRAPHY

J. N. Adams, *The Latin Sexual Vocabulary* (Baltimore, 1982).

J. N. Adams, 'Words for 'Prostitute' in Latin', *Rheinisches Museum für Philologie* 126 (1983), 321–58.

W. S. Anderson, *Ovid's Metamorphoses: Books 6–10* (Oklahoma, 1972).

M. B. Arthur, 'The Tortoise and the Mirror: Erinna *PSI* 1090', *Classical World* 74 (1980), 53–65.

M. B. Arthur, 'Cultural Strategies in Hesiod's *Theogony*: Law, Family, Society', *Arethusa* 15 (1982), 63–82.

D. F. S. Bailey, '*O Rem Ridiculam!*', *Classical Philology* 71 (1976), 348.

D. F. S. Bailey, *Martial. Epigrams*, 3 vols (Cambridge, Mass., 1993).

D. Bain, 'Six Greek Verbs of Sexual Congress', *Classical Quarterly* 41 (1991), 51–77.

B. Baldwin, 'Rufinus, *AP* v 60', *Journal of Hellenic Studies* 100 (1980), 182–84.

A.-J. Ball, 'Capturing a Bride: Marriage Practices in Classical Sparta', *Ancient History* 19 (1989), 75–81.

R. J. Ball, *Tibullus the Elegist: A Critical Survey* (Germany, 1983).

S. Barnard, 'Hellenistic Women Poets', *Classical Journal* 73 (1978), 204–13.

W. S. Barrett, *Euripides Hippolytos* (Oxford, 1964).

J. Barsby, *Ovid Amores I* (Bristol, 1973).

M. Beard and J. Henderson, 'With this Body, I Thee Worship: Sacred Prostitution in Antiquity', in: M. Wyke (ed.), *Gender and the Body in Ancient Mediterranean* (Oxford, 1998), 56–79.

C. Bennett, 'Concerning "Sappho Schoolmistress"', *Transactions and Proceedings of the American Philological Association* 124 (1994), 345–47.

W. Berg, 'Pandora: The Pathology of a Creation Myth', *Fabula* 17 (1976), 1–25.

P. Bing and R. Cohen, *Games of Venus: An Anthology of Greek and Roman Erotic Verse from Sappho to Ovid* (London, 1991).

S. Blundell, *Women in Ancient Greece* (London, 1995).

J. Boardman and E. La Rocca, *Eros in Greece* (London, 1978).

J. Booth, *Latin Love Elegy: A Companion to the Translations of Guy Lee* (Bristol, 1995).

J. Boswell, *Christianity, Social Tolerance and Homosexuality* (Chicago, 1980).

E. L. Bowie, 'Early Greek Elegy, Symposium and Public Festival', *Journal of Hellenic Studies* 106 (1986), 13–25.

C. M. Bowra, 'Erinna's Lament for Baucis', in: J. D. Denniston and D. L. Page (eds), *Greek Poetry and Life* (Oxford, 1936), 325–42.

J. Bremmer, 'An Enigmatic Indo-European Rite: Paederasty', *Arethusa* 13 (1980), 281–98.

F. Brenk, 'Hesiod: How Much a Male Chauvinist?', *Classical Bulletin* 49 (1973), 73–76.

D. F. Bright, *Haec Mihi Fingebam: Tibullus in His World* (Leiden, 1978).

B. J. Brooten, *Love Between Women: Early Christian Responses to Female Homoeroticism* (Chicago, 1996).

T. R. S. Broughton, *The Magistrates of the Roman Republic*, Vol. 1 (Atlanta, 1951, 1986).

C. G. Brown, 'Iambos', in: D. E. Gerber (ed.), *A Companion to the Greek Lyric Poets* (Leiden, 1997), 43–69.

R. D. Brown, *Lucretius on Love and Sex. A Commentary on De Rerum Natura IV.1030–1287* (New York, 1987).

S. Brown, 'Feminist Research in Archaeology: What Does it Mean? Why is it Taking So Long?', in: N. S. Rabinowitz and A. Richlin (eds), *Feminist Theory and the Classics* (London, 1993), 233–71.

A. Burnett, 'Desire and Memory (Sappho Frag. 94)', *Classical Philology* 74 (1979), 16–27.

S. M. Burnstein, *The Hellenistic Age from the Battle of Ipsos to the Death of Kleopatra VII* (New York, 1985).

L. Cahoon, 'The Bed as Battlefield: Erotic Conquest and Military Metaphor in Ovid's *Amores*', *Transactions and Proceedings of the American Philological Association* 118 (1988), 293–307.

F. Cairns, *Tibullus: A Hellenistic Poet at Rome* (Cambridge, 1979).

C. Calame, *The Poetics of Eros in Ancient Greece*, trans. J. Lloyd (Princeton, 1999).

A. Cameron, 'Asclepiades' Girl Friends', in: H. P. Foley (ed.), *Reflections of Women in Antiquity* (New York, 1981a), 275–302.

A. Cameron, 'Notes on the Erotic Art of Rufinus', *Greek, Roman and Byzantine Studies* 22 (1981b), 179–86.

A. Cameron, 'Strato and Rufinus', *Classical Quarterly* 32 (1982), 162–73.

D. A. Campbell, *Greek Lyric*. Vols. I–IV (Cambridge, Mass., 1992–1994).

W. A. Camps, *Propertius Elegies. Books I–II* (Cambridge, 1961–1967).

E. Cantarella, *Pandora's Daughters*, trans. M. B. Fant. (Baltimore, 1987).

E. Cantarella, *Bisexuality in the Ancient World*, trans. C. Ó Cuilleanáin (London, 1992).

J. S. Carnes, 'The Myth Which is Not One: Construction of Discourse in Plato's *Symposium*', in: D. H. J. Larmour, P. A. Miller and C. Platter (eds), *Rethinking Sexuality: Foucault and Classical Antiquity* (Princeton, 1998), 104–21.

R. W. Carrubba, 'A Study of Horace's Eighth and Twelfth Epodes.' *Latomus* 24 (1965), 591–98.

A. Carson, *Eros the Bittersweet: An Essay* (Princeton, 1986).

P. Cartledge, 'The Politics of Spartan Pederasty', *Proceedings of the Cambridge Philological Society* 207 (1981), 17–36.

P. Cartledge, 'Spartan Wives: Liberation or Licence?', *Spartan Reflections* (London, 2001), 106–126.

W. Castle, 'Observations on Sappho's *To Aphrodite*', *Transactions and Proceedings of the American Philological Association* 89 (1958), 66–76.

D. L. Clayman, 'Horace's Epodes VIII and XII: More than Clever Obscenity?', *Classical World* 69 (1975), 55–61.

D. Cohen, 'The Athenian Law of Adultery', *Revue Internationale des Droits de l'Antiquite* 31 (1984), 147–65.

D. Cohen, *Law, Sexuality, and Society: The Enforcement of Morals in Classical Athens* (Cambridge, 1991).

S. G. Cole, 'Greek Sanctions Against Sexual Assault', *Classical Philology* 79 (1984), 97–113.

K. M. Coleman, 'Fatal Charades: Roman Executions Staged as Mythological Enactments', *Journal of Hellenic Studies* 80 (1990), 44–73.

G. B. Conte, *Latin Literature: A History*, trans. J. B. Solodow (Baltimore, 1994).

F. O. Copley, 'The Structure of Catullus C.51 and the Problem of the *Otium*-Strophe', *Grazer Beitrage* 2 (1994), 25–37.

M. D. Corte, *Loves and Lovers in Ancient Pompeii*, trans. A.W. Van Buren (Salerno, 1976).

N. B. Crowther, 'Male "Beauty" Contests in Greece: The Euandria and Euexia', *L'Antiquitie Classique* 54 (1985), 285–91.

P. Culham, 'Ten Years After Pomeroy: Studies of the Image and Reality of Women in Antiquity', in: M. B. Skinner (ed.), *Rescuing Creusa: New Methodological Approaches to Women in Antiquity*, *Helios* 13 (1986), 9–30.

I. C. Cunningham, *Herodas. Mimiambi* (Oxford, 1971).

L. C. Curran, 'Gellius and the Lover's Pallor: A Note on Catullus 80', *Arion* 5 (1966), 24–27.

L. C. Curran, 'Rape and Rape Victims in the *Metamorphoses*', *Arethusa* 11 (1978), 213–41.

M. S. Cyrino, in: *Pandora's Jar: Lovesickness in Early Greek Poetry* (Lanham, 1995).

M. S. Cyrino, 'Heroes in D(u)ress: Transvestism and Power in the Myths of Herakles and Achilles', *Arethusa* 31 (1998), 207–42.

A. Dalzell, *The Criticism of Didactic Poetry: Essays on Lucretius, Virgil, and Ovid* (Toronto, 1996).

G. Davenport, *Archilochos, P. Colon. 7511* (1995), http://www.uky.edu/AS/Classics/archiloch.html

J. Davidson, *Courtesans and Fishcakes* (London, 1998).

A. J. Davison, 'A Marriage Song of Sappho's (S104 and 105)', in: *From Archilochus to Pindar: Papers on Greek Literature from the Archaic Period* (London, 1968), 242–46.

S. Deacy, 'The Vulnerability of Athena: *Parthenoi* and Rape in Greek Myth', in: S. Deacy and K. F. Pierce (eds), *Rape in Antiquity: Sexual Violence in the Greek and Roman Worlds* (London, 1997), 43–63.

J. de Luce, '"O for a Thousand Tongues to Sing": A Footnote on Metamorphosis, Silence, and Power', in: M. DeForest (ed.), *Woman's Power, Man's Game: Essays on Classical Antiquity in Honor of Joy K. King* (Wavconda, Illinois 1993), 305–21.

G. Devereux, 'Greek Pseudo-Homosexuality and the "Greek Miracle"' *Symbolae Osloenses* 42 (1968), 69–92.

G. Devereux, 'The Nature of Sappho's Seizure in *Fr.* 31 LP as Evidence of Her Inversion', *Classical Quarterly* 20 (1970), 17–31.

A. R. de Verger, 'Erotic Language in Pliny, *Ep.* VII 5', *Glotta* 74 (1997–1998), 114–16.

S. Dixon, *The Roman Mother* (London, 1988).

S. Dixon, *The Roman Family* (Baltimore, 1992).

K. J. Dover, *Aristophanes: Clouds* (Oxford, 1964).

K. J. Dover, 'Classical Greek Attitudes to Sexual Behaviour', *Arethusa* 6 (1973), 59–73.

K. J. Dover, *Greek Homosexuality* (London, 1978).

K. J. Dover, *Plato: Symposium* (Cambridge, 1980).

K. J. Dover, 'Two Women of Samos', in: M. C. Nussbaum and J. Sihvola (eds), *The Sleep of Reason. Erotic Experience and Sexual Ethics in Ancient Greece and Rome* (Chicago, 2002), 222–28.

P. duBois, 'Sappho and Helen', in: J. Peradotto and J. P. Sullivan (eds), *Women in the Ancient World: The Arethusa Papers* (New York, 1984), 95–105.

P. duBois, *Sowing the Body: Psychoanalysis and the Ancient Representations of Women* (Chicago, 1988).

P. duBois, *Sappho is Burning* (Chicago, 1995).

J. D. Duff, *T. Lucreti Cari. De Rerum Natura Liber Primus* (Cambridge, 1958).

R. Duncan-Jones, *The Economy of the Roman Empire*, 2nd ed. (Cambridge, 1982).

J. M. Edmonds, *Elegy and Iambus, with the Anacreontea*, 2 vols. (Cambridge, Mass., 1954).

M. L. Edwards, 'The Cultural Context of Deformity in the Ancient Greek World: "Let There Be A Law That No Deformed Child Shall Be Reared"', *Ancient History Bulletin* 10 (1996), 79–92.

A. G. Elliott, '*Amores* 1.5: The Afternoon of a Poet', in: C. Deroux (ed.), *Studies in Latin Literature and Roman History*, Vol. I (Brussels, 1979), 349–55.

E. Fantham, '*Stuprum*: Public Attitudes and Penalties for Sexual Offences in Republican Rome', *Echos du monde Classique* 35 (1991), 267–91.

E. Fantham, H. P. Foley, N. B. Kampen, S. B. Pomeroy and H. A. Shapiro, *Women in the Classical World* (Oxford, 1994).

C. A. Faraone, 'Aphrodite's KESTOS and Apples for Atalanta: Aphrodisiacs in Early Greek Myth and Ritual', *Phoenix* 44 (1990), 219–43.

C. A. Faraone, 'Sex and Power: Male-Targeting Aphrodisiacs in the Greek Magical Tradition', *Helios* 19 (1992), 92–103.

C. A. Faraone, *Ancient Greek Love Magic* (Cambridge, Mass., 1999).

P. Fedeli, *Catullus' Carmen 61* (Amsterdam, 1983).

J. Ferguson, *Juvenal. The Satires* (New York, 1979).

J. Ferguson, *Catullus* (Lawrence, KA., 1985).

W. Fitzgerald, 'Power and Impotence in Horace's Epodes', *Ramus* 17 (1988), 176–91.

H. P. Foley, 'Marriage and Sacrifice in Euripides' *Iphigenia in Aulis*', *Arethusa* 15 (1982), 159–180.

F. N. Forsyth, 'The Allurement Scene: A Typical Pattern in Greek Oral Epic', *California Studies in Classical Antiquity* 12 (1981), 107–20.

P. Y. Forsyth, 'The Gellius Cycle of Catullus', *Classical Journal* 68 (1972), 175–77.

B. O. Foster, 'Notes on the Symbolism of the Apple in Classical Antiquity', *Harvard Studies in Classical Philology* 10 (1899), 39–55.

M. Foucault, *The History of Sexuality*, Vol. 1, 'An Introduction', trans. R. Hurley (Harmondsworth, 1978).

M. Foucault, *The History of Sexuality*, Vol. 2, 'The Use of Pleasure', trans. R. Hurley (Harmondsworth, 1985).

M. Foucault, *The History of Sexuality*, Vol. 3, 'The Care of the Self', trans. R. Hurley (Harmondsworth, 1986).

L. Foxhall, 'Pandora Unbound: A Feminist Critique of Foucault's *History of Sexuality*', in: D. H. J. Larmour, P. A. Miller and C. Platter (eds), *Rethinking Sexuality: Foucault and Classical Antiquity* (Princeton, 1998), 122–37.

R. I. Frank, 'Catullus 51: *Otium* Versus *Virtus*', *Transactions and Proceedings of the American Philological Association* 99 (1968), 233–39.

E. A. Fredricksmeyer, 'On the Unity of Catullus 51', *Transactions and Proceedings of the American Philological Association* 96 (1965), 153–63.

P. Friedrich, *The Meaning of Aphrodite* (Chicago, 1978).

C. Fuqua, 'Tyrtaeus and the Cult of Heroes,' *Greek, Roman and Byzantine Studies* 22 (1981), 215–26.

T. Gantz, *Early Greek Myth: A Guide to Literary and Artistic Sources* (Baltimore, 1996).

R. Garland, *The Greek Way of Life: From Conception to Old Age* (Ithaca, 1990).

R. Garland, 'The Mockery of the Deformed and Disabled in Graeco-Roman Culture', in: S. Jäkel and A. Timonen (eds), *Laughter Down the Centuries*, Vol. 1, (Turku, 1994), 71–84.

S. Gaselee, *Achilles Tatius*, Revised ed. (Cambridge, Mass., 1969).

S. Georgoudi, 'Creating a Myth of Matriarchy', in: P. S. Pantel (ed.), *A History of Women in the West: From Ancient Goddesses to Christian Saints*, trans. A. Goldhammer (Cambridge, Mass., 1992).

D. E. Gerber, 'The Female Breast in Greek Erotic Literature', *Arethusa* 11 (1978), 203–12.

D. E. Gerber (ed.), *A Companion to the Greek Lyric Poets* (Leiden, 1997).

D. E. Gerber, *Greek Elegiac Poetry From the Seventh to the Fifth Centuries BC* (Cambridge, Mass., 1999a).

D. E. Gerber, *Greek Iambic Poetry From the Seventh to the Fifth Centuries BC* (Cambridge, Mass., 1999b).

A. Giacomelli, 'The Justice of Aphrodite in Sappho Fr. 1', *Transactions and Proceedings of the American Philological Association* 110 (1980), 135–42.

J. Glenn, 'Pandora and Eve: Sex as the Root of all Evils', *Classical World* 71 (1977), 179–85.

J. Godwin, *Catullus: Poems 61–68* (Wiltshire, 1995).

M. Golden, 'Slavery and Homosexuality at Athens', *Phoenix* 38 (1984), 308–24.

M. Golden, 'Pais, "Child" and "Slave"' *Acta Classica* 54 (1985), 91–104.

M. Golden, *Children and Childhood in Classical Athens* (Baltimore, 1990).

M. Golden, *Sport and Society in Ancient Greece* (Cambridge, 1998).

S. Goldhill, *Review of Feminist Theory and the Classics*, Bryn Mawr Classical Review 94.01.15, http://ccat.sas.upenn.edu/bmcr/1994/94.01.15.html

M. Goodman, 'Incest', in: S. Hornblower and A. Spawforth (eds), *The Oxford Classical Dictionary*, 3rd ed (Oxford, 1996).

G. P. Goold, 'The Cause of Ovid's Exile', *Illinois Classical Studies* 8 (1983), 994–107.

G. P. Goold, *Propertius. Elegies* (Cambridge, Mass., 1990).

A. S. F. Gow, *Theocritus*, 2 vols (Cambridge, 1952).

A. S. F. Gow and D. L. Page, *The Greek Anthology: Hellenistic Epigrams*, 2 vols (Cambridge, 1965).

A. S. F. Gow and D. L. Page, *The Greek Anthology: The Garland of Philip and Some Contemporary Epigrams*, 2 vols (Cambridge, 1968).

M. Gray-Fow, 'Pederasty, the Scantinian Law, and the Roman Army', *Journal of Psychohistory* 13 (1986), 449–60.

P. Green, 'Ars Gratia Cultus: Ovid and Beautification', *American Journal of Philology* 100 (1979), 381–92.

P. Green, 1994. *Ovid: The Poems of Exile* (Harmondsworth, 1994).

E. Greene, 'Re-figuring the Feminine Voice: Catullus Translating Sappho', *Arethusa* 32 (1999), 1–18.

R. D. Griffith, 'In Praise of the Bride: Sappho Fr.105 (A) L-P, Voight', *Transactions and Proceedings of the American Philological Association* 119 (1989), 55–61.

C. B. Gulick, *Athenaeus: The Deipnosophists*, Vol. II, Vol. IV, Vol. VI (Cambridge, Mass., 1928–1957).

J. P. Hallett, 'Sappho and Her Social Context: Sense and Sensuality', *Signs* 4 (1979), 447–64.

J. P. Hallett, 'The Role of Women in Roman Elegy', in: J. Peradotto and J. P. Sullivan (eds), *Women in the Ancient World: The Arethusa Papers* (Albany, 1984a).

J. P. Hallett, *Fathers and Daughters in Roman Society: Women and the Elite Family* (Princeton, 1984b).

J. P. Hallett, 'Female Homoeroticism and the Denial of Roman Reality in Latin Literature', *Yale Journal of Criticism* 3, (1989), 209–27.

S. Halliwell, 'Aristophanic Sex: The Erotics of Shamelessness', in: M. C. Nussbaum and J. Sihvola (eds), *The Sleep of Reason. Erotic Experience and Sexual Ethics in Ancient Greece and Rome* (Chicago, 2002), 120–42.

D. M. Halperin, 'Sex Before Sexuality: Pederasty, Politics, and Power in Classical Athens', in: G. Chauncey, M. Duberman and M. Vicinus (eds), *Hidden From History: Reclaiming the Gay and Lesbian Past* (Harmondsworth, 1989), 37–53.

D. M. Halperin, *One Hundred Years of Homosexuality and Other Essays on Greek Love* (London, 1990).

D. M. Halperin, J. J. Winkler and F. I. Zeitlin (eds), *Before Sexuality: The Construction of Erotic Experience in the Ancient Greek World* (Princeton, 1990).

E. M. Harris, 'Did the Athenians Regard Seduction as a Worse Crime than Rape?', *Classical Quarterly* 40 (1990), 370–77.

A. R. W. Harrison, *The Law of Athens*, Vol. 1 (Oxford, 1968).

W. C. Helmbold, E. L. Minar and F. H. Sandbach (trans.), *Plutarch's Moralia*, Vol. 9 (Cambridge, Mass., 1961).

A. A. R. Henderson, *P. Ovidi Nasonis. Remedia Amoris* (Edinburgh, 1979).

J. Henderson, 'The Cologne Epode and the Conventions of Early Greek Erotic Poetry', *Arethusa* 9 (1976), 159–79.

J. Henderson, *Aristophanes. Lysistrata* (Oxford, 1987).

J. Henderson, *The Maculate Muse: Obscene Language in Attic Poetry*, 2nd ed. (Oxford, 1991).

C. Henriksén, *Martial, Book IX. A Commentary*, Vol. 1 (Uppsala, 1998).

M. Henry, *Prisoner of History: Aspasia of Miletus and Her Biographical Tradition* (Oxford, 1994).

T. W. Hillard, 'The Sisters of Clodius Again', *Latomus* 32 (1973), 505–14.

R. J. Hoffman, 'Some Cultural Aspects of Greek Male Homosexuality', *Journal of Homosexuality* 5 (1980), 217–26.

A. S. Hollis, *Ovid. Ars Amatoria. Book I* (Oxford, 1980).

N. Holzberg, *The Ancient Novel: An Introduction*, trans. C. Jackson-Holzberg (London, 1986).

N. Holzberg, *Ovid. The Poet and His Work*, trans. G. M. Goshgarian (London, 2002).

K. Hopkins, 'The Age of Roman Girls at Marriage', *Population Studies* 18 (1965), 309–27.

S. Hornblower and A. Spawforth (eds), *The Oxford Classical Dictionary*, 3rd ed. (Oxford, 1996).

L. J. J. Houdijk and P. J. J. Vanderbroeck, 'Old Age and Sex in the Ancient Greek World', *WZ Rostock* 36 (1987), 57–61.

A. E. Housman, 'Praefanda', *Hermes* 66 (1931), 404–12.

P. Howell, *A Commentary on Book One of the Epigrams of Martial* (London, 1980).

T. K. Hubbard, *Homosexuality in Greece and Rome: A Sourcebook of Basic Documents* (Berkeley, 2003).

R. Hunter, *Theocritus and the Archaeology of Greek Poetry* (Cambridge, 1996).

M. E. Irwin, 'Roses and the Bodies of Beautiful Women', *Echos du Monde Classique* 13 (1994), 1–13.

R. C. Jensen, '"Otium Catulli tibi molestum est" Catullus 51', *Rheinisches Museum für Philologie* 113 (1970), 197–204.

C. Johns, *Sex or Symbol? Erotic Images of Greece and Rome* (Austin, 1982).

M. M. Johnson, 'Martial and Domitian's Moral Reform', *Prudentia* 29 (1997), 24–70.

M. M. Johnson and T. Ryan, 'Catullus' Epithalamia: Translation and Commentary. Part I: Catullus 61 – The Epithalamium of Junia and Manlius', *Classicum* 24 (1998), 36–46.

R. Just, *Women in Athenian Law and Life* (London, 1989).

N. M. Kay, *Martial Book XI: A Commentary* (London, 1985).

E. J. Kenney, *Apuleius. Cupid and Psyche* (Cambridge, 1990).

W. C. A. Ker, *Martial. Epigrams*, 2 vols (Cambridge, Mass., 1978).

E. Keuls, *The Reign of the Phallus: Sexual Politics in Ancient Athens*, 2nd ed. (Berkeley, 1985).

D. A. Kidd, 'The Unity of Catullus 51', *Journal of the Australian Universities Language and Literature Association* 20 (1963), 298–308.

M. Kilmer, 'Genital Phobia and Depilation', *Journal of Hellenic Studies* 102 (1982), 104–12.

M. Kilmer, *Greek Erotica on Attic Red-Figure Vases* (London, 1993).

A. O. Koloski-Ostrow and C. L. Lyons (eds), *Naked Truths: Women, Sexuality and Gender in Classical Art and Archaeology* (London, 1997).

G. L. Koniaris, 'On Sappho, Fr. 31 (L-P)', *Philologus* 112 (1968), 173–86.

D. Konstan, 'Introduction', in: D. Konstan (ed.), *Documenting Gender*, *Helios* 19 (1992), 5–6.

D. Konstan, 'Greek Friendship', *American Journal of Philology* 117 (1996), 71–94.

D. Konstan, *Friendship in the Classical World* (Cambridge, 1997).

W. A. Krenkel, 'Fellatio and Irrumatio', *WZ Rostock* 29 (1980), 77–88.

W. A. Krenkel, 'Tonguing', *WZ Rostock* 30 (1981), 37–54.

L. Kurke, 'Inventing the *Hetaira*: Sex, Politics, and Discursive Conflict in Archaic Greece', *Classical Antiquity* 16 (1997), 106–50.

L. La Follette, 'The Costume of the Roman Bride', in: L. Bonfante and J. L. Sebesta (eds), *The World of Roman Costume* (Wisconsin, 1994), 54–64.

A. Lardinois, 'Who Sings Sappho's Songs?', in: E. Greene (ed.), *Reading Sappho: Contemporary Approaches* (Berkeley, 1996), 150–72.

D. H. Larmour, P. A. Miller and C. Platter (eds), *Rethinking Sexuality: Foucault and Classical Antiquity* (Princeton, 1988).

M. R. Lefkowitz, *Heroines and Hysterics* (London, 1981).

M. R. Lefkowitz, 'Seduction and Rape in Greek Myth', in: A. E. Liaou (ed.), *Consent and Coercion to Sex and Marriage in Ancient and Medieval Societies* (Washington DC, 1993), 17–37.

M. R. Lefkowitz and M. B. Fant, *Women's Life in Greece and Rome*, 2nd ed. (Baltimore, 1992).

D. Leitao, 'The Legend of the Sacred Band', in: M. C. Nussbaum and J. Sihvola (eds), *The Sleep of Reason. Erotic Experience and Sexual Ethics in Ancient Greece and Rome* (Chicago, 2002), 143–69.

R. G. Levens, 'Catullus', in: M. Platnauer (ed.), *Fifty Years (and Twelve) of Classical Scholarship*, 2nd ed. (Oxford, 1968), 357–78.

S. Lilja, *Homosexuality in Republican and Augustan Rome* (Helsinki, 1983).

G. Lindberg, 'Hera in Homer to Ancient and Modern Eyes', in: S.-T. Teodorsson (ed.), *Greek and Latin Studies in Memory of Cajus Fabricius* (Sweden, 1990), 65–80.

J. Lindsay, *The Complete Poems of Catullus* (London, 1929).

W. M. Lindsay, *Festus: De Verborum Significatu quae Supersunt cum Pauli Epitome* (Hildesheim, 1965).

A. R. Littlewood, 'The Symbolism of the Apple in Greek and Roman Literature', *Harvard Studies in Classical Philology* 72 (1968), 147–81.

H. Lloyd-Jones, *Females of the Species. Semonides on Women* (London, 1975).

N. Loraux, *The Children of Athena: Athenian Ideas About Citizenship and the Division Between the Sexes*, trans. C. Levine (Princeton, 1993).

N. Loraux, *The Experiences of Tiresias: The Feminine and the Greek Man*, trans. P. Wissing (Princeton, 1995).

R. O. A. M. Lyne, *The Latin Love Poets from Catullus to Horace* (Oxford, 1980).

D. Macey, *The Many Lives of Michel Foucault* (London, 1993).

B. MacLachlan, 'Sacred Prostitution and Aphrodite', *Studies in Religion* (1992), 145–62.

B. MacLachlan, *The Age of Grace: Charis in Early Greek Poetry* (Princeton, 1993).

B. MacLachlan, 'Personal Poetry', in: D. E. Gerber (ed.), *A Companion to the Greek Lyric Poets* (Leiden, 1997), 133–220.

D. Mankin, *Horace: Epodes* (Cambridge, 1995).

M. Marcovich, 'Sappho Fr. 31: Anxiety Attack or Love Declaration?', *Classical Quarterly* 22 (1972), 19–32.

P. Marquardt, 'Hesiod's Ambiguous View of Woman', *Classical Philology* 77 (1982), 283–91.

J. D. Marry, 'Sappho and the Heroic Ideal', *Arethusa* 12 (1979), 71–92.

P. G. Maxwell-Stuart, 'Strato and the Musa Puerilis', *Hermes* 100 (1972), 215–240.

P. G. Maxwell-Stuart, 'Further Notes on Strato's Musa Puerilis', *Hermes* 103 (1975), 379–82.

E. S. McCartney, 'How the Apple Became a Token of Love', *Transactions and Proceedings of the American Philological Association* 56 (1925), 70–81.

L. K. M. McClure, *Sexuality and Gender in the Classical World* (Oxford, 2002).

W. C. McDermott, 'The Sisters of P. Clodius', *Phoenix* 24 (1970), 39–47.

T. McEvilley, 'Sapphic Imagery and Fragment 96', *Hermes* 101 (1973), 257–78.

T. McEvilley, 'Sappho, Fragment Thirty One: The Face Behind the Mask', *Phoenix* 32 (1978), 1–18.

B. F. McManus, *Classics and Feminism: Gendering the Classics* (New York, 1997).

A. M. Miller, *Greek Lyric: An Anthology in Translation* (Indianapolis, 1996).

J. F. Mitchell, 'The Torquati', *Historia* 15 (1966), 23–31.

G. Morgan, 'Aphrodite Cytherea', *Transactions and Proceedings of the American Philological Association* 108 (1978), 115–20.

G. W. Most, 'Sappho, Fr.16.6–7L-P', *Classical Quarterly* 31 (1981), 11–17.

D. Mountfield, *Greek and Roman Erotica* (New York, 1982).

P. Murgatroyd, *Tibullus I: A Commentary on the First Book of the Elegies of Albius Tibullus* (Natal, 1980).

O. Murray, 'The Greek Symposium in History', in: E. Gabba (ed.), *Tria corda: scritti in onore di Arnaldo Momigliano* (Como, 1983), 257–72.

O. Murray, (ed.), *Sympotica: The Papers of a Symposium on the Symposion* (Oxford, 1990).

M. Myerowitz, *Ovid's Games of Love* (Detroit, 1985).

C. Nappa, 'The Goat, the Gout, and the Girl: Catullus 69, 71, and 77', *Mnemosyne* 52 (1999), 266–76.

C. L. Neudling, *A Prosopography to Catullus* (Oxford, 1955).

A. G. Nikolaidis, 'Plutarch on Women and Marriage', *Wiener Studien* 110 (1997), 27–88.

J. D. Noonan, '*Mala Bestia* in Catullus 69.7–8', *Classical World* 73 (1979), 155–64.

H. M. North, 'The Mare, the Vixen, and the Bee: *Sophrosyne* as the Virtue of Women in Antiquity', *Illinois Classical Studies* 2 (1977): 35–49.

F. Norwood, 'The Riddle of Ovid's *Relegatio*', *Classical Philology* 58 (1963), 150–63.

J. H. Oakley and R. H. Sinos, *The Wedding in Ancient Athens* (Wisconsin, 1993).

D. Ogden, 'Homosexuality and Warfare in Ancient Greece', in: A. B. Lloyd (ed.), *Battle in Antiquity* (London, 1996), 107–68.

D. Ogden, *Magic, Witchcraft, and Ghosts in the Greek and Roman Worlds: A Sourcebook* (Oxford, 2002).

R. Omitowoju, 'Regulating Rape: Soap Operas and Self Interest in the Athenian Courts', in: S. Deacy and K. F. Pierce (eds), *Rape in Antiquity: Sexual Violence in the Greek and Roman Worlds* (London, 1997), 1–24.

R. Osborne, 'The Use of Abuse: Semonides 7', *Proceedings of the Cambridge Philological Society* 47 (2001), 47–64.

D. L. Page, *Sappho and Alcaeus: An Introduction to the Study of Ancient Lesbian Poetry* (Oxford, 1955).

D. L. Page, *The Epigrams of Rufinus* (Cambridge, 1978).

C. Paglia, 'Junk Bonds and Corporate Raiders: Academe in the Hour of the Wolf', in: *Sex, Art, and American Culture* (New York, 1992), 170–248.

T. D. Papanghelis, 'About the Hour of Noon: Ovid, *Amores* 1.5', *Mnemosyne* 52 (1989), 54–61.

H. N. Parker, 'Love's Body Anatomized: The Ancient Erotic Handbooks and the Rhetoric of Sexuality', in: A. Richlin (ed.), *Pornography and Representation in Greece and Rome* (Oxford, 1992).

H. N. Parker, 'Sappho Schoolmistress', *Transactions and Proceedings of the American Philological Association* 123 (1993), 309–51.

H. N. Parker, 'The Myth of the Heterosexual: Anthropology and Sexuality for Classicists', *Arethusa* 34 (2001), 313–62.

W. H. Parker, *Priapea: Poems for a Phallic God* (London, 1988).

P. J. Parsons, *The Oxyrhynchus Papyri*, Vol. XLII (London, 1974).

T. Passman, 'Out of the Closet and into the Field: Matriculture, the Lesbian Perspective, and Feminist Classics', in: N. S. Rabinowitz and A. Richlin (eds), *Feminist Theory and the Classics* (London, 1993), 181–208.

W. R. Paton, *The Greek Anthology*, 5 vols (Cambridge, Mass., 1948–1953).

C. B. Patterson, *The Family in Greek History* (Cambridge, Mass., 1998).

J. Penwill, 'Men in Love: Aspects of Plato's *Symposium*', *Ramus* 7 (1978), 143–75.

W. A. Percy, *Pederasty and Pedagogy in Archaic Greece* (Chicago, 1996).

C. B. Petropoulos, 'Sappho the Sorceress – Another Look at *Fr*. 1 (LP)' *Zeitschrift für Papyrologie und Epigraphik* 97 (1993), 43–56.

R. A. Pitcher, 'Martial and Roman Sexuality', in: T. W. Hillard, R. A. Kearsley, C. E. V. Nixon and A. M. Nobbs (eds), *Ancient History in a Modern University*, Vol. 1 (Sydney, 1998), 309–315.

A. J. Podlecki, *Plutarch: Life of Pericles* (Bristol, 1987).

A. J. Podlecki, *Perikles and His Circle* (London, 1998).

S. B. Pomeroy, *Goddesses, Whores, Wives, and Slaves* (New York, 1975).

S. B. Pomeroy, 'Supplementary Notes on Erinna', *Zeitschrift für Papyrologie und Epigraphik* 32 (1978), 17–22.

S. B. Pomeroy, 'Technikai kai Mousikai: The Education of Women in the Fourth Century and in the Hellenistic Period', *American Journal of Ancient History* 2 (1990), 51–68.

S. B. Pomeroy, (ed.), *Plutarch's Advice to the Bride and Groom and A Consolation to His Wife* (Oxford, 1999).

S. B. Pomeroy, *Spartan Women* (Oxford, 2002).

S. R. F. Price, 'Prostitution, sacred', in: S. Hornblower and A. Spawforth (eds), *The Oxford Classical Dictionary*, 3rd ed. (Oxford, 1999), 1263–64.

L. C. Purser, *The Story of Cupid and Psyche as Related by Apuleius* (New York, 1983).

M. C. J. Putnam, *Tibullus: A Commentary* (Oklahoma, 1973).

K. Quinn, *Catullus: An Interpretation* (London, 1972).

K. Quinn, *Catullus: The Poems*, 2nd ed. (London, 1973).

N. S. Rabinowitz, 'Introduction', in: N. S. Rabinowitz and A. Richlin (eds), *Feminist Theory and the Classics* (London, 1993).

W. H. Race, 'Sappho *Fr*. 16 L-P and Alkaios *Fr*. 42 L-P: Romantic and Classical Strains in Lesbian Lyric', *Classical Journal* 85 (1989), 16–33.

H. D. Rankin, 'Clodia II', *Acta Classica* 38 (1969), 501–506.

H. D. Rankin, 'Archilochus and Achilles', *Hermathena: H.W. Parke Festschrift* 118 (1974), 91–98.

H. D. Rankin, 'Catullus and the "Beauty of Lesbia" (Poems 43, 86 and 51)', *Latomus* 35 (1976), 5–11.

H. D. Rankin, *Archilochus of Paros* (New Jersey, 1977).

B. P. Reardon, 'Achilles Tatius and Ego-Narrative', in: J. R. Morgan and R. Stoneman (eds), *Greek Fiction: Greek Novel in Context* (London, 1994), 80–96.

K. J. Reckford, 'Desire and Hope: Aristophanes and the Comic Cartharsis', *Ramus* 3 (1974), 41–69.

J. D. Reed, 'The Sexuality of Adonis', *Classical Antiquity* 14 (1995), 317–47.

R. Rehm, *Marriage to Death: The Conflation of Wedding and Funeral Rituals in Greek Tragedy* (Princeton, 1994).

A. Richlin, 'Invective Against Women in Roman Satire', *Arethusa* 17 (1984), 67–80.

A. Richlin, 'Zeus and Metis: Foucault, Feminism, Classics', *Helios* 18 (1991), 160–80.

A. Richlin, *The Garden of Priapus: Sexuality and Aggression in Roman Humor*, 2nd ed. (Oxford, 1992a).

A. Richlin, (ed.), *Pornography and Representation in Greece and Rome* (Oxford, 1992b).

A. Richlin, 'Reading Ovid's Rapes', in: A. Richlin (ed.), *Pornography and Representation in Greece and Rome* (Oxford, 1992c), 158–79.

A. Richlin, 'Not Before Homosexuality: The Materiality of the *Cinaedus* and the Roman Law Against Love Between Men', *Journal of the History of Sexuality* 3 (1993a), 523–73.

A. Richlin, 'The Ethnographer's Dilemma and the Dream of a Lost Golden Age', in: N. S. Rabinowitz and A. Richlin (eds), *Feminist Theory and the Classics* (London, 1993b), 272–303.

A. Richlin, 'Foucault's *History of Sexuality*: A Useful Theory for Women?', in: D. H. J. Larmour, P. A. Miller and C. Platter (eds), *Rethinking Sexuality: Foucault and Classical Antiquity* (Princeton, 1998), 138–70.

E. Robbins, '"Every Time I Look at You . . .": Sappho Thirty-One', *Transactions and Proceedings of the American Philological Association* 110 (1980), 255–61.

E. Robbins, 'Who's Dying in Sappho *Fr.* 94?', *Phoenix* 44 (1990), 111–21.

E. Robbins, 'Sappho, Aphrodite, and the Muses', *The Ancient World* 26 (1995), 225–39.

E. Robbins, 'Public Poetry. 1. Alcman', in: D. E. Gerber (ed.), *A Companion to the Greek Lyric Poets* (Leiden, 1997), 223–31.

N. Robertson, 'The Origin of the Panathenaea', *Rheinisches Museum für Philologie* 128 (1985), 231–95.

J. E. Robson, 'Bestiality and Bestial Rape in Greek Myth', in: S. Deacy and K. F. Pierce (eds), *Rape in Antiquity: Sexual Violence in the Greek and Roman Worlds* (London, 1997), 65–96.

K. Rockwell, '*O Rem Ridiculam!*', *Classical Philology* 70 (1975), 214.

R. S. Rogers, 'The Emperor's Displeasure and Ovid', *Transactions and Proceedings of the American Philological Association* 97 (1966), 373–78.

W. Sale, 'Aphrodite in the *Theogony*', *Transactions and Proceedings of the American Philological Association* 92 (1961), 508–21.

A. Scafuro, 'Discourses of Sexual Violation in Mythic Accounts and Dramatic Versions of "The Girl's Tragedy"', *differences* 2 (1990), 126–59.

T. F. Scanlon, *Eros and Greek Athletics* (Oxford, 2002).

R. Seaford, 'The Tragic Wedding', *Journal of Hellenic Studies* 107 (1987), 106–30.

R. Seager, 'Venustus, Lepidus, Bellus, Salsus: Notes on the Language of Catullus', *Latomus* 33 (1974), 891–94.

C. Segal, 'Catullan *Otiosi*: The Lover and the Poet', *Greece and Rome* 17 (1970), 25–31.

C. Segal, 'Eros and Incantation: Sappho and Oral Poetry', *Arethusa* 7 (1974), 139–60.

C. Segal, 'Philomela's Web and the Pleasures of the Text: Ovid's Myth of Tereus in the *Metamorphoses*', in: H. Jones and R. M. Wilhelm (eds), *The Two Worlds of Poet: New Perspectives on Vergil* (Detroit, 1992), 281–95.

B. Sergent, *Homosexuality in Greek Myth*, trans. A. Goldhammer (London, 1986).

H. A. Shapiro, 'Eros in Love: Pederasty and Pornography in Greece', in: A. Richlin (ed.), *Pornography and Representation in Greece and Rome* (Oxford, 1992), 53–72.

A. R. Sharrock, 'The Drooping Rose: Elegiac Failure in Amores 3.7', *Ramus* 24 (1995), 152–80.

J.-A. Shelton, 'Pliny the Younger, and the Ideal Wife', *Classica et Mediaevalia* 41 (1990), 163–86.

D. Sider, 'Notes on Two epigrams of Philodemus', *American Journal of Philology* 103 (1982), 208–13.

D. Sider, *The Epigrams of Philodemos* (Oxford, 1997).

M. B. Skinner, 'Briseis, The Trojan War, and Erinna', *Classical World* 75 (1982), 265–69.

M. B. Skinner, 'Clodia Metelli', *Transactions and Proceedings of the American Philological Association* 113 (1983), 273–87.

M. B. Skinner, 'Classical Studies vs. Women's Studies: *duo moi ta noemata*', *Helios* 12 (1985), 3–16.

M. B. Skinner, 'Introduction', in: M. B. Skinner (ed.), *Helios Rescuing Creusa: New Methodological Approaches to Women in Antiquity* (1986), 131–38.

M. B. Skinner, 'Classical Studies, Patriarchy and Feminism: The View from 1986', *Women's Studies International Forum* 10 (1987), 181–86.

M. B. Skinner, 'Sapphic Nossis', *Arethusa* 22 (1989), 5–18.

M. B. Skinner, 'Nossis *Thelyglossos*: The Private Text and the Public Book', in: S. B. Pomeroy (ed.), *Women's History and Ancient History* (Chapel Hill, 1991a), 20–47.

M. B. Skinner, 'Aphrodite Garlanded: Eros and Poetic Creativity in Sappho and Nossis', in: F. di Pieria (ed.), *Rose di Pieria* (Bari, 1991b), 79–96.

M. B. Skinner, 'Ego mulier: The Construction of Male Sexuality in Catullus', *Helios* 10 (1993), 107–30.

M. B. Skinner, 'Zeus and Leda: The Sexuality Wars in Contemporary Classical Scholarship', *Thamyris* 3 (1996), 103–23, http://www.Stoa.org/cgni-bin/ptext?doc=Stoa:text:2002.01.0006.

J. M. Snyder, *The Woman and the Lyre: Women Writers in Classical Greece and Rome* (Carbondale, 1989).

A. H. Sommerstein, *Aristophanes: Acharnians* (Warminster, 1980).

P. A. Stadter, *A Commentary on Plutarch's Pericles* (Chapel Hill, 1989).

K. Stanley, 'The Rôle of Aphrodite in Sappho Fr. 1', *Greek, Roman and Byzantine Studies* 17 (1976), 305–21.

W. J. M. Starkie, *The Acharnians of Aristophanes* (London, 1909).

E. Stehle, *Performance and Gender in Ancient Greece: Nondramatic Poetry in its Setting* (Princeton, 1997).

J. Stern, 'Theocritus' *Epithalamium for Helen*', *Revue belge de philologie et d'histoire* 56 (1978), 29–37.

A. Stewart, 'Rape?', in: E. D. Reeder (ed.), *Pandora: Women in Classical Greece* (Princeton, 1995), 74–90.

A. Stewart, *Art, Desire, and the Body in Ancient Greece* (Cambridge, 1997).

E. S. Stigers, 'Retreat from the Male: Catullus 62 and Sappho's Erotic Flowers', *Ramus* 6 (1977), 83–102.

B. E. Stirrup, 'Techniques of Rape: Variety and Art in Ovid's "Metamorphoses"', *Greece and Rome* 24 (1977), 170–84.

J. P. Sullivan, 'Martial's Sexual Attitudes', *Philologus* 123 (1979), 288–302.

J. P. Sullivan, 'The Roots of Anti-Feminism in Greece and Rome', *Helix* 19 (1984), 71–84.

J. P. Sullivan, *Martial: The Unexpected Classic* (Cambridge, 1991).

D. A. Svarlien, 'Women, by Semonides of Amorgos (Poem 7)', http://www.stoa.org/diotima/anthology/sem_7.shtml

R. G. Tanner, 'Catullus LVI', *Hermes* 100 (1972), 506–08.

E. Thomas, 'Variations on a Military Theme in Ovid's *Amores*', *Greece and Rome* 11 (1964), 151–65.

R. F. Thomas, '"Death", Doxography, and the "Termerian Evil" (Philodemus, Epigr. 27 Page = A. P. 11.30)', *Classical Quarterly* 41 (1991), 130–37.

O. Thomsen, *Ritual and Desire: Catullus 61 and 62 and Other Ancient Documents on Wedding and Marriage* (Denmark, 1992).

D. F. S. Thomson, *Catullus* (Toronto, 1997).

B. S. Thornton, 'Constructionism and Ancient Greek Sex', *Helios* 18 (1991a), 181–93.

B. S. Thornton, 'Idolon Theatri: Foucault and the Classics', *Classical and Modern Literature* 12 (1991b), 81–100.

B. S. Thornton, *Eros: The Myth of Ancient Greek Sexuality* (Colorado, 1997).

J. Thorp, 'The Social Construction of Homosexuality', *Phoenix* 46 (1992), 54–65.

S. Treggiari, *Roman Marriage* (Oxford, 1991).

O. Tsagarakis, 'Some Neglected Aspects of Love in Sappho's *Fr.* 31 LP', *Rheinisches Museum für Philologie* 122 (1979), 97–118.

O. Tsagarakis, 'Broken Hearts and the Social Circumstances in Sappho's Poetry', *Rheinisches Museum für Philologie* 129 (1986), 1–17.

K. Tsantanoglou, 'The Memoirs of a Lady of Samos', *Zeitschrift für Papyrologie und Epigraphik* 12 (1973), 183–95.

J. Van Sickle, 'Archilochus: A New Fragment of an Epode', *Classical Journal* 71 (1975), 1–15.

A. Varone, *Erotica Pompeiana: Iscrizioni d'amore sui muri di Pompei* (Rome, 1995).

W. J. Verdenius, 'Tyrtaeus 6-7D: A Commentary', *Mnemosyne* 4 (1969), 337–55.

J.-P. Vernant, 'One . . . Two . . . Three: *Eros*', in: D. M. Halperin, J. J. Winkler and F. I. Zeitlin (eds), *Before Sexuality: The Construction of Erotic Experience in the Ancient World* (Princeton, 1990), 465–78.

B. C. Verstraete, 'Ovid on Homosexuality', *Echos du monde classique* 19 (1975), 79–83.

P. Veyne, 'Homosexuality in Ancient Rome', in: P. Ariès and A. Béjin (eds), *Western Sexuality: Practice and Precept in Past and Present Times* (Oxford, 1985), 26–35.

B. Vine, 'On the "Missing" Fourth Stanza of Catullus 51', *Harvard Studies in Classical Philology* 94 (1992), 251–58.

M. Waegeman, *Amulet and Alphabet: Magical Amulets in the First Book of Cyranides* (Amsterdam, 1987).

J. Walters, 'Making a Spectacle: Deviant Men, Invective, and Pleasure', *Arethusa* 31 (1998), 355–67.

P. Watson, 'Erotion: *Puella Delicata*', *Classical Quarterly* 42 (1992), 253–68.

M. L. West, *Hesiod: Theogony* (Oxford, 1966).

M. L. West, *Iambi et Elegi Graeci*, 2 vols (Oxford, 1971–1972).

M. L. West, *Studies in Greek Elegy and Iambus* (Berlin, 1974).

M. L. West, 'Erinna', *Zeitschrift für Papyrologie und Epigraphik* 25 (1977), 95–119.

M. L. West, *Greek Lyric Poetry* (Oxford, 1994).

A. L. Wheeler, 'Tradition in the Epithalamium', *American Journal of Philologie* 51 (1930), 205–23.

L. P. Wilkinson, 'Ancient and Modern: Catullus 51 Again', *Greece and Rome* 21 (1974), 82–85.

C. A. Williams, 'Greek Love at Rome', *Classical Quarterly* 45 (1995), 517–39.

C. A. Williams, *Roman Homosexuality: Ideologies of Masculinity in Classical Antiquity* (Oxford, 1999).

G. Williams, 'Poetry in the Moral Climate of Augustan Rome', *Journal of Roman Studies* 52 (1962), 28–46.

L. H. Wilson, *Sappho's Sweetbitter Songs: Configurations of Female and Male in Ancient Greek Lyric* (London, 1996).

S. F. Wiltshire, 'Catullus Venustus', *Classical World* 70 (1977), 319–26.

J. Winkler, 'Gardens of Nymphs: Public and Private in Sappho's Lyrics', in: H. Foley (ed.), *Reflections of Women in Antiquity* (New York, 1981), 66–71.

J. Winkler, *The Constraints of Desire: An Anthropology of Sex and Gender in Ancient Greece* (London, 1990a).

J. Winkler, 'Laying Down the Law: The Oversight of Men's Sexual Behaviour in Classical Athens', in: D. M. Halperin, J. J. Winkler and F. I. Zeitlin (eds), *Before Sexuality: The Construction of Erotic Experience in the Ancient Greek World* (Princeton, 1990b), 171–209.

T. P. Wiseman, *Catullan Questions* (Leicester, 1969).

T. P. Wiseman, *Cinna the Poet and Other Roman Essays* (Leicester, 1974).

T. P. Wiseman, 'Clodia: some imaginary lives', *Arion* 2 (1975), 96–115.

T. P. Wiseman, *Catullus and His World: A Reappraisal* (Cambridge, 1985).

D. E. W. Wormell, 'Catullus as Translator', in: L. Wallach (ed.), *The Classical Tradition: Literary and Historical Studies in Honor of Harry Caplan* (Ithaca, 1966), 187–201.

C. Zangemeister (ed.), *Inscriptiones Parietariae Pompeianae* (Berlin [= CIL IV, Supp. 1–3], 1871).

F. I. Zeitlin, 'Signifying Difference: The Myth of Pandora', in: R. Hawley and B. Levick (eds), *Women in Antiquity: New Assessments* (London, 1995a), 58–74.

F. I. Zeitlin, 'The Economics of Hesiod's Pandora', in: E. Reeder (ed.), *Pandora: Women in Classical Greece* (Baltimore, 1995b), 49–56.

INDEX